A HISTORY
OF
SEQUENCE
DANCING
AND
SCRIPT LIST

BY

T.A. WHITWORTH

First published 1995
by
T. A. Whitworth,
42 Newbold Back Lane, Chesterfield,
Derbyshire, S40 4HQ.

ISBN 0-9501927-4-0

British Library Cataloguing in Publication Data:

Whitworth, Thomas Alan

A History of Sequence Dancing and Script List

I. Title II. Guy, Derek

793.33

ISBN 0-9501927-4-0

Printed in Great Britain by:
Hillman Printers (Frome) Limited
Frome, Somerset,
BA11 4RW.

PREFACE

Although sequence dancing is a very popular form of social dance it has been largely neglected by dance historians. It is, by its very nature, a self-sufficient activity in that it has its regular attenders, repertoire of sequence dances, music and dance leaders. It requires little advertising or finance and is largely independent of the various ballroom associations. It is an absorbing pastime for those who like to dance but not particularly attractive to watch and is rarely featured in the press or on TV - it does not have the glamour of ballroom dancing.

The roots of sequence dancing lie deep in history and it was felt that some permanent record should be produced before memories fade and vital information is lost. Unlike ballroom dancing there are few outstanding figures like winners of world championships, great stylists, writers of textbooks and prominent members of institutions. The history of sequence dancing is largely enshrined in its dance scripts and the best approach seemed to be to list these scripts in chronological order with appropriate comments. A comprehensive list of this kind is also useful in helping to prevent the allocation of the same name to different sequence dances - a not infrequent occurrence!

Many problems arise in compiling such a list. There are thousands of sequence dances, some have inadequate scripts, others exist in various versions, different sequence dances bear the same name. Some dances have been lost in the mists of time; other dances, popular in the clubs, have no arranger, date or formal script. The arranger and performers of an award-winning dance may not be the same and it is not always possible to allocate credit for a particular dance fairly between a husband-wife couple or families of dancers such as the Finnigans and Roscoes.

The author and his associates have done their best to grapple with these problems and hope they have produced an accurate and balanced account which is fair to all.

CONTRIBUTORS

The text is based on a list of scripts compiled by Derek Guy which has been revised and extended by Ken Fuller and others. The author has coordinated the material, written the commentaries and prepared the book for publication.

DEREK GUY started ballroom and Latin dancing in 1939. After marrying his wife Betty in 1948 they both studied old-time dancing at the Tudor Dance School under George and Nora Shaw and Madge Wooding. They took further qualifications in old-time and modern sequence dancing after their family had grown up. Derek and Betty run regular sequence dances in their home town and act as resident dance leaders in hotels, Blackpool being their main base. Derek Guy is an engineer by trade but has been much involved with youth work and Age Concern; among his other interests are model engineering and chrysanthemum growing.

KEN FULLER is one of the small band of people in the Manchester area who helped to put modern sequence dancing on the map. Since 1956 he has been Secretary of the Manchester M.C's Club and has organised dances, led off the sequences and helped people where he could. As well as being a writer of many popular sequence dances, he is a dancer of no mean ability. In 1962 he and his then partner, Margaret, took first place in the NASD new dance competition with his Kingston Quickstep. He has recently been awarded the first Certificate of Merit for services to sequence dancing issued by the 'Sequence Dancing World' magazine.

T. A. WHITWORTH is a keen sequence dancer and a collector of dancing books; he has degrees in science, social psychology and research methods. His 'Modern Sequence Dancing for All' (1994), is a companion volume to the present work - it is a complete guide to the theory and practice of both old-time and modern sequence dancing.

CONTENTS

ACKNOWLEDGEMENTS

The cover picture is based on a photograph by *Heinz Lautenbacher* and is by courtesy of *Eaglemoss Publications Limited*. It shows Michael O'Callaghan and Emma Dodd performing the Mayfair Quickstep. In 1994 they received the Carl-Alan Award for Amateur Dancers (Sequence Section) at the Bognor Regis Festival.

Graphics, preparing the book for print and artwork was by *David Charlesworth* (Notions by Design) one Derbyshire's best known professional artists and designers.

My thanks are offered to *Mrs. Susan Baker* for type-setting the manuscript and advising on the layout, and to many others for advice, support and encouragement.

The book is dedicated to the dance leaders and teachers who give unsparingly of their time and expertise to provide enjoyment for the many.

To my wife, Margaret, with love

A. M. D. G.

AN
OVERVIEW
OF
SEQUENCE
DANCING

The Nature of Sequence Dancing - Dance Scripts

If you have seen or danced the Veleta, Military Two Step or St. Bernard Waltz you will have grasped the essentials of an old-time sequence dance. Two partners move in a more-or-less anti-clockwise direction round the dance floor performing a set sequence of steps which is often 16 bars in length - it is a type of round dance. All the dancers do the same dancing figures in the same order and the sequence of steps is repeated several times. Dances of this kind can always be described by a dance script which sets out how the dance should be performed - it is like the musical score for the musician. A concise form of the dance script for the Military Two Step appears below.

Military Two Step

Music: 'Washington Post' or ' Blaze Away'

Both face down line of dance. Man starts with his left foot, lady with her right foot.

Point outside foot forward counting 1 and 2.
Point outside foot backward counting 1 and 2.

March 3 steps forward and face about.	4 bars
Repeat in the opposite direction. Salute partner.	4 bars
Waltz with partner.	8 bars
	16 bars

A 16-bar sequence strikes a happy mean between a short dance which lacks variety and an extended sequence which is difficult to remember. Exceptions are the Barn Dance (8), Latchford Schottische (12), Maxina (24), Pride of Erin Waltz (32), Australian new vogue dances (32).

Any dance can be arranged in this form giving sequence dancing great flexibility and variety. Instruction by a teacher is not essential since the sequences can be learned by observation and practice; these dances have always been popular with the general public but less so with teachers of dancing! They are essentially dances for the common people rather than activities of a trained elite.

Dance Scripts and History

A vast amount of information resides in the dance scripts accumulated over more than a century - merely counting them measures the popularity of sequence dancing and shows what dances were in fashion at any particular time. Studying the scripts in more detail is an excellent method of tracing changes in types of dance, technique and dancing fashions.

Looking again at the Military Two Step we can see how scripts have changed over the years. Notice that the music is specified but not the time signature (6/8) or tempo (56 bpm). The arranger of a sequence would often write the music and in many cases dance and music would have the same name as in the Veleta and Maxina. Modern sequence dances, in contrast, are performed to many different melodies although novelty dances sometimes have their own music. Always having the same tune for a dance brings back memories and helps in timing the steps but it may become boring if the dance is performed too frequently.

The script of the Military Two Step in this text is rather brief and does not set out the steps individually - a more modern version in 'Sequence Dancing' (1989) by Michael Gwynne is 4 times as long with a script of equal length for the lady. Some old scripts are no more than 'memory joggers' to remind an accomplished dancer of a sequence that he has seen and danced many times. A modern script is a set of detailed instructions for someone to execute the dance who might never have seen it performed. Each 4-bar section will have a heading which lists the figures which are to follow, and details will be given of foot orientations, timing and sometimes footwork (heel or toe, etc.). Some versions have a separate script for the lady's steps and scripts of Latin-American dances will include hand movements and specify a variety of holds. Old-time dances were constructed from a relatively small range of figures (10 at the most) compared with some 20-40 for a modern slow foxtrot. All these factors make the modern scripts longer - and perhaps more difficult to follow!

As a second example, consider two popular dances written at about the same time - the Mayfair Quickstep by Frank Short (1956) and the Broadway Quickstep by Edith Farmer (1957). The Mayfair Quickstep starts in open hold and has walks and solo turns - figures commonly found in saunters and old-time tangos. It is really more of a swing than a quickstep and is often used as an alternative to the Sindy Swing for progressive dances. The Broadway Quickstep, in contrast, is modern in almost every respect and in modified form is used as a teaching dance by the ISTD. Modern quickstep figures are used and ballroom hold is maintained throughout. A comparison of scripts for the two dances shows clearly the differences between an early and a late form of the quickstep.

Origins of Ballroom and Sequence Dancing

Ballroom and sequence dancing are closely related in that they use the same dancing figures, music and technique and, indeed, the higher reaches of sequence dancing are largely controlled by the Official Board and the various ballroom associations. Ballroom dancing is a form of go-as-you-please dancing in that the order of dancing figures is decided by each couple - there is no script. If in a foxtrot you see everyone turning at different times this is a ballroom slow foxtrot - if all turn together it is a sequence foxtrot. The freedom of the individual ballroom dancer to choose his own order of steps has far-reaching consequences which are examined in Chapter 5.

In looking for origins, however, similarities are more important than differences - these are that both forms are round dances for couples moving in an anti-clockwise direction round the ballroom and ballroom hold is often used (partners facing; man's right arm round lady's waist; left arm holding lady's raised hand). The waltz, introduced into England at Almack's London ballroom in 1812, is the first dance to have these characteristics. Originally there was considerable 'daylight' between the partners, as is often found in the social and sequence dancing hold of today. In modern ballroom dancing close body contact is essential for the man to lead his partner; this 'English style' dates from the formation of a ballroom branch of the ISTD in 1924. Hence, origins are 1812 for the early ballroom waltz and 1924 for the modern style of dancing.

Sequence dancing has its roots in the square dances for four couples of previous centuries. Round dances for individual couples began to appear in the Victorian era (1837-1901). One of F. J. Mainey's lists for this period has 65 round sequence dances including two steps, barn dances and sequence schottisches, polkas and mazurkas. A good case could be made out for the La Varsovianna (1850 or earlier) being one of the first popular 16 bar sequence dances of this type. It has elements of the polka-mazurka (redowa) and is danced in waltz rhythm with a step and point at 4-bar intervals. Performed to the proper music and with correct movements of arms, body and head, it is a pleasure to behold. Allen Dodworth is said to have taught the old form of this dance in the USA in 1853. It still appears on programmes of old-time sessions of today. Dancing at this time was very popular among the upper classes and Queen Victoria used to lead off in the Quadrilles at the state balls in Buckingham Palace. With the death of the Prince Consort in 1861 she never danced again in public and dancing became less fashionable among the elite. Formal dances like hunt and state balls began to be replaced by lavish parties in the larger private houses. The standard of dancing deteriorated and many just 'walked through' the dances instead of using the proper old-time technique.

At the turn of the century social dancing became more and more popular with working people and many assembly halls were built. These had a large room with a polished floor and a few smaller ancillary rooms. Then (as today) a teacher of dancing organised the programme of dances and provided the music in one form or another. Round sequence dances came into favour and many dance historians take Arthur Morris's Veleta of 1900 as a starting point. Thus this form of sequence dancing had its early beginnings in the 1850's becoming widely popular after 1900.

From Ballroom to Sequence Dancing

Any dance worthy of the name has characteristic groups of steps called 'dancing figures'. When a new dance appears there are differences in the steps and technique used by individuals but if the dance is more than a passing fancy it will eventually acquire a repertoire of dancing figures standardised by some committee and used for teaching purposes. These dancing figures are the 'building bricks' for dances. In ballroom dancing each pair will use them to make a dancing pattern of their own; in sequence dancing the arranger will put his figures together (possibly with figures from other dances) to make a pleasing 16-bar sequence which all will perform.

Most sequence dances are constructed from figures which have been developed originally from free-choice ballroom dances and there is thus often a time lapse between the appearance of a new dance and its conversion to sequence form. Perhaps we shall see a multitude of sequence salsas and lambadas if these dances stay the course! Not all sequence dances arise from go-as-you-please ballroom dances in this way. In old-time dancing there is a pool of figures, such as the twinkle, step and point, four step and rotary turn. These can be put together to make glides, strolls, sways, swings, etc. which have no corresponding ballroom equivalent and no standard figures of their own. Sequence gavottes and minuets arise from square (or circle) dances. Novelty dances are sometimes devised to fit a particular tune, e.g. the Lambeth Walk.

Classification of Sequence Dances

In inventive dance competitions for new sequence dances, the Official Board (OBBD) awards prizes in three areas -old-time, modern and Latin American. Each style has its own particular technique and the aspiring sequence dancer has to be something of a jack-of-all-trades performing competently in all three modes!

Old-Time Dances

The dates in the first column give some idea of when the dances first appeared in the UK in ballroom (free-choice) style.

	Dance Type	**Early Sequence Forms**
1812	Waltz O/T	Veleta (1900)
1840	Mazurka	Marie Mazurka (1906)
1844	Polka	Berlin Polka (1894)
1849	Schottische	Highland Schottische (1855)
		Barn Dance (1880)
	Two Step	Washington Post (1889)
		Military Two Step (1904)
	Gavotte	Butterfly Gavotte (1907)

The technique for these dances is based on ballet. Steps are taken more on the ball of the foot rather than the heel and the calf muscles are in a state of tension. Feet are placed at an angle in one of the five basic ballet positions. Full rotary turns are used in the waltz and these are taken more on the spot. Apart from the gavotte they tend to be vigorous dances played at fairly fast tempos.

1912	Tango O/T	Royal Empress Tango (1922)
1914	Foxtrot (early)	On Leave Foxtrot (1917)
1922	Blues	Lingering Blues (1929)
	Glide	Gainsborough Glide (1950)
	Parade	New Empress Parade (1956)
	Saunter	Yearning Saunter (1919)
	Stroll	Festival Stroll (1953)
	Sway	Islington Sway (1950)
	Swing	Majong Swing (1959)

These dances are performed with a natural walking action and more use is made of the heels; the feet are in parallel position, not at an angle. It will be seen from the dates that several of these styles became popular in the old-time revival which followed the second world war.

Modern Dances

1914	Foxtrot	Alana Foxtrot (1967)
1922	Waltz (Mod)	Waltz Marie (1948)
1929	Quickstep	Broadway Quickstep (1957)
1935	Tango (Mod)	Morecambe Tango (1948)

Modern dances have standard dancing figures and a clearly defined technique. In the 'English style' ballroom hold is used and body contact maintained at all times; there is no pronounced movement against the line of dance. In the modern waltz, foxtrot and quickstep much attention is devoted to rise and fall, sway, footwork and contrary body movement.

Modern waltzes are played at a slower tempo than old-time waltzes and the feet are parallel rather than at an angle. Early modern waltzes, foxtrots and quicksteps often display some old-time characteristics - solo and rotary turns, step and point, squares, etc.

Modern tangos have a special hold; longer steps are taken and movements are more staccato than in the old-time tango. There are exaggerated, quick turning movements of the head and other parts of the body.

(The Viennese Waltz is another modern dance but there is no true sequence quick waltz based on this dance.)

Latin-American Dances

Latin-America comprises those parts of South and Central America, Mexico and the Caribbean Islands which have Spanish or Portuguese as their official language. Dances from these areas have a strong, compulsive rhythm and are readily adapted to sequence form.

1916	Paso Doble	Paso Madrid (1964)
1930	Samba	Samba Zeeta (1950)
1943	Jive	Peppermint Jive (1970)
1948	Cuban Rumba	Rumba Royal (1964)
1954	Cha Cha Cha	Jacqueline Cha Cha Cha (1961)
1958	Bossa Nova	Broadway Bossa Nova (1969)

The paso doble (Spanish Two Step) is played to brisk marching music. The man represents the matador, the lady is his cape, there is no bull!

The samba is an up-dated version of the strenuous Brazilian Maxixe (1912-1914) which used to be very popular in the USA; it is danced with a characteristic samba bounce.

Both the jive and cha cha cha are danced to triple beat rhythms with chassés occurring at regular intervals. Steps for the cha cha cha and rumba are very similar with the chassé figure being replaced by a single step in the rumba.

The bossa nova has some elements of the rumba and samba - there are not many sequence forms of this dance.

A Time Scale for Sequence Dancing

Most of the remainder of this book deals with scripts year by year and it is very easy to lose track of the general pattern in a mass of detail. The following sections describe briefly the contents of the remaining chapters.

Chapter 2 The Early Years (Up to 1945)

This covers the first period of great popularity of old-time sequence dancing. Old-time dances were converted to sequence form and some modern dances were beginning to appear.

Before 1910	The waltz, schottische, polka, mazurka, gavotte and minuet were adapted to sequence form; two steps and barn dances became popular.
1910-1924	More modern dances such as the tango, saunter, foxtrot, blues and one step were arranged in sequence form.
1924-1945	Sequence dancing suffered a temporary lapse from favour although it continued in the the north of England and Scotland. Social dancing became mainly go-as-you-please; the English style of modern ballroom dancing was developed.

Chapter 3 Years of Transition (1946-1974)

Old-time/sequence dancing had a great revival after the war and many new sequence dances (and some square dances) were arranged. Dancing technique was refined and the range of dancing figures extended. Modern waltzes danced at a slower speed in ballroom hold became more popular than old-time waltzes. Foxtrots lost their saunter-like characteristics and became the smooth gliding ballroom-type dances of today. Quicksteps replaced one steps and two steps were less in evidence. Latin-American dances like the rumba, cha cha cha and jive were added to the repertoire. By 1960-1965 clear differences had emerged between old-time and modern sequence dancing and the ballroom dancing associations became involved. New sequence dances were appearing at an alarming rate.

Chapter 4 The Modern Era (1975 and after)

A period of relative stability but not we hope stagnation!

The Official Board (now the British Council of Ballroom Dancing) took tighter control of inventive dance competitions. All new (official) sequence dances must now be winners of events licensed by the BCBD. At the present time there are 15 competitions with prizes in the modern, old-time and Latin-American sections making a total of 45 new official dances each year.

The list of prizewinners in official competitions at the end of the chapter should help to avoid allocating names already in use to new sequence dances.

Chapter 5 Sequence Dancing in Perspective

Differences between ballroom and sequence dancing are discussed and their implications explored. Old-time, social and modern forms of sequence dancing are considered in more detail.

THE
EARLY YEARS
(UP TO 1945)

INDEX OF DANCES FROM 1850-1945

Introduction

Most of the scripts from this early period are unusual in that they have been revised, modified and assessed by a later generation of dancers. Sequence dancing was very popular from 1900 to 1924 but was then largely replaced by free-choice dances in which there was no agreed sequence - partners and individuals chose their own steps and style of performance. When interest in old-time dancing revived in the late 1940's most of the great dancing masters had either died or retired or forgotten their sequence skills. The scripts were still there but they were much shorter and contained less detail than those of today - they were more like reminders to the experts (memory joggers) than precise instructions on how to perform the dances. A. J. Latimer went to great trouble to produce two 'bouquets' of authentic scripts of old-time dances in the 1940's. Bill Botham (of Bilmay Script Service fame) considered that only 36 out of the total of 126 dances described were 'danceable' from the descriptions given. Teachers thus had to fill out these sketchy instructions and often conflicting versions appeared. Large numbers of these dances were presented to the general public at dances, in books and on radio and TV. Certain of those dances became favourites and still form a valuable part of the repertoire of the old-time dancing of today. Most of these scripts are named in the lists which follow along with prize winners and other dances of historical importance.

The dance scripts for the period are now considered in chronological order. Where possible arrangers of dances and the home towns are included. Prizes won at the various dance festivals are indicated using the abbreviations listed below:-

BATD	British Association of Teachers of Dancing
NATD	National Association of Teachers of Dancing
UKAPTD	United Kingdom Alliance of Professional Teachers of Dancing
ESTD	Empire Society of Teachers of Dancing
MATD	Midland Association of Teachers of Dancing
Blackpool	Blackpool Festival

Certain rules have been adopted to help in preparing the alphabetical lists of dances in various parts of the book:-

(a) The title of the sequence is placed in front of the type of dance,

    e.g.   Square Tango, Butterfly Gavotte

If the type of dance normally comes first, this is indicated by placing this in square brackets,

    e.g.   Tango Serida becomes Serida [Tango]

             Valse Superbe becomes Superbe [Valse]

This rule is not followed for titles like Waltz of the Bells.

(b) Round brackets are used in some titles to add extra information and the prefix 'The' is omitted from most dances,

    e.g.   Devonia becomes Devonia (Waltz)

             Chin Chin becomes Chin Chin (One Step)

             Desmond (Jasmine) Blues indicates two alternative names for the same sequence.

             The Cazaret becomes Cazaret

(c) 'O/T' is used for old-time, 'Mod' for modern in some dances.

Waltzes before 1950 are almost all old-time and any exceptions are described as modern (Mod). After 1950 waltzes are placed under 'Old-Time' and 'Modern' headings.

Old-time and modern tangos are not distinguished in all cases.

Up to 1899

1850 La Varsovianna
1855 Highland (Balmoral) Schottische (a Scottish dance)
1868 Gavotte Schottische, Edward Humphrey (London)
1880 Military Schottische (Barn Dance)
1886 Pas de Quatre, Edward Humphrey (London)
1889 Washington Post (Two Step)
  " Pennsylvania Two Step
1894 Alsatian and Berlin Polkas, Karl Kapps
1895 Carnival (a square dance), H. R. Johnson (London)
1898 Victoria Cross (Two Step), James Finnigan (Manchester)
  " Gordon Schottische, William Thomson Jnr., 1st BATD

La Varsovianna is a typical sequence dance of the 19th century with hopping steps rather than the smooth gliding movements of today - Major Cecil Taylor describes it very aptly as a first cousin to the mazurka. This Polish dance has great charm when correctly performed to the proper music - it was included at one time in medal tests by the ISTD. It has a characteristic pause after each half turn with special movements of arms, body and head; tuition by an expert is necessary to bring out the full flavour of the dance.

The schottische is a type of hopping waltz in 2/4 or 4/4 time played at a slower tempo than the polka - it is sometimes known as the German polka. 'Schottische' is German for 'of Scotland' and the dance may have affinities with this country. The Highland Schottische is a vigorous sequence version, still popular in Scotland today; the Military Schottische was known in the USA as the Barn Dance since it was often performed to 'Dancing in the Barn'. Several other barn dances are listed in the following pages; the Pas de Quatre is a barn dance for two couples. The arranger of this dance and the Gavotte Schottische was Edward Humphrey who ran a dancing academy at the Cavendish Rooms in London. His son, Walter E. Humphrey, launched the 'Dancing Times' in 1894 - this was reissued after a break in 1909 and is still the leading dance newspaper; he also issued a London Ballroom Guide which provided accurate information on new dances and matters of current interest.

The 'Washington Post' march was written by J. P. Sousa in June 1889 for a school prize-giving arranged by the newspaper of the same name. The two step danced to this march became so popular that 'Washington Post' became a synonym for the two step in Europe; the Pennsylvania Two Step is a simpler version of the dance.

The 'Victoria Cross' danced to music of the same name by Gustav Howig is one of a number of military two steps. They are danced to brisk marching music with the air of the parade ground and include military salutes.

The polka is a vigorous dance in 2/4 time which was all the rage in the 1840's. Its basic figure is three steps and a hop. The Berlin Polka is a simpler form of the Alsatian Polka in which the chasses in the final section are replaced by 4 bars of the ordinary polka. Elements of these dances are found in the square dance called the Carnival - its author, H. R. Johnson, was a founder member of the British Association of Teachers of Dancing and its President in 1894.

1892 Formation of the British Association of Teachers of Dancing. Prizes were awarded annually by BATD for new sequence dances. Karl Kapps was musical director from 1893-1902; he was made an honorary life member in 1904. James Finnigan joined the association in 1898.

1894 Opening of the Tower Ballroom in Blackpool.

1897 Gramophone records were used to promote songs. Many records appeared after the sensational success of Caruso's recordings of arias in the USA in 1903. The development of the sapphire point in 1912 meant that needles did not need to be changed so frequently.

1897 Some 3,000 dancers could now be accommodated in the Empress Ballroom of the Winter Gardens in Blackpool.

1904 The Palace Ballroom (previously the Alhambra) became Blackpool's third major ballroom - it had a lift which was something of a novelty in those days! Blackpool has always been a favourite venue for dance festivals and conferences.

1900-1904

1900 Veleta, Arthur Morris (Leeds)
1901 Classic, A. H. Brown, 1st Prize BATD
1902 Avena, A. H. Brown, 1st Prize BATD
   "   Fylde Waltz, Tom Almond (Darwen), music by Karl Kapps
1903 Carlina Square Dance, James Finnigan (Manchester)
   "   Eclipse, A. H. Brown
1904 Eva Three Step, Sydney Walter Painter (Snr.)
   "   Raw Recruit (Two Step), Miss (or James) Finnigan
   "   Military Two Step, James Finnigan (Manchester)
   "   Athenium Waltz, S. Bishop (Kilburn)
   "   Chamberlain Valsette, F. Honey (London)
   "   Duchess Barn Dance, A. E. Brown (Blackpool)
   "   Dinky Two Step, A. E. Brown (Blackpool)
   "   Divina (Waltz), D. W. D'Vine (Dublin)

Arthur Morris's Veleta of 1900 did not win a prize at the BATD festival but was an immediate success with the general public; he followed it with the Empire Veleta, Veleta Polka and Carlton Veleta. There are also Derby, Japanese and Tango Veletas and a Veleta Square Dance. Would the inventor recognise his original dance as we dance it today? Arthur Morris lived for many years at Veleta Cottage in Leeds; he was a musical director of BATD (with C. Harris) from 1903 to 1916. The Divina Waltz listed above is described as a new Veleta with all forward movements.

A. H. Brown was president of BATD in 1899. Two of his other dances are the New Skating Waltz and the Lancer Cotillon.

Sydney Painter of Manchester was a large man but very light on his feet; he named the Eva Three Step after his daughter. It was a stately dance in 4/4 time consisting of three steps followed by a point in various directions; it had allemandes and the partners were sometimes in bower position. In Scotland it is played to tunes like 'The Duke of Atholl' and 'Bonnie Dundee' in 6/8 time without using the bower position. It is often performed elsewhere as a jolly marching dance with stamping of feet or hand claps. As Edward Scott would say, "Tempora mutantur!"

The Fylde Waltz of Tom Almond has some attractive and unusual features - it is regarded as one of the neatest of the old-time waltzes. It is now a championship dance (although not in the original OBBD list). It is popular also among the general run of sequence dancers which is not always the case with championship dances. The Esperano Barn Dance (1907) and Oriental Mazurka are two more of his arrangements.

James Finnigan of Manchester and his daughters Florence and Ethel (Mrs. Kerrigan) will always be associated with two steps performed in military fashion. As well as the Victoria Cross (1898) he composed Over the Top (1918) and the Marine Four Step (1911) - named after the Marine Gardens in Portobello, Edinburgh. Some of his other dances are the Carlina Square (1903), Corona Waltz, Hopscotch Schottische (1913), Empire Barn Dance, Jazz Twinkle (1919) and L'Espagnolita (1920). He was MC for a time at the Empress Ballroom, Blackpool and Chairman of the adjudicators there for the festivals of 1921, 1921, 1922; he died in 1923. The Waltz Amelia by Florence Finnigan was very popular in Scotland; it is danced to music of the same name by S. Cunnington. Some authorities attribute it to her father, James Finnigan.

1901 Death of Queen Victoria (born 1819; became queen in 1837). Her consort, Prince Albert, died in 1861.

1903 Formation of the Manchester Association of Teachers of Dancing; this became the Empire Society of Teachers of Dancing (ESTD) in 1938. In 1961 this joined with the Midland Association of Teachers of Dancing (MATD) to become the Dance Teachers' Association (DTA). In 1967 there was a further amalgamation with the International Dance Masters' Association (IDMA) to become the International Dance Teachers' Association (IDTA).

1903 Formation of the United Kingdom Alliance of Professional Teachers of Dancing (UKAPTD, or UKA).

1904 Formation of the Imperial Society of Teachers of Dancing (ISTD). Major C. H. Taylor was President (except for a brief period) from 1904 to 1945; he was also General Secretary from 1932 to 1943. Victor Silvester and Alex Moore and have both held high office in this association.

1905-1908

1905   Eddy Waltz, H. Wilkinson (Huddersfield)
   "   Le Militaire, J. H. Stirling
   "   Moonie, J. H. Randall (Swindon)
1906   Braw Laddie Two Step, A. J. Latimer (Barnet)
   "   Marie Mazurka, A. J. and Marie Latimer (Barnet)
   "   Josephine Mazurka, A. E. Brown (Blackpool)
   "   Princess Ena Quadrille, A.E. Brown (Blackpool), 1st BATD
1907   Hurndilla, W. F. Hurndall (South London)
   "   Empress Promenade Waltz, A. E. Brown (Blackpool)
   "   County Cotillon, Major Cecil H. Taylor (Leeds)
   "   Donnybrook Party Dance, W. F. Hurndall (South London)
   "   La Mascotte, H. Bloodworth, 1st NATD
   "   Esperano Barn Dance, T. Almond (Darwen), 1st BATD
   "   Georgian Waltz, R. B. Kennedy (Lanark)
   "   Royal Two Step, A. E. Brown (Blackpool)
   "   Zerlina Waltz, F. E. Freeborn, 1st BATD
   "   Butterfly Gavotte, Mme A. Collier
1908   Boston Two Step, Tom Walton, 1st BATD
   "   Doris Waltz, J. H. Bickerstaffe
   "   Belgrave Waltz, G. F. Childs
1902/8   Imperial Waltz, James Powell (Kensington), 1st BATD

The mazurka is a fast Polish military-style dance in triple time, popular in ballrooms since the 1850's; it is danced with stamping of feet and clicking of heels. Of its many steps only the *pas de mazurka* survives in the sequence dances; this involves hopping on one foot and whipping the other foot behind in low aerial position. All hopping steps can be made simpler (and less attractive) by replacing the hop by a step - this often occurs in mazurkas, polkas, and schottisches in sequence form. The Oriental Mazurka (T. Almond) and Polka Mazurka are other dances of this period; the Varsovianna, Der Styrien and the Hurndilla have mazurka elements. The Empress Mazurka (David Rollinson, 1954) is possibly the most popular sequence mazurka. The polonaise is another Polish dance of this period. Its stately music is well-suited to the grand parades used at the start of formal dancing occasions. La Czarina by A. E. Brown is a popular sequence dance arranged to polonaise music.

The gavotte is the oldest and slowest of the popular sequence dances of today. In the French courts (1650 onwards) it was a lively circle 'kissing' dance which often followed the minuet. The main step used in sequences is the *pas de gavotte* which consists of a step, close and a point to low aerial position. The Gavotina by Charles D'Albert is another popular dance of this period. It has 16 bars of gavotte in 2/4 time followed by 16 bars of waltzing in triple time; it has a backward *pas de gavotte*. The Butterfly Gavotte became very popular after its inclusion in the 'Take Your Partners' radio programme in March 1950.

La Mascotte took first prize as a novelty dance in 1907 and is sometimes played at 33 bpm. It is really a type of gavotte and is now a championship dance performed at the gavotte tempo of 24 bpm. H. Bloodworth was a member of the executive council of NATD.

The Boston Two Step is based on the *pas de basque* said by Edward Scott to be one of the most beautiful steps used in dancing. It is a championship dance which appears in a more boisterous form at many social dances.

James (Jimmie) Powell of Kensington was a famous teacher of champions who attributed much of his success to the Imperial Waltz. He kept it secret from all but his pupils but eventually entered it at the BATD Congress of 1908 winning first prize. (He was President of BATD in 1905.) It has always been considered to be a good teaching dance since it contains the *pas de valse* forward and backward, solo turns and other waltz figures. There is some mystery about this dance as A. J. Worrall writing in the 'Dancing Times' of 1960 said that an Imperial Waltz by J. Powell won 1st prize at the BATD conference of 1894.

1907 The National Association of Teachers of Dancing (NATD) was formed as the Southern Dance Teachers' Association in 1907; it was the first association to institute medal awards for ballroom dancers in 1932.

1909 - 1912

1909 Latchford Schottische, Mme. M. Oldbury, 1st BATD
"   La Rinka (Skating Waltz), W. F. Hurndall (South London)
"   Superbe [Valse], Charles W. Gardner, 1st NATD
"   Fillebrook Waltz, A. J. and Marie Latimer (Barnet)
"   Navy Two Step, Mme. Emily Jones (Bolton)
"   Bonnie Lassie (Party Dance), Mr. Webb, 2nd NATD
1910 La Rosa (Waltz), George Chester (London), 1st NATD
"   Minuet [Waltz], R. M. Crompton
"   Helbe Two Step, James Stewart (Edinburgh)
"   Truro Gavotte, A. J. Latimer (Barnet)
"   Colorado Two Step, described by Billy Smith
1911 Pride of Erin Waltz, C. S. Wood (Edinburgh), 1st BATD
"   Mississippi Dip, C. S. Wood (Edinburgh)
"   Marine Four Step, James Finnigan (Manchester)
1912 Florentine Waltz, G. Birkenshaw (Chesterfield)
"   Mascot One Step, H. R. Johnson (London), BATD
"   Empress One Step, A. J. Latimer (Barnet)
"   Carlton, Master Eric Law Hurndall (London)
"   Dorothy Waltz, D. McLeod, 1st UKAPTD
"   1912 Tango

The Latchford Schottische is a popular 12 bar sequence still used in old-time championships. The schottische ending is usually replaced by bars of waltzing. Victor Silvester thought it had some similarities to the Butterfly Gavotte (1907). Bill Botham's 'Guide to Music for MC's and Band Leaders' published for FSDI says, "The Latchford Schottische, La Mascotte, Gainsborough Glide, Butterfly Gavotte and Eva Three Step are all gavotte in style and nearly all gavotte music can be used ... ".

La Rinka is an example of a 'skating' waltz. Long gliding steps are used and the partners often use a crossed-hands hold in side-by-side position to simulate the actions of skaters. French waltzes tended to be more languid and feminine and were played at a more deliberate pace than their Viennese counterparts - a typical example being 'Les Patineurs' (The Skaters) written by Emile Waldteufel. The Skaters Waltz, New Skating Waltz (A. H. Brown) and Rinking (1939) are other sequences of this type.

C. S. (Charles) Wood (born in 1875) taught dancing all over the world for more than 70 years. Often known as 'Professor' he was a dancing master in the old style. He wore tails and white gloves when teaching and controlled his students by whistle and baton. He once stopped the band at a formal dance when the dancers were going astray in his Pride of Erin Waltz! He was a dancer of great artistry. One demonstration dance he made famous (with his partner, Miss Alice Ross) was the Spanish Fandango. The fandango is a Spanish dance in 3/4 time which goes faster and faster but stops at intervals when the dancers stand like statues; there is much snapping of fingers and shaking of castanets - not an ideal dance for a 16-bar sequence! Wood's dance is performed to 'Fandango Espagnole' by Ray Downes and has hopping steps and stamping of feet; it is really a party dance to put life into the proceedings.

The Mississippi Dip listed above is a type of one step but dances well to rag-time music although you need your partner's support for the dip! It is said that tunes like 'On the Mississippi' and 'California Here I Come' had more to do with its success rather than the dance itself. Nowadays it is sometimes played at quickstep tempo as a fun dance on festive occasions. Dances of this type are forerunners of the modern quickstep. Other dances by C. S. Wood are the Queen's Waltz (1920) and Cavendish Two Step (1949).

Professor Wood was MC for a time at the Marine Gardens in Portobello near Edinburgh. This was an early version of a modern leisure centre set in extensive gardens on the shores of the Firth of Forth; the ballroom added a year later in 1910 was half the size of a football pitch. (This ballroom closed in 1939 never again to be used for dancing.) James Finnigan's Marine Four Step listed above takes its name from this complex. The dance itself is in military style with 3 marching steps and a point (or sometimes a hop) taken both forward and backwards. Why it is called a four step is something of a mystery - the Eva Three Step has a series of three steps and a point and is called a three step! There are relatively few sequence three steps and four steps; one of F. J. Mainey's lists has the Cara Five Step!

The one step in its original form was a smooth walking dance in 2/4 time. With the introduction of ragtime music, however, rhythm and trotting steps were introduced and a host of 'animal' dances appeared such as the bunny hug, turkey trot and camel walk. The one step tended to lose its identity, although still appearing on dance programmes; it had become the rag - a form of one step played to syncopated rhythms. A great exponent of the one step in all its variations was Vernon Castle (real name Vernon Blyth) - he has been described as the 'Father of Modern Dancing'. He and his wife Irene revolutionised the social dancing scene in America from 1910 to the middle period of the Great War producing dances such as the Castle Walk, Castle House Rag, Castle Tango and Castle Lame Duck. Before 1910 much emphasis was placed on steps; afterwards bodily rhythm became the driving force with foot-tapping tunes that urged people onto the dance floor. As Vernon Castle says: "The Waltz is beautiful, the Tango is graceful, the Brazilian Maxixe is unique. One can sit quietly and listen to them all; but when a good orchestra plays a 'rag' one has simply got to move. The One Step is the dance for rag-time music."

Many dance historians say that the one step displaced the two step at this time but this is certainly not the case for sequence dancing. The two step is now the only common dance in 6/8 played to a marching rhythm and still adds welcome variety to sequence dancing programmes. The one step in contrast has largely disappeared although some of its elements appear in the modern quickstep. A modern script list shows almost 100 two steps including the Grenadier Two Step (1993) with only 7 one steps.

The tango has somewhat disreputable origins in South America. As the 'Argentine tango' it became very popular in London from 1910-1914 when 'tango teas' were all the rage. At this time it had many steps and dancers hardly progressed round the ballroom floor, which made it an ideal dance for small drawing rooms and restaurants. The 1912 tango listed above is a sequence dance from this period. The tango fell from favour during the war but reappeared in a more acceptable form from 1919 onwards (see later).

1913 Hop Scotch Schottische, James Finnigan
" Vestris (Minuet), W. Robertson (Montrose)
" King's Waltz, A. E. Brown (Blackpool)
" Freda Waltz, Alfred Smith (Oldham)
" Georgian Gavotte, Tom Almond (Darwen), 1st BATD
" St. Bernard Waltz, Billy Smith (Glasgow)
1914 L'Inspiration Gavotte, Mrs. H. G. Roscoe (Mansfield)
" Devonia (Waltz), A. Lugg (Croydon)
" Killarney Two Step, Billy Smith (Glasgow)
1915 Rose of Killarney Waltz, Billy Smith (Glasgow)
" Loyalty Waltz, Fred Moore
1907/15 Gay Gordons
1916 De Triomphe [Valse], C. J. Daniels
" Saunter, A. J. Latimer (Barnet)
1917 Chrysanthemum Waltz, James Telford and A. Bell
" Maxina, Mme. A. Low-Hurndall (South London), 1st BATD
" On Leave Foxtrot, Mary Cheshire (Burton-on-Wirral)
" Sovereign Two Step, Alfred Smith
" King's Paso Doble, W. F. Hurndall (South London)

The minuet is a slow stately dance for couples, dating from the 17th century. It is performed to music in 3/4 time with emphasis on each beat; it is however light and delicate as opposed to the strong style of the mazurka. The *pas de minuet* is a small step in which the feet are hardly raised from the floor; the bow and curtsey at the beginning of the dance are deeper than usual. The Vestris minuet above is named after the family of great ballet dancers. Auguste Vestris (born Paris in 1760) was considered to be one of the greatest male dancers of all time. The Chamberlain Valsette (1904) has minuet movement in both first and second parts. Of the handful of sequence minuets the Royal Minuet (1947) is the most popular.

The Waltz Minuet (1910) has 10 bars of minuet followed by 32 bars of waltzing which is then repeated. The Minuet Lancers was a popular square dance in Victorian times. It was danced to Lancers music but in minuet fashion with deeper salutations and a pause on the last beat of every bar.

The St. Bernard Waltz (Knock-Knock dance) is still featured in the social dancing sessions of today, becoming popular again after 1937. Its arranger, Billy Smith, was President of the Scottish MC's Association in 1962 when he was 83 years old. On behalf of this association he compiled a book of scripts in the 1950's which included the St. Bernard Waltz. Among the 6 other dances bearing his name is the 'Pride of Erin Waltz - arranged by Billy Smith 1913'. There is some mystery here as this waltz is usually attributed to C. S. Wood of Edinburgh (see earlier).

The Gay Gordons is a marching dance in 6/8 time, often danced in Scotland and at tea dances. It starts in Maxina hold with the man slightly behind the lady with the same hands held above shoulder height - both face down the line of dance. There is some disagreement about its history: some give a date of 1907 and music by G. H. Record; others state August 1915 with music by James Scott Skinner originally called the Gordon Highlander's March.

The Maxina by Mme. Low-Hurndall is a 24 bar sequence dance with music of the same name written by M. Bissonade and W. F. Hurndall. It is said to have some elements of the Brazilian Maxixe (or Maxiste) which is a vigorous dance with graceful sways and low dips. The Maxixe was the third most popular dance in the USA in 1914 and is the parent of the modern samba. The Maxina was written off by many authors of early textbooks but is still danced today. To paraphrase Mark Twain - reports of its demise have been greatly exaggerated!

Mr. W. F. Hurndall from South London was a dance teacher who managed to overcome the handicap of an artificial leg. He arranged and wrote the music for several sequence dances which he was able to demonstrate very effectively. Some of his dances are the Donnybrook Party Dance (1907), the Hurndilla (1907) and the Popular Jazz (1919). He also produced a new version of the Maxina in 1920 which caused considerable confusion. His King's Paso Doble listed above was much before its time; the script says at one point that the partners look at one another with a defiant Spanish expression!

1918-1919

1918 Ladbroke, George Chester
  "   Over the Top (Two Step), James Finnigan (Manchester)
  "   Jazz Dance, W. A. Worrall (Gillingham)
  "   Dinky One Step
  "   Honeymoon Parade, C. J. Daniels
  "   Tantivita (Two Step), B. Durrans (Oldham)
  "   Carina Waltz, Tom Hayton (Manchester)
1919 Tango Waltz, C. J. Daniels
  "   Moonlight Saunter, C. J. Daniels
  "   Yearning Saunter, Harry Boyle
  "   Popular Jazz, W. F. Hurndall (South London)
  "   Jazz Twinkle, James Finnigan (Manchester)
  "   Cazaret, B. Durrans (Oldham), 1st BATD
  "   Jazzina, A. E. Brown (Blackpool)
  "   Hula Yale Blues
  "   Bradford Progressive Barn Dance, C. J. Daniels
  "   Delight [Valse], J. H. Bickerstaffe (Blackpool)
  "   Demure [Waltz], J. H. Bickerstaffe
  "   Eulalie Waltz, J. H. Bickerstaffe (Blackpool)

The Ladbroke is an unusual dance in 4/4 time still performed today which starts with partners side-by-side in a maxina hold; there is a Scottish Ladbroke (1957) by Ralph Ward (London). La Rosa (1910), the London Tango and Glen Mona are other dances by George Chester.

The Dinky One Step is still a popular party dance. Like the Square Tango, Eugene Tango, Donella Tango and Evening Waltz, its origins are uncertain - perhaps like Topsy it 'just growed'. The Jazz dances listed above are really syncopated one-steps (rags) - forerunners of the modern foxtrot and quickstep. The Jazz Twinkle is the most popular of these early dances; it was standardised by the Official Board in a somewhat modified form.

The Cazaret is danced to the music of the same name by Armand Falk. It is a sequence based on waltz figures adapted to slow music in common time.

It is sometimes said that a poor dancer cannot tell a waltz from a tango! By taking 1 step to 3 beats in 3/4 time, however, it is possible to introduce gliding tango steps into a waltz and Charles Daniel's Tango Waltz starts in this way. La Valsa (1921) is another example of a hesitation waltz; this type of dance was popular in the USA when the Boston was in full swing. An old-time tango like the Tango Serida can be performed to Viennese Waltz music to give an element of variety on festive occasions.

The name 'saunter' was suggested by P. J. S. Richardson of the 'Dancing Times' for a dance of foxtrot type in which steps were made "without hurry and without jumping". A. J. Latimer's Saunter was the winner of a 'Dance News' competition held in 1916 to devise a dance to fit the dreamy, relaxed played by some American bands; it was danced to 'Underneath the Stars'. Saunters were based on a slow, leisurely walk coupled with the better figures of the foxtrot. They provided a restful, smooth alternative to the more vigorous dances with hopping and jumping steps which were the order of the day. Saunters are particularly suited to the older dancers, only tangos and waltzes being more popular in the clubs today. The Moonlight Saunter was an early championship dance which was revised as the London Moonlight Saunter by W. F. Hurndall in 1920. The Yearning Saunter is still taught and danced and exists also in a party version.

Charles Daniels arranged more than 50 dances from 1915 to 1945 including the Palais Glide (1928). Some of C. J. Daniels prize-winners are the Celebration Waltz, Moonlight Waltz, Valse Divine (1923) and Valse Tres Bon; Pom Pom, Society and Whitley Foxtrots; Carnival Two Step, Jollity Parade, International Blues, Parisienne Tango Saunter, Tangena and All Change Walk (1939). His popular Bradford Barn Dance is named after his dance school held in the Bradford Hall in Swindon; it is sometimes known as the Canadian Barn Dance. He was President of the Northern Counties Dance Teachers' Association in 1930 and compiled a book of dance scripts for the old-time revival. His son, Gilbert, carries on the family traditions.

Several of the 1920 dances above are arranged by the Blackpool rivals A. E. Brown and J. H. Bickerstaffe. Blackpool has been the leading northern holiday resort for many years and with its Tower, Empress, Palace and other ballrooms it is ideal for large-scale dancing events. The first Blackpool Dance Festival took place in the Empress Ballroom of the Winter Gardens in 1920 with Albert Brown as MC. There were competitions for new sequence dances based on the waltz, the two step and the foxtrot - a day being devoted to each style. Each couple had to submit a script and music and demonstrate their dance before the adjudicators and the MC. Eventually first, second and third winners were chosen and the dances taught first to the assembled teachers and later to the general public at the evening ball. Apart from gaps in 1928 and the war years, this festival has been a major event for both ballroom and sequence dancers over the years. The festival is now run by the Blackpool Tower Company and is held for a week during the middle of October.

The first winner of the old-time sequence dance competition after the war was Mr. C. M. Farmer with his Festival of Britain Waltz in 1950; when the modern section was included in 1965 the winning dance was the Sylvellen Waltz by Mr. S. Burrows of Haydock.

Some of A. E. Brown's dances are: Dinky Two Step (1904), Duchess Barn Dance (1904), Princess Ena Quadrille (1906), Josephine Mazurka (1906), Empress Promenade Waltz (1907), Royal Two Step (1907), King's Waltz (1913), Jazzina (1919), New Empress Waltz (1920), Queen's Waltz (1920), Tangino (1921), New Skating Waltz, Luna Waltz, Waltz Edna, Sylvan Tango, Tanks Saunter and Tingle Tangle. A. E. Brown was MC at the Empress Ballroom for 16 years up to 1922; he was Vice President of BATD in 1904.

J. H. Bickerstaffe was his rival at the Tower Ballroom. Some of his dances are: Doris Waltz (1908), Valse Delight, Waltz Demure and Eulalie Waltz (all 1919), Dapper Dandy Foxtrot, Dorina Waltz and Queen's Waltz (all 1920), Florida Waltz (1921), Sweet Steps Waltz and Tower Tango.

1920

1920 Square Tango
- " Gipsy Tango I, C. J. Daniels, NATD
- " Gipsy Tango II, Arthur Wantling (Manchester)
- " Gipsy Tango III, John Evans and Miss Millicent Clayton
- " Chicago Maze, Mme. Collyns (Stockport), 1st UKAPTD
- " Toledo Waltz, W. A. Worrall (Gillingham), BATD
- " Parma Waltz, Miss N. C. Locke (Sunderland), BATD
- " London Moonlight Saunter, W. F. Hurndall (Sth London)
- " New Maxina, W. F. Hurndall (South London)
- " Ritz, H. R. Johnson (London), BATD
- " L'Espagnolita, James Finnigan (Manchester)
- " Queen's Waltz I, A. E. Brown (Blackpool)
- " Queen's Waltz II, J. H. Bickerstaffe (Blackpool)
- " Queen's Waltz III, C. S. Wood (Edinburgh)
- " New Empress Waltz, A. E. Brown (Blackpool)
- " Dappy Dandy Foxtrot, J. H. Bickerstaffe (Blackpool)
- " Dorina Waltz, J. H. Bickerstaffe (Blackpool)
- " Elita [Valse], H. G. Roscoe (Mansfield), 1st Blackpool
- " Festival Two Step, H. G. Roscoe, 2nd Blackpool

The foxtrot was an off-shoot of the one step and rag arriving from America in 1915. Opinions are divided as to whether it resembled the trotting steps of a fox or took its name from the stage routines of Harry Fox. Foxtrots were played in 4/4 time and consisted at that time of a slow, springy walk (2 beats) and a trotting step (1 beat). Sometimes the music had a break when the partners bent the knee and raised one foot backwards. Faster tempos were used than today and steps were often exaggerated when the music became lively. By 1925 the dance began to separate into a slow foxtrot and a faster foxtrot-cum-Charleston, now known as the quickstep. Early sequence slow foxtrots were similar to saunters in having elements of the waltz and tango and being performed to music of a relaxed nature without too much accent on the beats. The modern sequence slow foxtrot did not gain official recognition until the late 1960's. (The first booklet of 23 sequence dances for competition purposes issued by the Official Board in 1966 did not contain a modern version of the slow foxtrot.)

1921-1922

1921 Lilah [Valse], Adela Roscoe (Notts), 1st Blackpool
" Bluebird Waltz, Arthur Lister (Blackpool)
" El Chucó
" Tangino, A. E. Brown (Blackpool)
" La Valsa, George C. Howard (Barnsley), 2nd BATD
" Hesitango (Hesitation Waltz), A. J. Latimer (Barnet)
" Broadway Foxtrot, Miss N. C. Locke, 1st BATD
" Florida Waltz, J. H. Bickerstaffe (Blackpool)
1922 Royal Empress Tango, Adela Roscoe, 1st Blackpool
" Lola Tango, Arthur Wantling (Manchester), ESTD
" Magique [Valse], Miss N. C. Locke, 2nd BATD
" Chin Chin (One Step), Malcolm Munro and Mary Daly
" Progressive Waltz I, A. J. Latimer (Barnet)
" Mona Foxtrot, Tom Hayton, 1st BATD

After the war the tango came back again into favour as a simple dance with fewer steps. Rudolph Valentino gave it a great fillip with his films 'The Four Horsemen of the Apocalypse' and 'The Sheik' in 1921 and the 'Son of the Sheik' in 1926. These inspired the writing of at least 6 Gipsy sequence tangos. The popular Square Tango (1920) is more of a saunter to tango music and the Lola and Royal Empress Tangos have more real tango style. The modern tango with its staccato rhythm and rapid head movements can be said to date from 1935 when Freddie Camp from Germany electrified the dancing world with his new dancing style at the Open British Championships. He had an extraordinary capacity for 'exploding from stillness'. Modern tangos are played in milonga rhythm with an insistent beat and 'brighter' melodies.

Tom Hayton from Manchester joined BATD in 1904 and was President in 1933; he died in 1948. He was a dapper little man and it was said that what he didn't know about old-time dancing was hardly worth knowing. He was well-known for his work as steward at the Blackpool festivals. Two of his other dances are the Esme Waltz and the Carina Waltz (1918).

1922 The Allied Dancing Association (ADA) was founded by Malcolm Munro of Liverpool.

1923-1929

1923 Cosmo, A. J. Latimer (Barnet)
" Divine [Valse], C. J. Daniels, 1st Blackpool
" Feline Trot, A. J. and Marie Latimer (Barnet)
" Foxette, W. Lugg (Croydon)
" L. A. Blues, A. J. Latimer (Barnet)
" Simplicity Waltz, E. Matthewman (Pontefract), BATD
" Supreme [Waltz], A. J. Latimer (Barnet), BATD
1924 Nadine [Valse], H. G. Roscoe (Mansfield), 1st Blackpool
" Bluette, A. J. Latimer (Barnet), BATD
" Baltilat, A. J. Latimer (Barnet)
" Ayanden [Valse], A. J. Latimer (Barnet)
" New Valse, E. Matthewman (Pontefract)
1925 Tutankamen Dream Tango, 1st Blackpool
" Chinese Tango, 2nd Blackpool
" Linda Foxtrot, Adela Roscoe (Notts), 3rd Blackpool
1926 Charlestrot, A. J. Latimer (Barnet)
1919/26 Pom Pom Foxtrot, C. J. Daniels, 1st Blackpool
1927 Yale Blues, Major C. H. Taylor
1928 Hezito (Waltz), W. A. Greenwell, 1st BATD
" Palais Glide (Line Party Dance), C. J. Daniels
1929 Lingering Blues, Adela Roscoe (Notts)
" Otas Waltz, Charles B. Selby (North London)

At least four members of the Roscoe family from Mansfield, Nottinghamshire were members of BATD, joining dates being H. G. 1904, Mrs. H. G. (Mme. A. E.) 1909, daughter Edna 1925, daughter Adela 1936. Mr. H. G. Roscoe won at Blackpool with Waltz Elita (1920) and Waltz Nadine (1924). Mme. Adela Roscoe won with Waltz Lilah (1921) and the Royal Empress Tango (1922) (dancing with H. A. Clifton); she was third in 1925 with Linda Foxtrot. The daughter, Miss Adela Roscoe, dancing with Cyril Farmer was British Professional Ballroom Champion in 1937 and 1938. As well as the Lingering Blues (1929) she was the arranger of many other sequence dances in the 1950's (see later).

The Otas Waltz was named after the 'Old-Time and Sequence' clubs conducted by Charles Selby. It became popular again in 1951 after its inclusion in old-time radio programmes.

The blues is similar to the foxtrot but has a characteristic lilting step and the music has more accent on the four beats. Great efforts were made to promote the blues as a ballroom dance. Go-as-you-please (non-sequence) dances included Blues Trot (Mary Blake, 1923); Imperial Blues (M. Camille de Rhynal, 1923); Yale Blues (Major Cecil H. Taylor, 1927); Charleston Blues (Victor Silvester, 1933). (The Yale Blues seems to have appeared first as a sequence dance - a reversal of the usual process of ballroom first, sequence form later.) The blues never really took off as a ballroom dance but it survives today (without the lilt) as the slow social rhythm dance. Alex Moore, dancing with his sister Avis, won the open competition at the 'Blues Ball' organised by the 'Dancing Times' in 1923. Blues in sequence form have remained popular over the years - at least 90 scripts being available. The Lingering Blues (1929) is still played in the clubs; one of the latest is the Aqua Blues (1994). Some early dances such as the Manhattan Blues and Georgella Blues (1951) are played at a faster quickstep tempo.

The early 1920's were a time of reaction against the formal dances of the past and go-as-you-please dances such as the Shimmy (1919), Charleston (1922) and Black Bottom (1926) became fashionable. Everyone danced in their own style and there were many freak steps which impeded (and sometimes harmed) fellow dancers. The Imperial Society of Teachers of Dancing (ISTD) formed a Ballroom branch in 1924 in an attempt to bring order out of the chaos. A committee was set up to standardise dancing figures and technique. The members were Miss Josephine Bradley, Miss Eve Tyngate Smith, Miss Muriel Simmons, Mrs. Lisle Humphries and Mr. Victor Silvester. From their deliberations over several years emerged the 'English style' of ballroom dancing with its rise and fall, sway, footwork, contrary body movement and standard figures; close body contact is maintained at all times so that the man can lead his partner and give a good line. This technique applies mainly to the modern waltz, quickstep and slow foxtrot (and to a lesser extent the modern tango). This technique for the 'standard four' is the approved style for the modern sequence dancer.

The foundations of modern sequence dancing (as distinct from old-time) were laid in 1928 by Miss Belle Harding. She ran a famous dancing school in Kensington and, after teaching Victor Silvester, she employed him as an instructor and professional partner. She was a woman of considerable vision and organising ability and did much to make the tango and foxtrot popular in their early years. Phyllis Haylor has sketched her as a dowager holding a lorgnette! From 1928 onwards she ran courses for professional teachers at which modern dances like the waltz, tango and foxtrot were performed in 16 bar sequences. Many teachers from the north attended these sessions including Malcolm Munro of Liverpool - the founder of ADA. Miss Harding was well before her time - it was not until the 1960's that the modern sequence style received widespread official recognition.

1923 Dance music broadcast by the BBC more for entertainment than for dancing. Henry Hall, Jack Hylton, Jack Payne and Ambrose became household names.

1925 Formation of the Northern Counties Dance Teachers' Association (NCDTA). It was known originally as the Northern Professional Dance Circle.

1929 Formation of the Official Board of Ballroom Dancing (OBBD); this consisted of representatives from the recognised dancing associations with some independent members. In 1975 the name was changed to the British Council of Ballroom Dancing (BCBD). At the present time corporate members are: Allied Dancing Association, Ballroom Dancers' Federation, First Leisure Corporation PLC, English Amateur Dancers' Association, Butlin's Ltd., British Association of Teachers of Dancing, Imperial Society of Teachers of Dancing, International Dance Teachers' Association, Mecca Ltd., National Association of Teachers of Dancing, Northern Counties Dance Teachers' Association, Scottish Amateur Ballroom Dancers' Association, Scottish Dance Teachers' Alliance, United Kingdom Alliance, Welsh Alliance of Teachers of Dancing, Welsh Amateur Dancers' Association, Dance Promoters Association.

1930-1936

1930 Blue Bell Waltz, Walter James Carvill
" Tapper, Adela Roscoe (Notts), 1st Blackpool
1931 City Blues, Billy Lang
1932 Serenata, Albert Cowan (Manchester), 1st Blackpool
" Marina Waltz, Danny MacMillan
" La Fanatique Tango, John Pitt
1933 Trixie Tango, J. Comensey
" San Francisco Blues, Bobby Steward
1934 Robertina (or Roberta) Tango, J. McIntyre
1936 Swingtime
" Blue Rhythm, Frank Handford, 1st Blackpool

Mr. Albert Cowan (1 of 9 brothers) ran a dance school in Moss Side, Manchester. He was for many years Chairman of the Old-Time Committee of the Official Board and he acted as adjudicator at the Blackpool and Star Championships on numerous occasions. His Serenata has proved to be a versatile dance being played in 4/4 time (28 bpm), 2/4 time (38 bpm) and 6/8 time (56 bpm). The Emperor Waltz (1949) was another of his dances. He died in February 1978 at the age of 91.

Swingtime was inspired by the film of the same name with music by Jerome Kern; Fred Astaire and Ginger Rogers gave their usual marvellous performances. The sequence dance was adapted to fit the song 'A Fine Romance'. Swingtime was very popular in the Manchester district, particularly in the Coronation Ballroom in Belle Vue. This ballroom was part of the Zoological and Botanical Gardens, rightly called the 'Playground of the North' - it was the venue for the Area finals of the Butlins Veleta Competition and many other important events. Dancers came from far afield to enjoy the music, dancing and fireworks. It took an early part in the revival with the famous Fred Bonelli and his orchestra playing for old-time dancing every Tuesday and Thursday from 1941 onwards. A fire in 1958 destroyed three ballrooms (and Bonelli's priceless collection of music) but they were restored in 1960 on a truly magnificent scale - there was underfloor lighting with colour effects, floors of Canadian maple and excellent bar facilities.

1937-1945

1937 V8, Cyril Bourne (Nottingham), 1st Blackpool
1938 Dream Waltz, Major Cecil H. Taylor
" Hoop-a-La, Alec Hooper, 1st Blackpool
" Palais Stroll, Alec Hooper
" 1938 Polka
1939 All Change Walk, C. J. Daniels
" Rinking (Skating Waltz), Major Cecil H. Taylor (Leeds)
1940 Blue Danube Waltz, F. J. Mainey
1944 Fascination Waltz I, Dora Reid, 1st ESTD, Hayton Trophy
1945 Swingola (O/T Waltz) ('Cruising Down The River')

Alec Hooper's Hoop-a-La was a foretaste of things to come - it was a sensational winner at the Blackpool Festival of 1938. It was played originally at a tempo intermediate between that of the modern foxtrot and quickstep. It had a Merry-go-Round (a propelled pivot turn), a Breakaway (a fallaway with a cross) and a Ritzy Stroll (a zig-zag to the right). In the clubs it was often played in quickstep time with a spin turn replacing the propelled pivot.

F. J. Mainey was a prominent architect of the old-time revival (see later). It is said that he once had an uncomfortable experience with his Blue Danube Waltz. It had become the fashion to replace the usual 2 or 4 bar introduction of early waltzes (for the dancers to set their rhythm) by greatly extended introductions for the concert waltzes. On this occasion the orchestra gave the full treatment and the dancers had to wait for a while to get into action!

1930 Formation of the International Dancing Masters' Association (IDMA) by the amalgamation of The English Association of Dancing Masters, The Universal Association of Teachers of Dancing, The Premier Association of Teachers of Dancing and the Yorkshire Association of Dancing Masters. In 1967 it merged with the Dance Teachers' Association to become the International Dance Teachers' Association (IDTA).
1932 Formation of Scottish MC's Dancing Association (SMCDA).
1934 Formation of Scottish Dance Teachers' Alliance (SDTA).

Social Dancing in the 1940's

Ballroom dancing became very popular in the late 1930's - there were programmes on the radio (and later on TV) and textbooks were written by Victor Silvester, Alex Moore and others. The dancing figures, techniques and tempos of the modern waltz, foxtrot, quickstep and tango had been standardised and there were many more competitions. Social dancing became a popular pastime, particularly for young adults. The dance became the place to meet everyone and (along with the cinema) became part of the courtship ritual. There were many dancing sessions with live music which later became a welcome distraction for service personnel on leave. Programmes consisted of the standard four dances with simple sequence dances to give variety - Barn Dance, Veleta, Military Two Step, St. Bernard Waltz and newer novelty dances like the Lambeth Walk and Hokey Cokey; there were Paul Jones and excuse-me dances to encourage change of partners. This pattern persisted until the late 1940's when free-style dances like the jive, rock 'n' roll and twist began to take over from the standard four.

Among the more mature dancers, sequence dancing was coming back into favour. Belle Vue in Manchester had old-time sessions in 1941 and 'Those Were The Days' started on BBC in 1943. F. J. Mainey started his International Sequence (Old Time) Dance Circle in 1944 and the Midland Association of Teachers of Dancing in 1945 could report the existence of a "thriving Old-Time section". By the end of the war the old-time 'boom' was well on its way and dances with a more modern flavour and timing were beginning to emerge. Some sessions were old time, others popular sequence, but most were a mixture of the two styles; some MC's had dancing qualifications, others were gifted amateurs with 'a following'. The gradual emergence of the modern form of sequence dancing from this state of confusion is dealt with in the following chapter. (Modern sequence dancing was recognised as a separate classification by the Official Board in 1965 and a handbook containing 23 modern sequence dances for competition purposes appeared in 1966.)

Novelty Dances

Novelty or fun dances provide an element of gaiety on festive occasions. They are simple line, square or circle sequences readily performed by all. They often involve imitative actions with hands, arms and body and usually have their own music. A few well-known dances of this period are described below.

1928 Palais Glide, C. J. Daniels. Rows of dancers link arms behind in side-by-side position and perform an 8-bar sequence of kicking and ronde steps.

1937 Lambeth Walk, steps by Adele England, music by Noel Gay. This dance is adapted from the Lupino Lane show, 'Me and My Gal'. It has the swaggering Cockney walk, slapping of knees and shouts of "Oi".

1938 Chestnut Tree, Adele England and C. L. Heiman.

1938 Knees Up Mother Brown, Adele England, music by Harris Weston and Bert Lee.

1939 Boomps-a-Daisy, Annette Mills - sister to John Mills, the actor. She was a Charleston champion and manipulator of 'Muffin the Mule' on TV.

1939 Sequence Conga, 'I came, I saw, I conga'd [conquered]' from veni, vidi, vici. The dancers move forward in a long snake with hands on waist of person in front doing 3 steps and a sideways kick in unison.

1942 Cokey Cokey (Hokey Cokey in UK), Jimmie Kennedy, "You put your left arm out ... ". This dance, based on a traditional melody, came over with Canadian troops during the war; it may be performed in lines, circles or loose ballroom hold.

Books:- Old Time and Novelty Dances (1944), Major Cecil H. Taylor, Dancing Times Limited;
Party Dances (1993), Nancy Clarke, IDTA.

Square Dances

Square dances are sequence-style dances for sets of 4 couples facing one another across a square. They are sometimes called 'set' dances although this term is sometimes used to mean dances like the Dashing White Sergeant, Sir Roger de Coverley or the Siege of Ennis where the dancers form up in two lines.

In square dances the Master of Ceremonies acts as caller using certain key phrases such as "set to partners" or "advance and retire". Sometimes all the couples are in action; at other times one or two couples will dance while the rest look on. A dance such as the Lancers has five sections and will take about 20 minutes - old-style cotillons had many sections and might last for 1-2 hours!

Quadrilles This name has roots suggesting both 'four' and 'square' and it is sometimes used as a general term for square dances. The dance came to England from France in the early 19th century. There are many quadrilles - one version has been standardised by the Official Board; the Princess Imperial Quadrille was danced at the Blackpool festival in 1953.

Lancers This is a type of quadrille dating from 1820 which was popular in London ballrooms from 1850 onwards. A rowdy, boisterous version of the dance is known as the Kitchen Lancers.

Cotillon *(or cotillion)* Many dances in the 19th century ended with a cotillon in which the hostess chose the figures - it was more of a game than a dance and could take up considerable time. Its most popular form today is the Waltz Cotillon in which the waltz plays a major part. Arthur Morris arranged a Royal Cotillon; Major C. H. Hart's County Cotillon of 1907 was revived in 1950.

Caledonians A popular square dance in which all dancers are more frequently occupied. It consists of 5 figures the first of which is danced twice, the remainder 4 times.

A Select List of Old-Time Dances

A very useful selection of popular old-time sequence dances was produced by Albert Cowan in 1947 on behalf of the Official Board of Ballroom Dancing (a body established in 1928 to co-ordinate the activities of the various dancing associations). A committee of experts spent many hours in selecting and standardising the dances listed below; details are taken from the second completely revised edition of 1950.

Championship Dances: Waltz, Veleta (1900), Military Two Step (1904), Boston Two Step (1908), Royal Empress Tango(1922) Latchford Schottische (1909), Lola Tango (1922), Moonlight Saunter (1919), Destiny Waltz (1949).

Waltzes: Carina (1918), Chrysanthemum (1917), Devonia (1914), Doris (1908), Florentine (1912), Fylde (1902), Hesitation (1947), Imperial (1902-8), King's (1913), La Rinka (1909), La Rosa (1910), Tango (1919), Superbe (1909), Viennese Sequence Waltz, Pride of Erin (1911).

Tangos: Donella, Square (1920).

Barn Dances: Barn (1880), Esperano (1907).

Misc: Dinky One Step (1918), Eva Three Step (1904), Gay Gordons (1907/1915), Glen Mona, Highland Schottische (1855), Hurndilla (1907), Jazz Twinkle (1919), Ladbroke (1918), Marine Four Step (1911), Maxina (1917), On Leave Foxtrot (1917), Oriental Mazurka, Serenata (1932), Yearning Saunter (1919).

Square Dances: Caledonians, Carnival (1895), Lancers, Quadrilles, Waltz Cotillon.

The Viennese Sequence Waltz by Jack Mercer was originally called the Viennese Waltz - the name was changed to avoid confusion with the quick ballroom waltz.

Index of Early Sequence Dances (Up to 1945)

Gavottes

Butterfly, 1907
Gavotina, p.19
Georgian, 1913
La Mascotte, 1907
L'Inspiration, 1914
Truro, 1910

One-Steps

Chin Chin, 1922
Dinky, 1918
Empress, 1912
Mascot, 1912
Cosmo, 1923

Barn Dances

Barn, 1880
Bradford (Canadian Progressive), 1919
Duchess, 1904
Empire, p.17
Esperano, 1907
Pas de Quatre, 1886

Mazurkas

Der Styrien, p.18
Marie, 1906
Josephine, 1906
La Varsovianna, 1850

Oriental, p.17, 18, 38
Polka Mazurka, p.18

Polkas

Alsatian, 1894
Berlin, 1894
1938 (Polka), 1938

Square Dances

Caledonians, p.37, 38
Carlina Square, 1903
Carnival, 1895
County Cotillon, 1907
Lancer Cotillon, p.16
Lancers, p.37, 38
Minuet Lancers, p.23
Princess Ena Quadrille, 1906
Quadrilles, p.38
Royal Cotillon, p.37
Veleta, p.16
Waltz Cotillon, p.38

Miscellaneous

All Change Walk, 1939
Avena, 1902
Baltilat, 1924
Blue Rhythm, 1936
Bluette, 1924
Bonnie Lassie (Party), 1909

Boomps-a-Daisy, 1939
Carlton, 1912
Castle Walk, p.22
Castle House Rag, p.22
Castle Lame Duck, p.22
Cazaret, 1919
Charlestrot, 1926
Chestnut Tree, 1938
Chicago Maze, 1920
Classic, 1901
Cosmo, 1923
Donnybrook Party Dance, 1907
Eclipse, 1903
El Chuco, 1921
Eva Three Step, 1904
Feline Trot, 1923
Foxette, 1923
Gay Gordons, 1907/15
Glen Mona, p.25, 38
Hokey Cokey, 1942
Honeymoon Parade, 1918
Hurndilla, 1907
Hoop-a-La, 1938
Jazz Dance, 1918
Jazz Twinkle, 1919
Jazzina, 1919
Jollity Parade, p.26
King's Paso Doble, 1917

Knees Up Mother Brown, 1938
La Czarina, p.18
Ladbroke, 1918
Lambeth Walk, 1937
Le Militaire, 1905
L'Espagnolita, 1920
Maxina, 1917
Marine Four Step, 1911
Mississippi Dip, 1911
Moonie, 1905
New Maxina, 1920
Palais Glide, 1928
Palais Stroll, 1938
Park Parade, 1938
Popular Jazz, 1919
Ritz, 1920
Sequence Conga, 1939
Serenata, 1932
Spanish Fandango, p.21
Swingtime, 1936
Tangena, p.26
Tangino, 1921
Tapper, 1930
Tingle Tangle, p.27
Vestris (Minuet), 1913
V8, 1937

Nos. of Dances up to 1945

Old-Time Waltzes	76	Schottisches	6
Two Steps	18	Gavottes	6
Tangos	18	Mazurkas	6
Square Dances	12	Barn Dances	7
Foxtrots	8	One-Steps	5
Blues	7	Polkas	3
Saunters	6	Miscellaneous	60
			238

THE YEARS OF TRANSITION (1946 – 1974)

INDEX OF DANCES FROM 1975-1994

INTRODUCTION

Wars are periods of great upheaval and social change. The new attitudes and different life styles are reflected in the patterns of social dancing, particularly in the post-war years. The first world war produced a reaction against the values of the old society, and dancing became free and easy in contrast to the somewhat artificial technique taught by the old dancing masters. The second world war produced almost the opposite effect - so much change had occurred that everyone was looking for order and stability and something to put a little gaiety into the rather dismal aftermath of the war. The older generation in particular began to take up the dancing habits of their youth. This development was so rapid and unexpected that it took the teachers of old-time dancing by surprise - they had to look out their notes and try to remember what they had taught in the past. Old-time sequence dancing had survived in the northern clubs and in Scotland but there were relatively few centres elsewhere. Many thought that the revival would be short-lived but more and more people flocked to the dance halls. The old dances came back into favour and new sequence and square dances were arranged. The dancing associations made great efforts to put things on a firm foundation by standardising the best dances and bringing teaching methods up-to-date. As time passed the 'modern' style of sequence dancing gained ground and by the 1960's there were considerable differences between old-time and modern sequence dancing sessions. While no-one can really be said to have initiated the revival in old-time dancing there were a select few who did much to help it on its way. In the main these were people who had access to wide audiences by writing books or articles, broadcasting, providing script services, holding office in a dancing institution, arranging dances or by organising large-scale dancing events. The contributions of some of these key figures are set out in the following pages.

F. J. Mainey was the founder and director of the International Sequence Dance Circle (ISDC) in the early 1940's. His Easter dancing festivals at Blackpool and Autumn festivals at Prestatyn (and later at Douglas in the Isle of Man) were organised with characteristic flair and proved to be memorable occasions for all. He had many scripts of old-time dances and ran a script service. In 1946 he formed the Old Time Teachers of Dancing Association (OTTDA or OTDA) which conducted medal tests for amateurs in old-time dancing. His handbook, published in 1953, is a mine of information on the old-time style.

'Old Time Dancers' Handbook', F. J. Mainey, Herbert Jenkins, 1953

A. J. Latimer was a dancing master of the old school - some of his earlier sequences are the Marie Mazurka (1906), Braw Laddie Two Step (1906) and Truro Gavotte (1910). He was President of the BATD in 1932 and was the first MC of the radio programme 'The Good Old Days' with music provided by the Harry Davidson Orchestra from 1943 onwards. He went to great trouble to obtain authentic descriptions of the old dances although these were often rather brief and lacking in essential information. In June 1948 he published some of these dances (originally on the back of sheet music mainly by Francis Day and Hunter); this was followed by a second volume:-

'A Bouquet of Old Time Dances', Danceland Publications
'A Second Bouquet of Old Time Dances', Danceland Publications

Major Cecil H. Taylor was a Leeds dancing master with family dancing traditions extending more that 150 years. He was in great demand as an adjudicator and sat on many important committees. As president of the ISTD for more than 30 years he did much to establish the power and reputation of this society - in particular he was one of the moving spirits in the setting up of the Ballroom Branch in 1924. His dances include the County Cotillon introduced at the Berlin Congress of 1907, Yale Blues (1927), Dream Waltz (1938), Rinking (1939), Waltz Caprice (1952) and Progressive Quadrilles. He wrote a very useful book:-

'Old Time and Novelty Dances', Major Cecil H. Taylor, Dancing Times Ltd., 1948

Victor Silvester (dancing with Phyllis Clarke) won the world professional championship in 1922 and 1923. He was a man of many talents with charm, energy, ideas and great organising ability. He made thousands of broadcasts on radio and TV and was known the world over; he was active in the dancing world for more than 50 years until his death in 1978. He formed a strict tempo dance orchestra in 1934 which provided music for the BBC Dancing Club from 1941 onwards; from 1948 the public were able to see him as well as hear him in the BBC Television Dancing Club. Although he is best known for his 'Modern Ballroom Dancing' (latest version 1993) he made valuable additions to the literature of sequence dancing:-

'Old Time Dancing', Herbert Jenkins, 1948
'Sequence Dancing', Herbert Jenkins, 1950
'Old Time and Sequence Dancing', Barrie and Jenkins, 1980
'More Old Time Dances', Herbert Jenkins, 1951
'The Complete Old Time Dancer' (with Walter Whitman),
Herbert Jenkins, 1967

Edward Scott was a well-known teacher and a prolific writer on both the technique and background of dancing at the turn of the century. His many books include *'Dancing as an Art and Pastime' (1892), 'Dancing' (1894) and 'The New Dancing as it should be' (1910).* His *'ABC of Dancing'* has scripts for the Highland Schottische, Washington Post, Alsatian and Berlin Polkas and the Versa. His style was rather circumlocutory and he was much given to classical allusions. He served on the first committee sponsored by the 'Dancing Times' in 1920 to standardise the steps of the various dances.

Other books containing scripts of older dances are:-

'Old Time Favourite and Modern Dances', Frances Day and Hunter, 1939
'The Book of Popular Old Time and Sequence Dances', 1950's, compiled by Billy Smith, (Scottish MC's Dancing Association)
'Old Time Dancing', John R. Gillespie, C. Arthur Pearson, 1947
'Old Time and Sequence Dances', Official Board of Ballroom Dancing, 1947 (revised 1950)
'How and What to Dance', Geoffrey D'Egville, C. Arthur Pearson, various editions, 1919-1941

New Sequence Dances

Some dances are arranged by committees for teaching or competition purposes while others are produced to celebrate special events or to add variety to the programmes. Most dances appear, however, as entries to inventive dance competitions. Winning a prize does not ensure that a dance will be popular with the dancing public as the skills of the demonstrators, luck and other factors enter into the final equation. The Waltz Babette, arranged by Arthur Lightfoot of Leeds in 1968, is a delightful modern waltz with its own music which is still popular today although it only came third in the OBBD competition of the year - many winners have been forgotten in 2 or 3 months!

Nevertheless winning a competition does enhance the status of a dance and its performers and where possible details of prizes won have been entered in the lists. It might be thought that institutions awarding prizes over the years might have a complete list of winners - this may be so in some cases but these records are not usually available to independent historians. The data in these lists has been taken from the scripts themselves, dancing journals and textbooks and is of necessity incomplete. Scripts of modern dances are often arranged so that the man's steps fit on one side of a page for ease of duplication. When space is at a premium details of the prize won (and sometimes the date and arranger) are left out and this is one reason for awards being omitted in some cases. Certain abbreviations have been used to save space in the lists:-

BATD 1893	British Association of Teachers of Dancing
ISTD 1904	Imperial Society of Teachers of Dancing
NATD 1907	National Association of Teachers of Dancing
NCDTA 1925	Northern Counties Dance Teachers' Association
ADA 1922	Allied Dancing Association
IDMA 1930-67)	International Dancing Masters' Association
IDTA 1967)	International Dance Teachers' Association

UKAPTD (or UKA) 1903	United Kingdom Alliance of Professional Teachers of Dancing
SDTA 1934	Scottish Dance Teachers' Alliance
SDTA	Sequence Dance Teachers' Association
OBBD 1929-85 ⎞ BCBD 1985 ⎠	Official Board of Ballroom Dancing British Council of Ballroom Dancing
MATD 1920-61	Midland Association of Teachers of Dancing
ESTD 1938-61 ⎞ DTA 1961 ⎠	Empire Society of Teachers of Dancing Dance Teachers' Association
ISDC 1944	International Sequence Dance Circle Ltd.
OTDA 1946	Old Time Teachers of Dancing Association
SMCDA 1936	Scottish MC's Dancing Association
FSDI 1952	Federation of Sequence Dance Instructors
FSDI 1956	Fellowship of Sequence Dance Instructors
Manc. MC's 1953	Manchester MC's Club
ASDT 1953	Association of Sequence Dance Teachers
NASD North 1957	National Alliance of Sequence Dancing
NASD Yorks.	National Association of Sequence Dancing
YSDF 1956	Yorkshire Sequence Dancing Federation
SDF London 1959	Sequence Dancing Fellowship (London)

Names like Blackpool, Filey and Prestatyn indicate prizes won at festivals at these places. These events were organised by dancing associations, magazines and commercial organisations such as Mecca or Butlins. Festivals spread over several days require one or more large ballrooms with plentiful accommodation for visitors - these are commonly found in seaside resorts and holiday camps rather than big cities like London and Birmingham.

The use of a dash instead of the arranger's name indicates that no name appears on the script and it has not been possible to find this from other sources.

1946-1948

1946 Ansdella Waltz (O/T), Walter Mastin, 1st ISDC Blackpool
  "   Fascination [Tango], Fred and Ada Holmes (Sheffield)
  "   Dutch Foursome, F. J. Mainey, 1st Dance News
  "   Breakaway Blues, A. Roscoe/F. Fitzgerald,ISDC Blackpool
1947 Progressive Waltz, Adela Roscoe (Nottingham)
  "   Royal Minuet, Adele England
  "   Hesitation Waltz I, Ronald Hanmer (music)
  "   Wedding Waltz, Isabel Barr and A. H. Nichols
  "   Starlight Saunter, Fred Holmes (Sheffield), 1st MATD
  "   Tip Toe Two Step, Ada Holmes (Sheffield), 3rd MATD
1948 Morecambe Tango, E. Macdonald, 1st NATD
  "   Rio Tango I, Fred Holmes (Sheffield), 2nd MATD
  "   Capri I [Tango], Adela Roscoe (Nottingham)
  "   New Inspiration Gavotte, Adela Roscoe (Nottingham)
  "   Marie I [Waltz] (Mod), Joe Senior (Stretford)
  "   Silver Wedding Waltz (Mod), Joseph J. Patterson
  "   Magenta [Tango] I, Arthur Wantling, 1st ESTD
  "   Cavalcade [Waltz] (Mod), Marjorie Wantling, 1st ESTD
  "   Malayan Tango, Vyner Gomez, Blackpool
  "   June Waltz (O/T), Miss P. M. Davey, ESTD
  "   Ballin the Jack, Len Colyer and Doris Brace, ESTD

F. J. Mainey's Dutch Foursome is still danced today. It is a progressive dance for sets of two couples facing each other in a circle round the ballroom. It has a Dutch Glee Dance (16 bars), Waltz Square (16 bars), Dutch Mill (8 bars) and concludes with 8 bars of waltzing. It is often performed to 'Little Hollanders' written by *J. W. Tattersall* and it has some affinities to the Spanish Waltz.

Adela Roscoe's Breakaway Blues is still taught to beginners and performed in the clubs; confusion sometimes arises when couples do not use the correct diagonal alignment. She added 'New' to the title of her 'Inspiration Gavotte' to distinguish it from her mother's gavotte of 1914 of the same name. Adela won the British Ballroom Championship dancing with Cyril Farmer in 1937 and 1938 and up to 1945 the Roscoe School of Dancing in Nottingham was largely concerned with teaching ballroom dancing. She had however a great love for old time dancing and was well-trained in its theory and technique. When the revival started after the war she joined forces with Freddie Fitzgerald and in 1946 the school was moved from Bridlesmithgate to the Astoria Ballroom. The pair began to lecture, teach and demonstrate the old-time sequence style to the leading teachers of the day. From 1948 onwards they travelled the country giving courses and adjudicating at both old-time and modern festivals. In 1954 they retired from this work to take over the Palais in Mansfield (Adela's home town). Between 1948 and 1952 they produced some 20 new sequence dances.

'Ballin the Jack' by Len Colyer and Doris Brace was a dance based on the original tune written in 1913 by Chris Smith; it was supposed to simulate the action of a skittle player.

Fred and Ada Holmes of Sheffield produced many new sequence dances of high quality from 1947 to 1952 when they were in great demand; they won nearly a dozen prizes in this period (mainly from the Midland Association of Teachers of Dancing). After a break caused by illness they were again winners with the White Rose (Modern) Waltz (1956) and the White Rose Saunter (1956). As is often the case their Tango Fascination (1946) and Variety Foxtrot (1949) which did not win prizes were the most popular with the dancing public.

The Waltz Marie is sometimes said to be the most popular of all sequence dances; it was given great publicity in Manchester by one of the arranger's friends, Len Meadows. It was one of the first examples of a modern waltz being played at a slower tempo (29-31 bpm) than the old-time waltz (40-44 bpm). Steps were taken more on the heels with a walking action and the turns were only 3/4 compared with the full rotary turn in the old-time waltz; this produced a diagonal mode of progression down the line of dance. Unfortunately it is danced in different ways, particularly with the first turn and following steps; some versions have an allemande for the lady to achieve some old-time flavour. This was the only truly modern sequence waltz to be featured in Harry Davidson's BBC programme 'Those Were The Days' (1943 onwards).

1949

1949   Serenade I [Saunter], Miss Dorothy Bullars (Doncaster)
"   Rosary Waltz, Fred Holmes (Sheffield), 1st MATD
"   Palais Merry Go Round, Ada Holmes, 3rd MATD
"   Variety Foxtrot, Fred Holmes (Sheffield)
"   Vienna [Waltz], Adela Roscoe (Nottingham)
"   Variety Rumba, Edward Burke
"   University Waltz, Netta Brooke (Wandsworth)
"   Harry Lime Foxtrot, Henry Clarke
"   Sherrie Saunter, Nancy Clarke (Rhyl), 1st IDMA
"   Destiny Waltz, W. Compton
"   Emperor Waltz, Albert Cowan (Manchester)
"   Cavendish Two Step, C. S. Wood, Danceland Trophy

The rumba is a very old dance with its roots in Africa and Cuba. The American or square rumba dates from 1931. The Cuban Rumba (1948) is now used by ballroom dancers; the Variety Rumba is an early example of a sequence form of this dance.

The University Waltz was inspired by the remarkable boat race of that year. It was danced to 'Song of the River' by Archibald Joyce. Netta Brooke served for some time on the Executive Council of BATD and was an examiner for ISTD.

The Harry Lime Foxtrot is still taught and danced today. Demonstrated by Henry Clarke and Mae Dickens it was an outstanding success at the ISDC Festival at Blackpool. The music from the film 'The Third Man' featured the unforgettable zither playing of Anton Karas. Henry Clarke (who died in 1951) arranged several other dances about this time including the Cuckoo Waltz (1950), Lancelot Two Step (1951), Delilah Waltz and Elizabeth Tango (1951) (named after his wife). 'Henry Clarke' and 'Elizabeth Clarke' trophies were competed for at ISDC festivals in the Isle of Man. Elizabeth Clarke was at one time President of the OTDA. Three of her ISDC prize-winning dances are the Caroline Waltz (1953), Crinoline Waltz (1954) and Isle of Man Two Step (1957); she died in 1976.

Old Time Sequence Dancing Associations

When interest in old-time dancing began to revive in the 1940's F. J. Mainey was well-prepared to play a major role in its development. He had much experience of running old-time dances in the Liverpool area in the 1930's, he had a large collection of scripts and music and above all he was a person of vision and determination. When he moved to the Blackpool area during the war he found that his old-time dancing sessions were an instant success and the movement soon spread to other areas. He had some fears (quite rightly as it turned out) that the modern style might take over and he formed two organisations to promote and preserve the purity of the old-time style of dancing.

International Sequence (Old Time) Dance Circle (ISDC)

The Thornton Cleveleys Sequence Dance Circle formed by F. J. Mainey in 1944 had the following objectives: (a) to promote Old Time dancing; (b) to foster Old Time dancing under its correct title of sequence dancing; (c) to encourage modern youth to take up sequence dancing. Many more circles were formed and eventually the ISDC came into being - by 1949 there were branches in more than 20 countries. Writing in his 'Crinoline' journal in 1953 F. J. Mainey stated that the ISDC was "the world's largest dance organisation".

Festivals and group events have always been important in promoting a sense of unity among enthusiasts for old-time dancing. Following the first rally in Blackpool in 1944 the annual festival had to move from Blackpool to Filey and then to Prestatyn to accommodate the increasing numbers. From 1957 to 1985 it was held in the Isle of Man where more than 2,000 dancers would assemble to enjoy the pageantry, dancing and competitions; Bridlington has been one of the venues in recent years. When F. J. Mainey died in 1960 the festival was organised by Harry and Jess Ashworth; in the 1970's responsibility passed to Stuart and Audrey Singleton (née Ashworth). Although the ISDC is authorised to hold inventive dance competitions (now old-time, modern and Latin American) it has never been a full member of the OBBD.

Old Time Teachers of Dancing Association (OTDA)

This organisation provided training and medal tests for amateurs in the old-time style - it is said to have been the last society to drop the Lancers from its associateship syllabus. It was formed after a series of meetings in Blackpool convened by F. J. Mainey in 1946. H. D. Brittain was the representative from the Official Board and he was elected President with W. Mastin as Secretary. Both these officers died 5 years later - possibly through overwork. Presidents were elected annually, Mrs. Ashworth being the second President; Will Ranwell (6 years) and Ray Hemming (8 years) were the longest-serving holders of this office. There were Northern, Midland, Southern, East Anglian and South Western areas; the Midland was the last survivor ceasing its activities in April 1993. Inventive dance competitions were held from the 1950's for the Brittain Shield (old-time) and more recently the Jack Smith Trophy (modern) - many of the award winners appear in the lists.

The Old Time Society

The 'Old Time Society' is the 'Society for the Preservation and Appreciation of Old Time Music and Dancing' formed at Cliftonville in Kent in February 1984 with 50 founder members; it now has more than 1,000 subscribers. A regular newsletter is sent to members giving news of current events, dance club reports and items of general interest. Bryan Smith was President of the Society from its inception to his untimely death on 23rd January, 1995. He had been active in musical and dancing circles for almost 50 years having toured the music halls, performed on cruise liners and played with the BBC Radio 2 Ballroom Orchestra for the programme 'Sequence Time' for more than 15 years. Another great driving force in the Society has been Fred Boast who has been Secretary and Vice President since the early days. He was a schoolmate of Bryan Smith and they both lived in the same street in Addlestone, Surrey. Fred and his wife Jo have been active in the dancing world for many years and have raised much money for charities. Both Fred Boast and Bryan Smith have received the Certificate of Merit for services to sequence dancing sponsored by the 'Sequence Dancing World' magazine.

PRESENTED IN 1950

Waltzes (Old-Time) (1950)

Coquette	Maurice Smart (music)	
Cuckoo	Henry Clarke	
Empress I	Adela Roscoe (Nottingham)	
Genora	Nora Shaw (Rotherham)	
Jacqeline	George Shaw (Rotherham)	
Killarney	Florence Newbegin	1st NCDTA
Majestic I	Jim and Freda Williams	
Martine [Valse]	Arthur Ives	
Oakley	Stan and Vi Ross	3rd ISTD
Princess Anne	Capt. A. H. Lemon (Oxford)	1st ISDC
Starlit	Alfred Belcher	DanceLand
Suzanne [Waltz]	George Shaw	
Tudor	George Shaw and Madge Wooding (Rotherham)	MATD
Windsor	George Shaw and Madge Wooding (Rotherham)	MATD Morgan Cup

Waltzes (Modern) (1950)

Festival	Cyril Farmer	
Gwynne Circle	Michael Gwynne (Bournemouth)	
Marguerite I [Waltz]	Margo Alderman	IDMA

Tangos (1950)

Ameleon	Leon Peers (Crewe)	
De Reve	Moray Cooper	
Del Rosa	Len Banks (Ashton-under-Lyme)	ESTD
Enchanteur	Doris Allan (Stanmore)	ISDC
Le Breton	James Wilson (Glasgow)	
Lilvina	Miss M. Greening (Castleford)	
Margharita	Adela Roscoe and Freddie Fitzgerald (Nottingham)	
Matador	Fred and Ada Holmes (Sheffield)	
Star I	Miss Vera Mathews (Cardiff)	1st IDMA
Tudor	Royce H. Anderson (High Wycombe)	
White Rose	Ada Holmes (Sheffield)	1st Danceland Trophy

Saunters (1950)

La Rita	Bill and May Botham (Wythenshawe)	
September	Ada Holmes (Sheffield)	2nd MATD
Stroll Along	Moray Cooper	
Superbe	Gerald Bullen (Southport)	1st ADA
Twilight	Bill Botham (Wythenshawe)	

Two Steps (1950)

Baghdad	Frederick Rovery
Gaiety	Gerald Bullen
Imperial (Progressive)	Mr. Meredith
Regency	Fred and Ada Holmes
Rosetta	———

Blues (1950)

Blues Glide	———
Georgella	Stella and George Berwick
Serenata	———

Miscellaneous (1950)

Bolerico	Johnny Pitt	
Chin Chin (One Step)	Malcolm Munro	'In a Pagoda'
Empress Walk	Adela Roscoe	
Festival Square Dance	Michael Gwynne	
Gainsborough Glide	Marjorie Fairley (Edinburgh)	1st OBBD
Islington Sway	R. W. Penford (Islington)	
Kenjan Maze	Frank Short (Birmingham)	1st ESTD Hayton Trophy
Kentucky Parade	Adela Roscoe	
Maryland Foxtrot	Stan Powell	
Masquerade	Fred and Ada Holmes	
New Charleston	Tom Brown (Catterick Garrison)	
Pier Parade	Fred and Ada Holmes	
Savoy Schottische	F. J. Mainey	ISDC
Skiffle (Novelty)	Leslie Lewis	
Swing Patrol	Adela Roscoe	
Twilight Minuet	Adela Roscoe	
Zeeta Samba	Alex Moore (name of his dance studio)	

A number of dances in the 1950 list belong to the early foxtrot group, being played in 4/4 time at 32-34 bpm with steps based on a walking action using figures such as points, twinkles. The Islington Sway arranged by R. W. Penford of the Islington Old Time Club takes its name from the side chassés and sways in bars 10-14; the Blues Glide (still danced today) has certain steps taken with the gliding action of a skater. The Stroll Along Saunter is played more slowly at 24 bpm and has some figures with the feet at an angle.

The Georgella Blues (1950) is an example of a blues played at a faster quickstep tempo of 46 bpm. The Manhattan Blues arranged by Isobel MacDonald of Edinburgh (date unknown) is another popular blues played at this speed; it was originally 12 bars in length but in due course 4 more bars were added to make the standard 16.

PRESENTED IN 1951

Waltzes (Old-Time) (1951)

Adelphi	Stan Ross	1st BATD
Babette	Arthur Lightfoot (Leeds)	3rd OBBD
Eclipse [Waltz]	Frank Short (Birmingham)	1st ESTD Hayton Trophy
Fascination [Waltz]	Fred Holmes	2nd Mecca Streatham
Hesitation II	John E. Evans	
La Margarette [Waltz]	John Collinson	1st ISDC
Lilac	Alfred Halford (Preston)	1st OBBD
Louise	Claude Millward	
Petite [Valse]	Dick and Jan Telford (North Shields)	NCDTA
Rainbow I	Adela Roscoe and Freddie Fitzgerald	
Ramon [Waltz]	Maurice Fletcher	2nd ISTD
Saturday	Capt. A. H. Lemon (Oxford)	2nd OTDA
Waltz of Britain	F. J. Mainey	

Waltzes (Modern) (1951)

Festival of Britain	Alfred Halford (Preston)	1st Blackpool
Jacqueline	Bert Finlay (Kirkaldy)	
Magenta	Michael Gwynne (Bournemouth)	
Symphony	Adela Roscoe and Freddie Fitzgerald	

Tangos (1951)

Bon Bon	———	
Butterfly	Millicent Clayton	
Dolores I	Stan Ross	1st NATD
Elizabeth	Henry Clarke	
Fantasy [Tango]	Freddie Fitzgerald (Nottingham)	
Fiesta I [Tango]	Maurice Smart (music)	
La Dell	Guy Waddell	
Marietta [Tango]	Bill Wait (Liverpool)	1st ADA
Marquita	Sylvester and Ellen Burrows (Haydock)	2nd ESTD
Progressive	Adela Roscoe and Freddie Fitzgerald	
Vee	Norman Olbery	2nd IDMA

Saunters (1951)

Dream	Vera Matthews (Cardiff)	1st IDMA Blackpool
Minx	———	
Promenade I	———	
Seaside	Miss Marjorie Wantling (Manchester)	1st Blackpool

Foxtrots (1951)

Freda	Fred and Ada Holmes (Sheffield)	2nd MATD
Swanee	Guy Waddell	

Two Steps (1951)

Anniversary (Progressive)	Frank Short (Birmingham)
Lancelot	Henry Clarke
Maxwell	Doris Allan
Terry (Progressive)	J. Preece
Thames (Progressive)	George Moore

Schottisches (1951)

Hedley	John A. Marston	OTDA Brittain Shield
Road to the Isles I		2nd NCDTA
Shirley	Henry Whiteside	1st ISTD

Miscellaneous (1951)

Chadwick		
Ivory Quickstep	S. Powell (Dudley)	
Park Promenade	Henry Whiteside	1st NATD
Vermilion Charleston	James Wilson (Glasgow)	

Arthur and Martine Ives [Valse Martine (1950)]

The Ives came from a village near Harrogate but moved to the London area to further their professional careers; they had dancing lessons from George Mott (of NDS fame) at the Wharfedale School of Dancing in Otley.

Of their various dances the Valse Martine has proved one of the most popular. It is a waltz in the old-time manner which includes a type of bower position in which the partners rotate round one another in loose ballroom hold with joined hands raised above the lady's head. The bower position dates back to at least 1716 and is found in early versions of the Eva Three Step (1904) and J. B. Arkley's Crown and Coronet Waltz. It is also found in Edward Scott's Versa of the 1890's and the first Hesitation Waltz of Miss Alice Martin. There was a strong French influence in old-time and ballet dancing and this is reflected in the use of 'valse' rather than 'waltz' - notice also the 'Le' Breton Tango (1950) and 'La' Rita Saunter (1951) by other arrangers. Many other dances by Arthur and Martine Ives appear in the following lists.

Alfred Halford [Festival of Britain Waltz, Lilac Waltz (1951)]

Alfred Halford of Preston was a ballroom dancer and examiner who took a great interest in sequence dancing. His Lilac Waltz is still a championship dance since it is ideal for teaching the rise and fall of the waltz style; It is sometimes used as an elimination sequence dance in the clubs for a prize since it is simple enough for most dancers to follow and is readily picked up when the music starts again. The Festival of Britain, opened on 2nd May, 1951, is commemorated by his modern waltz of the same name (and also by F. J. Mainey's old-time Waltz of Britain). Dancing with Marjorie Robinson Alfred Halford had several successes in the British Professional Old Time Dancing Championship 1954 (Jnt. 1st), 1955 (1st), 1957 (2nd) and he was a Carl Alan award winner; he died in 1992. Some of his other dances are the Tango Scintilla (1955), Lotus Waltz (1957), Pauletta Two Step (1957) and Grosvenor Waltz (1960).

Captain A. H. Lemon [Princess Anne Waltz (1950), Saturday Waltz (1951)]

The birth of Princess Anne on 1st August, 1950 inspired his old-time waltz of the same name - royal permission was given for the use of the title. This waltz starts with the partners in side-by-side position and most steps are taken 'on the same foot' - both man and lady start with the right foot. His other arrangements include the Carfax Waltz (1955), Sunset Saunter (1957) and the Lindy Loo Quickstep (1960).

Bill Wait [Tango Marietta (1951)]

Bill Wait has been prominent in Liverpool and North Wales circles since 1951 being associated with the ISDC festivals in Prestatyn and the Isle of Man. His dances usually have a modern flavour and show considerable originality. Some of the titles of his dances were constrained by ISDC rulings and this may not have helped their popularity. His modern Patricia Waltz (1954) is still popular and was used as a competition dance. Many of the dances by Bill and Rose appear in the lists, the latest being Dot's Two Step (1968).

Frank Short [Kenjan Maze (1950), Waltz Eclipse (1951), Anniversary Progressive Two Step (1951)]

Frank Short of Birmingham has produced many sequence dances of high quality and originality, winning many prizes in the 50's and 60's; his Broadway Quickstep (1957) and Bermuda Foxtrot (1965) are still danced today. His Kenjan Maze (1950) was considered to be well in advance of its time. It is danced in Maxina hold with man's and lady's steps being the same throughout - it has several locksteps before this figure became really fashionable. (F. J. Mainey's list of early dances has a Chicago Maze (1920).) In 1951 he again won the Hayton Trophy with his Waltz Eclipse and his Anniversary Two Step was featured on Harry Davidson's BBC programme 'Those Were The Days'. Nearly 20 of his dances appear in the lists up to 1971.

PRESENTED IN 1952

Waltzes (Old-Time) (1952)

Caprice	Major Cecil H. Taylor	
Cynthia	Jose Cowell	
Embassy I	Phyllis and Bill Groves	1st ISTD
Kentucky	James A. Wilson	
Nannette [Waltz]	Phyliss Ratigan	
Primrose	Vi Ross (Watford)	1st Danceland Trophy
Prince Consort	Bill Lipthorpe and Vi Hamilton	Joint 1st ODTA
Rainbow II	Frank Short (Birmingham)	
Springtime I	W. Morton and F. Wallace	1st NCDTA
Sunbeam	Adela Roscoe and Freddie Fitzgerald	
Victoria	W. Morton and F. Wallace	1st NCDTA

Waltzes (Modern) (1952)

Everlasting	Fred and Ada Holmes (Sheffield)
Lullaby I	Mr. Lindsay (Dunfermline)
Melody	Fred and Ada Holmes (Sheffield)
Merry Widow Waltz of 1952	Guy Waddell
Tennessee	Sylvester and Ellen Burrows (Haydock)

Tangos (1952)

Blue I	Bill Hall (Stretford)	3rd ESTD
Blue II	Guy Waddell	
Camellia	Eric Stonehouse (Stockport)	1st ESTD
Diana(e) [Tango]	Freddie Fitzgerald	1st NATD
Eduanita [Tango]	Edward Mitchell (Southend-on-Sea)	
Enchantment [Tango]	Fred Holmes (Sheffield)	2nd MATD
Glenmore	John Dryden	
Invitation	David Higgs	
Jubilee	Alfred Halford (Preston)	1st UKAPTD
Leona	Florence Newbegin	1st IDMA
Midnight	Gilbert and Elizabeth Daniels	
Red Carnation	Josef Jones	4th IDMA
San Remo [Tango]	Gilbert Daniels (South Shields)	

Two Steps (1952)

Filey Festival	Nora Bray (Huddersfield)	1st Danceland Trophy
Military Prog.	S. G. Fielding	

Two Steps (1952) (continued)

Millicent	Millicent Barrett	
Royal	Joe Stead (Blackpool)	3rd Blackpool
Trafalgar	Alfred Halford (Preston)	1st Danceland Trophy

Gavottes (1952)

Crinoline	Mme. Patricia Enderby (Sheffield)	
Elizabethan	Adela Roscoe and Freddie Fitzgerald	
Hazel	Harry Greenwood and T. Edney (Bradford)	
Janina	Raymond Bailey (Macclesfield)	2nd NATD
La Marguerite	Miss Christine Cousins	
Wesford	Winifred Sharp	2nd ISTD

Saunters (1952)

Clarendon I	Stan and Vi Ross (Watford)	2nd BATD Chester Trophy
Lullaby	Adela Roscoe and Freddie Fitzgerald	
Parisienne Tango	C. J. Daniels	2nd Filey
Silver I	Miss Queenie M. Clements	

Blues (1952)

Bohemian	Bill and May Botham (Wythenshawe)	
Charleston	(Michael Gwynne)	
Marie	L. Winmill	1st IDMA
Mona Lisa	Frank Short (Birmingham)	

Foxtrots (1952)

| Pins and Needles | Jack Dowling | 1st Blackpool |
| Princess | Stan Powell (Woodley) | |

Miscellaneous (1952)

American Quickstep	Nancy Clarke (Rhyl)	
Duetto		
Gay Schottische	Adela Roscoe and Freddie Fitzgerald (Nottm)	
Kingsley Glide (Progressive)	T. Edney	
Lancashire Square Dance	Harry Swindells (Manchester)	
Marguerite Mazurka	R. White	
Marigold Schottische	Ethel Hardy	2nd NCDTA
Moonlight Mazurka	Peter Light	
Princess Progressive Square Dance	Jack McInnes	
September Sway	Mr. M. Collinson	1st ISDC
Tipsy Two	Nancy Clarke (Rhyl)	1st Blackpool (O/T)

The Embassy Waltz (1952) is memorable in that to compete Bill Groves had to travel some 300 miles by road to Filey from a convalescent home where he was recovering from a serious illness. The music was arranged and recorded by Harry Davidson and broadcast with Bill and Phyllis in the studio.

The Charleston Blues (1952) is an alternative to the Manhattan Blues and Mississippi Dip. It lies somewhere between the old-time and modern styles having a half square and some Charleston movements. Tom Brown's New Charleston (1950) and the Vermilion Charleston (1951) by James Wilson are other dances in this genre.

The Tipsy Two (1952) is an unusual winner of a Blackpool Old Time Festival. It is played to music in common time at 44/46 bpm and has elements of the cakewalk and one-step; it features hand claps and 'tipsy' chassés.

The Duetto (1952) is a 16 bar sequence with gavotte features which can be used as a simpler alternative to La Mascotte for teaching purposes since there are no bars of waltzing.

Bill Botham [Twilight Saunter (1950), La Rita Saunter (1950), Bohemian Blues (1952)]

Bill Botham was one of the most influential figures in the development of modern sequence dancing. He established a script service, formed various dancing institutions and published articles in newspapers and magazines. Trained in old-time dancing by Tom Hayton, he was one of the first to realise the great potential of the modern style. By 1948, ably assisted by his wife, May, he was a most successful MC and teacher in the Manchester area. He had a weekly feature in the 'Manchester City News' called 'On with the Dance' which nearly always included a dance script. In 1953 Bill and May published some 48 of these dances in the 'MC's Handbook of Old Time and Sequence Dances'; this was reissued in 1987 by North Star Publishers (*P.O. Box 20, Otley, West Yorkshire, LS21 2SA*). This volume included 10 of their own dances, notably the Bilmay Two Step with its *dos à dos*, and May's Manchester Waltz.

Bill and May Botham arranged more than 30 dances but never entered them for inventive dance competitions as they had reservations about the judging methods used. Bill said his dances were arranged "just for fun - sometimes my own, sometimes for other people's". Their best-known dances were the Bilmay Two Step, Manchester Waltz, Tango Marcelle (1954) and Kerry Quickstep (1956).

Michael Gwynne [Magenta Waltz (1951), Kitchen Rag (1953)]

Michael Gwynne was a ballroom dancer of great technical ability who did much to develop sequence dancing - from 1950 onwards he provided dancers with a monthly letter and script service. His scripts were very detailed, often giving lady's steps separately - technique, amounts of turn and orientations were also included.

Although he was an authority on old-time dancing he welcomed the more modern arrangements, seeing them as the "old-time championship dances of tomorrow". In 1965 his slow modern Magenta Waltz (1951) was voted as the most popular of all modern sequences by the readers of 'Dance News'; his Kitchen Rag (1953) is a form of one step adapted to ragtime music. Some of his other dances are Ronde Tango (1958), Black Magic Tango (1959), Dancers Waltz (1960), Janette Waltz (1962), Alassio Tango (1962) and Aztec Quickstep (1962).

He produced two very useful collections of scripts of 'new' dances in the early 1950's:-
'The New Dances', 1952
'Second Book of New Dances', 1955

Michael Gwynne's comprehensive and authoritative manual (in revised form) is still in print today:-
'Old Time and Sequence Dancing', Pitmans, 1950
'Sequence Dancing', Pitmans 1971; 2nd Ed., H. & C. Black, 1985

The original title is more apt since the second edition contains no scripts later than 1970 and no Latin-American sequence dances. It has 30 pages of old-time theory but no treatment of the modern style.

PRESENTED IN 1953

Waltzes (Old-Time) (1953)

Beatrice	Fred Porritt	1st BATD Worrall Trophy
Caroline	Elizabeth Clarke	Prestatyn ISDC
Choristers	F. J. Mainey	
Coquet	Miss Marjorie Gwynne-Bell	1st Blackpool
Corinthian	Gerald Bullen (Southport)	
Coronation	Committee of ESTD	
Du Barry [Waltz]	Frank Short (Birmingham)	3rd ESTD Hayton Trophy
Edmora	Mrs. Barbara Smith	1st IDMA
Everest	Miss Nessie Moore	IDMA
Gloria	Nora Bray (Huddersfield)	
Mermaid	Jack Jay	
Merry Widow	ESTD Committee	
Prince of Wales	W. Riley	1st ISDC Prestatyn
Princess Margaret	Frank Noble and Nora Bray	1st NATD Handley Shield
Queen Elizabeth (Viennese)	Victor Silvester and Alex Moore	
Queen's Own	Jacqueline de Gaux	
Regal	Bill and May Botham	
Silver Wedding	Molly Affleck (Seaborn)	2nd NCDTA
Waltz for the Queen	Sydney Thompson	
Wessex	Jack Jay	

Waltzes (Modern) (1953)

Be Mine	Jacqueline Jay	
Renown [Waltz]	R. Nicholson (Manchester)	
Westminster	Alfred Halford (Preston)	1st Blackpool
Wyoming I	Peter Light (Stoke-on-Trent)	

Saunters (1953)

Coronation I	Miss Jessie Ives and Mr. L. Brice	1st NCDTA
Coronation II	Albert Cross	
Elizabeth	Malcolm Denbigh (St. Helens)	
Lover's	Mr. and Mrs. A. Billington	ESTD
Rendezvous [Saunter]	Doreen Young	IDMA
Royal	Holland Brockbank	1st BATD Chester Trophy

Tangos (1953)

Balmoral	Audrey Sylvester and John Eke	1st ISTD
Caprice I [Tango]	Arthur and Martine Ives	

Tangos (1953) (continued)

Celebration [Tango]	F. W. R. Calder	
Coronation	———	
Crown	R. H. Anderson	
Hesitante [Tango]	S. G. Fielding (Maidenhead)	
Maria I [Tango]	E. Mitchell	
Marlyn	Joe Maxwell	
Ricardo	Sam Clegg and Len Meadows	
Sebastian I	F. Whitely	MATD
Windsor	Audrey Sylvester and John Eke	

Two Steps (1953)

Brittania		
Carnival	A. Ives	
Coronation	Mona Rogers (Liverpool)	
Elizabeth I	Clarice Winmill (Risca, Monmouthshire)	
Equality	Gillian Bourne	
Liberty	Raymond Bailey (Macclesfield)	1st OBBD Filey
Pride of Britain	Frank Noble and Nora Bray	Prize
Trixie	Claude V. Best (Luton)	
Windsor	Clarice Winmill (Risca, Monmouthshire)	3rd IDMA

Blues (1953)

Bewitching	Joan Daniels	
Carefree	Kathie Stead (Blackpool)	3rd Blackpool
Graftonian	Sylvester and Ellen Burrows (St. Helens)	

Miscellaneous (1953)

Autumn Foxtrot	Madame Pat Enderby	
Avon Foxtrot	G. H. Fletcher (Redditch)	
Birthday Schottische	Harold Goddard	
Coronation Glide	F. J. Mainey	
Coronation Polka	Frank Noble and Nora Bray	Prize
Elizabeth of England (March-Minuet)	Nora Bray	1st Danceland Trophy
Festival Stroll	Nora Bray (Huddersfield)	2nd Blackpool
Kitchen Rag	Michael Gwynne (Bournemouth)	
Liverpool Twinkle	J. Rogers	1st ADA
Princess Gavotte	Phyllis Groves	2nd Blackpool
Queen's Quadrilles	Jack Crossley	
Rodney Schottische	Gerald Bullen	
Teatime Foxtrot	———	

This year produced many dances with titles commemorating the coronation of HM Elizabeth II on 2nd June, 1953. These included coronation saunters and a waltz, tango, polka and glide; Elizabeth, Westminster, crown and royal also appeared in the dance names. Elizabeth of England (1953) by Nora Bray was written to music of the same name by Haydn Wood. It was a march-minuet in 4/4 time which danced well to gavotte music.

The Beatrice Waltz (1953) was written by Fred Porritt. He was a superb organiser and committee man and was President of the BATD on 10 occasions between 1952: he died in 1976.

The Britannia Two step is a dance for 3 partners (usually 1 man and 2 ladies) which possibly dates from before 1953. Like the Courtesy Two Step (1956) and Social Two Step (1958) it is useful for teaching purposes or where men are in short supply (a so-called Mormon dance). The Dashing White Sergeant is another threesome dance popular in Scotland; it dates from the 19th century although its music is much older.

The Queen Elizabeth Waltz (1953) was arranged by Victor Silvester and Alex Moore with music by Victor Silvester and his pianist Ernest Wilson. The recommended tempo of 54 bpm falls between that of the old-time waltz (42) and the Viennese Quick Waltz (60). Like the Yale Blues (1927) of Cecil Taylor, it can be adapted to non-sequence by using each 4 bar section as an amalgamation.

The old-time Coronation Waltz (1953) devised by the Executive Council of the ESTD contains some hopping steps - these were not at all uncommon in sequence waltzes of the Victorian era.

Two square dances in the old style are The Queen's Quadrilles (1953) and Imperial Waltz Quadrilles (1957) by Jack Crossley of London. The Tango Magenta II (1954) and Tango Maria II (1956) are two more of his dances.; his Portchester Saunter (1958) was demonstrated on BBC TV. He has a Tina Tango (1963) not to be confused with the dance of the same name by Ted and Ethel Grundy - a prizewinner in 1986.

Script Lists

F. J. Mainey had one of the best collections of early scripts and music. One of his lists (price 6d) prepared for ISDC members in 1950 contained over 700 dances in alphabetical order. There were 193 old-time waltzes, 65 tangos, 46 foxtrots (and saunters) and 35 two steps; many dances had names such as Arizona, Delphine and Viola which gave no indication of the nature of the dance.

John E. Evans (Secretary of the Empire Society) operated a script service in Wales which used some of F. J. Mainey's material. When John died in the late 1940's Michael Gwynne extended the collection and improved the scripts by giving the tempo, amount of turn and correct hold; above all he set out the lady's steps in detail. He offered a monthly service to members somewhat similar to that offered by Alex Moore for ballroom dancers. One of his lists has from Volume 1 (April 1950) to Volume 16 (April 1965) with dances listed month by month. Holland Brockbank became a partner in the service in 1967 taking over on Michael Gwynne's retirement in 1972. Ten years later Percy Lane formed the Brockbank-Lane Script Service with Holland Brockbank acting as consultant. Ron Lane gave up his career in the Ministry of Defence in April 1987 to join his father and took charge following Percy's sudden death in December 1988. A list produced in 1983 still has the dances arranged month by month but now all the waltzes, quicksteps and other dances are collected together although volume numbers are still used. This is the best script list covering the period from 1950 to the present day; other scripts not included in the catalogue may also be obtained.

George Mott of Otley had a large collection of scripts which included many Manchester (unofficial) dances - these are still available from Northern Dance Services. Scripts of dances winning recent inventive competitions are obtainable from the Brockbank-Lane Script Service, North Star Publishers and David Bullen Enterprises. Derek Arnold of North Star Publishers also advertises collections of scripts of both modern and old-time dances.

PRESENTED IN 1954

Waltzes (Old-Time) (1954)

Constance [Valse]	Edward Sharman (Welwyn Garden City)	1st BATD Chester Trophy
Crinoline	Elizabeth Clarke	1st Prize Prestatyn
Edelweiss I	B. M. Edney	2nd IDMA (SE)
Friendly (Progressive)	B. M. and T. Edney	
Imperial Jubilee	Miss Winfred Sharpe	1st ISTD
Iona	Ivy G. Harrison	3rd MATD
Lyndale	Sylvester and Ellen Burrows (Haydock)	1st ADA
Marietta [Waltz]	Olive J. Adley	
Trecarn [Valse]	A. Ives (Clapham)	2nd Dance News
Treecia	Phyllis Senior	3rd IDMA
Viennese Flirtation	Eva Swain and Eddie Ghys	2nd OBBD Filey

Waltzes (Modern) (1954)

Moderna	Rene Buckley	
Paradise	Doreen Mack (Manchester)	
Patricia	Bill Wait	
Shadow	Frank Short (Birmingham)	2nd ESTD

Tangos (1954)

Belmont	Fred Hollings (Accrington)	
Buchanan	C. G. Skidmore	2nd ISTD
Carmenita	Adela Roscoe (Nottingham)	
Delano	F. Noble (Huddersfield)	2nd IDMA
Golden I	Doreen Mack (Manchester)	
Golden Festival	John and Ida Hill (Liverpool)	
Havana	Eileen Bowers	
Louetta	John Evans	1st UKAPTD
Madrid [Tango]	Bill Wait (Liverpool)	2nd ADA
Magenta II [Tango]	Jack Crossley (London)	1st OBBD Filey
Maladetta [Tango]	George and Nora Shaw	
Marcelle [Tango]	Bill and May Botham (Wythenshawe)	
Serenade	Miss Joan Field	3rd NCDTA
Temptation [Tango]	Len Banks (Manchester)	
Tongo	Gilbert and Elizabeth Daniels	
Trelawney	Stan Ross (Watford)	1st BATD Worrall Trophy
Vienna [Tango]	Arthur Jones and Joan Wright (Manchester)	

Two Steps (1954)

Highland I	Joe Stead (Blackpool)	3rd Blackpool
Lightning	Joan Field (Sunderland)	
Marlborough	Miss Doreen Edwards (Halifax)	2nd Blackpool
Piccadilly	Audrey Sylvester (Potters Bar)	4th ISTD
Prince of Wales	Bill Wait (Liverpool)	1st ISDC Prestatyn
Queen's	Bill and Phylis Groves	.

Blues (1954)

Delaville	Sylvester and Ellen Burrows (Haydock)	1st Danceland Trophy
Desmond (Jasmine)	———	
Empress	James Brook	1st IDMA
Sapphire	Molly Affleck	1st NCDTA
Twelfth Street	H. Vickers	

Saunters (1954)

Elise	Miss Elsie Brook	
Seaburn	Gilbert and Elizabeth Daniels	
Sefton	Robert Wright	2nd NCDTA
Southern	Miss Queenie Clements	1st IDMA
Woodland	Frank and Rose Calder (Leicester)	

Miscellaneous (1954)

Blackpool Schottische	Nora Bray (Huddersfield)	Blackpool Award
Edwina Foxtrot	Miss Edith Hurst	1st MATD
Empress Mazurka	David Rollinson (Birmingham)	1st Blackpool
Gaiety Gavotte	Doreen Young (Bristol)	
Hengist Glide	———	
Silhouette	Gerald Bullen (Southport)	
Victorian Gavotte	Arthur Lightfoot (Leeds)	1st ESTD Hayton Trophy

Edward Sharman of Welwyn Garden City dancing with his wife was awarded the BATD Chester Trophy for his Valse Constance (1954). He was the first blind person on record to win and teach a dance at a festival. In 1957 he had a second success with the Floral Waltz.

The Empress Mazurka came top of a poll of 91 old-time dances in 1992 attracting 15 votes (Manhattan Blues - 13, Wedgewood Blue Gavotte - 13, Crinoline Gavotte - 11).

PRESENTED IN 1955

Waltzes (Old-Time) (1955)

Allendale	Frank Noble and Nora Bray (Huddersfield)	1st Dance News
Bluebell	George Moore	2nd IDMA (SE)
Carfax	Captain A. H. Lemon (Oxford)	1st OTDA Brittain Shield
Continental	Tom White	
Dunedin	Marjorie Fairley (Edinburgh)	2nd UKAPTD
Eileen	Rose Wait (Liverpool)	2nd ADA
Gardenia [Waltz]	Molly Affleck	
Katrina [Waltz]	Miss Cathie Stephenson	2nd Blackpool
Lorna	Hilda Farrow	
Pink Lady	Jack Dowling	
Rendezvous	Jean Bailey (Macclesfield)	3rd IDMA
Roaming in the Gloaming	Bill Wait (Liverpool)	1st ADA
Serene [Waltz]	Phyllis Adams (Swindon)	1st BATD Worrall Trophy
Tulip	Frank Short (Birmingham)	2nd ESTD Hayton Trophy

Waltzes (Modern) (1955)

Charmaine I [Waltz]	Terry Drogan (Droylsden)
Cresta I	Jacqueline de Gaux
Diane I [Waltz]	Wilf Green (Manchester)
Melrose	Fred Hollings (Accrington)
Moonglow	David Sarre (Guernsey)
Serene [Waltz]	Charles E. Stocks
Windermere II	Jim and Freda Williams (Llandudno)

Tangos (1955)

Alexandra	Eric Stonehouse and Marjorie Wantling	1st ESTD Hayton Trophy
Barcelona [Tango]	John and Ida Hill (Liverpool)	
Berkeley	Arthur Ives (London)	3rd ESTD
Hevony	Vyner Gomez	1st MATD
La Pree	——	
Prince of Wales I	Bill Wait (Liverpool)	1st ISDC Prestatyn
Romero I [Tango]	Colin Skidmore (Glasgow)	3rd ESTD
Ronde I	Colin Skidmore (Glasgow)	3rd ESTD
Royale [Tango]	Miss D. Stockbridge (Manchester)	Blackpool Finalist
Scintilla [Tango]	A. Halford	1st OBBD Filey
Toledo I	Frank Short (Birmingham)	3rd ESTD

Two Steps (1955)

Alabama	Edith Hurst (Sheffield)	1st MATD
Caribbean	Jan Telford (North Shields)	3rd NCDTA
Flirtation	———	
Jasfyl	Phyllis Adams (Swindon)	1st BATD Chester Trophy
Marigold	Pauline Collins	
Melody	Joyce Simonds (Lancashire)	1st UKAPTD
New Rig	Florence Newbegin	1st IDMA
Nicholas	Alfred Halford (Preston)	3rd Blackpool
Olympia	Nora Bray (Huddersfield)	1st IDMA
Thanet	George Moore (Westgate)	1st IDMA (South)
Unity	Arthur Lightfoot	1st BATD

Saunters (1955)

Crinoline	Bill Botham (Wythenshawe)	
Gossip	Eva Swain (Acton)	
Kingsway	Stan Ross (Watford)	1st ISTD
Saucy	Jack Jay	
Wentworth	Michael Gwynne	

Gavottes (1955)

Georgette	Ivy Fraser	1st IDMA (SE)
Godetia	Mr. and Mrs. Edney	

Miscellaneous (1955)

Alkirk Quickstep	Arthur Jones	1st FSDI
April Foxtrot	Sylvester and Ellen Burrows (Haydock)	
Caribbean	Gilbert Daniels	2nd NCDTA
County Schottische	Frank Noble and Nora Bray	Prize
Darktown Strutter (Quickstep)	———	
Gaumont Foxtrot	Mrs. Muriel Gladwin (Morecambe)	2nd NATD Blackpool
Harlequinade	Gerald Bullen (Southport)	
Karen Blues	Leslie Winmill (Risca, Monmouthshire)	1st IDMA
Mambo Italiano	Jan Telford (North Shields)	1st NCDTA
Nelfield Quickstep	———	
Regency Stroll	Gerald Bullen (Southport)	
Royal Mazurka	Frank Noble and Nora Bray	1st NATD Handley Trophy
Strutter (Party)	Mr. Clarry Clarke (Rhyl)	1st Blackpool
Tantro	Bob Cleave (Bramfield)	

Associations for Promoting Modern Sequence Dancing

By 1955 the old-time boom was well established but a look at the lists will show more dances appearing with a modern flavour. Some dance leaders stuck rigidly to old time while others included modern sequence dances in their programmes. There was some rivalry between MC's in an attempt to maintain numbers. Then, as now, sequence dancing was a democratic process in which dancers voted with their feet - if they didn't like the programme they moved somewhere else. Another source of division was between the qualified professionals and the gifted amateurs who had never taken a lesson from an expert. The wiser heads realised, however, that some degree of cooperation between leaders would be to the good of all. F. J. Mainey had established the ISDC and the OTDA for old-time sequence dancing but there were no institutions catering for the modern style.

In this climate some keen sequence dancers were moved to set up their own 'unofficial' organisations. These ranged from informal gatherings of MC's on a regular basis to the more highly developed institutions which provided their members with scripts gave advice on dancing matters, organised competitions and ran their own journals. Some had branches in various parts of the country and details of new dances soon spread throughout the UK. Setting up bodies of this kind is not as easy as it might appear, particularly if some type of newsletter or journal is to be produced. Someone needs to collect the information, write articles, get the material into print, advertise for members and collect subscriptions. There is also the problem of jockeying for power and the friction which often seems to arise when committed people meet together. Again in the 1950's printing and duplicating was not so easy as they are today. Eventually things began to settle down and some of the organisations have survived to the present day. In several cases their presidents, chairmen or secretaries have held office for more than 20 years - persistence is a common characteristic of sequence dancers!

Bill Botham was instrumental in establishing some modern sequence dancing institutions which have lasted to the present day - he was the 'F. J. Mainey' of the modern style. Born in Sheffield in 1891 he moved about a great deal but operated mainly in the Manchester region (and in Portsmouth for a time). He was a small man of tremendous energy and enthusiasm who held strong views which he could express very clearly. He made some enemies in the dancing hierarchy but was generally respected for his abilities and sincerity. Although he lived to be over 70 he was a semi-invalid for much of his life suffering great pain when he rose in the morning. His wife May was a great companion and partner -as Lady Contra she produced a regular page in his journal dealing with the more feminine aspects of dancing. After his death she continued his work, turning up when she could to present the May Botham Trophy at the SDF competitions.

Federation of Sequence Dance Instructors

The launch of the Bilmay Script Service by Bill Botham in 1949 was followed by the setting up of the FSDI in 1952. This was an organisation which sought to bring together unattached MC's and others who felt that the existing societies did not cater for their needs. Fellowship was open to members of 6 month's standing on passing a suitable examination and there was also an associate grade. Members received the monthly 'Sequence Dancers' Journal' (from 1954) and had access to the script service; postal tuition and advice on all aspects of sequence dancing (including suitable music and records) were also available. In 1957 a merger with the 'Association of Sequence Dance Teachers' (ASDT) and two other organisations produced the 'Federation of Sequence Dancing' which in turn became the 'National Alliance of Sequence Dancing' (NASD). Terry Drogan was Chairman from the first meeting becoming President later; he resigned in 1961 due to poor health. Jack Richardson was Secretary of the NASD in 1960 and later became Chairman. He resigned in 1968 being succeeded by Miss Agnes Whitham. NASD (North) held its 34th annual ball in Wigan in 1994. It was a sister club to the Manchester MC's club and Ken Fuller was Chairman of both. Their activities and the journal 'Focus' will come to an end in 1995.

NASD (Yorks) is known as the National Association of Sequence Dancing; it was still holding inventive dance competitions in 1992 (1st, Westaway Waltz by D. M. Simpson; 2nd and 3rd, Kirsty's Waltz and Poppy Quickstep by Jack and Flo Howard of Barnsley).

Fellowship of Sequence Dance Instructors

For various reasons Bill Botham launched a 'fellowship' in addition to his 'federation' in 1956. Of several sections established in 1959, the London branch was particularly successful becoming known as the 'Sequence Dance Fellowship' (see following section). The fellowship society journal 'Sequence Dance World' printed originally by Stan Smith of Hove contained scripts, news of meetings, articles by Bill and May Botham and much informed comment. Bill Edwards took over the production in 1968 changing the name to 'Focus'. From 1984 onwards Ken Fuller has arranged it for publication and provided most of the copy; it will cease printing in 1995. Each issue contained several dance scripts (mainly 'unofficial' in the later years) and reports of meetings of bodies such as the NASD and Rother Valley MC's Club.

Sequence Dancing Fellowship (SDF, London)

Bill Botham had moved from Manchester to Portsmouth in 1956 and with the help of Freddie and Mary Wilkins of Edmonton he was to establish a London branch of the FSDI in January 1958. When the federation amalgamated with the NASD the members decided to 'go it alone' and formed the 'Sequence Dancing Fellowship' in December 1959. Freddie Wilkins was President until 1961 followed by John Morgan who retired in 1987. John Lampwell (who joined in 1970) is now President and Chairman. Inventive dance competitions for the May Botham Trophy (any sequence) were held from 1957 to 1991 and from 1969 to 1991 for the Blundell Trophy (any old-time sequence dance). Charles and Doris Blundell joined the Fellowship in 1960 - Charles was Vice Chairman until his death in 1968. Mrs. Jean Harvey is the longest-serving member joining in 1956; she was Secretary for many years. Some of her SDF winning dances are the Quickstep Mary Rose (1982), Riverside Saunter (1988) and Kamar Waltz (1991).

Manchester MC's Club

This club was formed in March 1953 after an initial meeting of Bill Botham, Bill Hunter, Arthur Jones and Arthur Shawcross; in the early days monthly meetings were held in Salford. Ken Fuller was appointed Honorary Secretary in 1956 and has the remarkable record of almost 40 years service in the post. In recent years he has also been Chairman and producer of the magazine 'Focus' which has been the main source of 'unofficial' dances. Chairmen of the club in order of succession have been Terry Drogan (1956), Walter Schofield (1960), Bill Hunter (1965), Jim Dalton (1968), Joe Sayer (1977). The club was affiliated to FSDI in 1956 and merged with the Northern Area of NASD in 1991; the final meeting was held in May 1995. An annual ball has been held every year since 1957.

Yorkshire Sequence Dance Federation (YSDF)

Founder members in January 1967 were George Mott, Hilda Cowling, Frank Smith and Joan Elstub. Jack Richardson joined a month later and was elected Chairman - he was still in office in 1985. This was the year of Jack and Elsie's golden wedding and they were made life members of YSDF.

Over the years the YSDF has organised many social events for sequence dancers in Leeds, York, Harrogate, Rotherham and elsewhere. The Federation was noted for its high standards and efficient organisation. One outstanding function is the 'Sunday Special' at the Spa Royal Hotel in Bridlington which consists of lunch followed by 6 hours of sequence dancing and demonstrations. This attracts more than 800 dancers and has run continuously for 24 years. The Federation did, for a time, run its own inventive dance competitions with handsome trophies; it has raised considerable sums for charity. Much of its success may be attributed to Miss Joan Elstub who has been Secretary from 1967 to the present day. As well as being a good administrator she has considerable journalistic talent - several of her articles have appeared in the 'Focus' magazine. Her dances include the Aramis Tango (1975), Waltz Fascination (1976) and Waltz Jennette (1977).

PRESENTED IN 1956

Waltzes (Old-Time) (1956)

Aldora	Alex Napier	3rd IDMA (SE)
Ambassador	Stan Ross (Watford)	1st BATD Worrall Trophy
Britannia	Lew and May Miles (Carshalton)	
Candlelight	Sylvester Burrows (St. Helens)	1st UKAPTD
Chartreuse	Joyce Briggs	2nd Blackpool
Fiona	Nora Capps	1st NCDTA
Halloween	Doris Ions (Newport, Monmouthshire)	2nd IDMA
Inspiration	Rita Pover (St. Helens)	1st IDMA
Laurain	Laura Wray (Hove)	
Olympia [Waltz]	A. Halford (Preston)	1st MATD
Rock 'n' Roll	Bill Wait (Liverpool)	1st ISDC Prestatyn
Silvern	Syliva and Holland Brockbank	2nd BATD
Waltheof	Frank Warren and Vi Clifton	

Waltzes (Modern) (1956)

Bettina	Bill Wait (Liverpool)	
Cathrine (Catherine) [Waltz]	Arthur Shaw (Sheffield)	
Markette [Waltz]	(New Zealand)	
Norma	Norman Knowles	
Riversdale	Jon Evans	1st UKAPTD
Ronde	Jacqueline Jay	
Terre [Waltz]	Terry Drogan (Droylsden)	
Variety	Jack Rogers (Liverpool)	3rd ADA
White Rose I	Frank Noble and Nora Bray	1st ESTD Hayton Trophy
White Rose II	Fred Holmes	MATD

Two Steps (1956)

Alexander	Frank Noble and Nora Bray	1st NATD Handley Shield
Alhambra (Progressive)	Mrs. Ivy Harrison	
Courtesy	J. Chandler (Coventry)	
Holiday	B. L. Jay	2nd Prestatyn
Honeywell	Kay Ranwell	2nd OTDA Brittain Shield
Lancastrian	Bob Dale (Dukinfield)	2nd ESTD
Rene	Miss Arline Slighy	MATD Finalist
Vanity	Martine and Arthur Ives (London)	
Waverley	Maurice Fletcher (Long Eaton)	1st OBBD

Foxtrots (1956)

Dreamtime	Terry Drogan (Droylsden)	
Empire	Terry Drogan (Droylsden)	
Hasel	Freddie and Mary Wilkins (Edmonton)	5th Dance News
Melody I	W. Hunter (before 1953)	
Melody II	(Birkenhead)	
Invicta	George Moore	
Sherwood	Terry Drogan (Droylsden)	
White Rose	Fred Holmes (Sheffield)	

Tangos (1956)

Beryl [Tango]	———	
Carlton	E. Riley	
Cherie [Tango]	Maurice Fletcher (Long Eaton)	1st ISTD
Ecstasy [Tango]	Bill Wait (Liverpool)	
Ivena	Ivy Fraser	2nd IDMA (SE)
Maria II [Tango]	Jack Crossley (London)	1st Danceland Trophy

Saunters (1956)

Broadway	Doris Westaway	1st Dance News
Empire	Rita Pover (St. Helens)	3rd ESTD
Prince of Wales	Bill Wait (Liverpool)	1st ISDC
Regalia [Saunter]	Stan and Vi Ross (Watford)	1st BATD Chester Trophy
Rock & Roll	Frank Noble and Nora Bray	3rd IDMA
Stuart	Mrs. Ingham	2nd ISDC Prestatyn
White Rose	Fred and Ada Holmes (Sheffield)	2nd MATD

Schottisches (1956)

Glydella	Doreen Young (Bristol)	
Mayfair	Joe and Kathie Stead (Liverpool)	Blackpool Finalist
Vanity Fair	Frederick Rovery (Oxford)	

Quicksteps (1956)

| Kerry (Kwickstep) | Bill Botham | |
| Mayfair | Frank Short (Birmingham) | |

Miscellaneous (1956)

Carioca Samba (Rumba)	(Liverpool)	
Cyrann Gavotte	Cyril Saunders and Anne Hobbs	3rd Prestatyn
Embassy Blues	Betty Dyce	
Kathryn Mazurka	Maurice Vallance and Kathleen Bonner	2nd Dance News Slough

Miscellaneous (1956) (continued)

La Brooke	(New Zealand)	
Margarette [Samba]	Ken Fuller (Worsley)	
Nanette Gavotte	Frank Short (Birmingham)	4th IDMA
New Empress Parade	Frank Noble and Nora Bray	1st Blackpool
Patricia Quickstep	George Hague (Stockport)	
Virginia Reel	(An American Square Dance)	

La Brooke and Markette (1956) are 32-bar sequences popular in New Zealand. In the scripts there are 8 sections with headings such as 'balance and go right' and 'wheel round and go forward' - expressions used in American square dancing.

Maurice Fletcher's Waverley Two Step (1956) is used as an old-time championship dance; his Tango Cherie (1956) has both old-time and modern features.

Frank Noble and Nora Bray [Alexander Two Step (1956), Rock 'n' Roll Saunter (1956), New Empress Parade (1956)]

This couple from Huddersfield were the leading prize-winners of the day gaining some 25 awards from 1952 to 1960. Their dances covered a wide range of styles and were often fitted to popular tunes of the day. They demonstrated these with superb showmanship and great attention to detail. Their popular Wedgewood Blue Gavotte (1959) is now a championship dance.

Stan and Vi Ross [Ambassador Waltz (1956), Saunter Regalia (1956)]

Stan and Vi Ross of Watford have won many inventive dance competitions particularly with old-time waltzes, tangos and saunters. They have placed more emphasis on their prize-winning dances and some dozen of these appear in the lists from 1950 to 1960; their Tango Sebastian (1960) received great acclaim. They have been examiners for NATD and adjudicators; Stan was a book reviewer/writer for 'Dancing Times'.

PRESENTED IN 1957

Waltzes (Old-Time) (1957)

Alice	Mrs. B. Hale (Ealing)	
Around the World (Progressive)	———	
Belverdere I	Bob Dale (Manchester)	3rd ESTD
Blue Sapphire	Miss D. Stockbridge (Manchester)	
Cavalcade	Marjorie Wantling (Manchester)	
Champagne	Frank Short (Birmingham)	
Debut	George and Ann Nixon (Blackpool)	1st OBBD Filey
Empress II	Mrs. Ethel Dunn	
Eveline	Ellis Greenfield (Manchester)	
Floral	Edward Sharman	1st BATD Worrall Trophy
Fredericka	Fred Sellars (Scarborough)	
Glen Maye (Glenmayne)	Jim Brook (Morley, Leeds)	IDMA (Merit)
Heather	Iris Kempsell (Edmonton)	1st ISTD
Ken San	A. Perke (Bolton)	
Lotus	Alfred Halford (Preston)	1st Blackpool
Louise [Valse]	Bill and Phyllis Groves	
Majestic II	Jim and Freda Williams	
Mayfair	Margaret Lawrence	1st Woolwich DTA
Missouri	Mr. B. H. Buchanan	
Moonlight	Eric Stonehouse (Stockport)	Joint 3rd Blackpool
Pirouette [Waltz]	Anita Dewidar	
Rainbow III	Bob Dale (Manchester)	Joint 1st ISDC IOM
Richmond	Frank Noble and Nora Bray (Huddersfield)	1st IDMA
Trudie	Ellis Greenfield (Manchester)	
Valentine	Betty Dyce (Loughton)	

Waltzes (Modern) (1957)

Adoration I	Terry Drogan (Droylsden)	
Adoration II	Bill Botham (Wythenshawe)	
Anna Maria	Maurice and Eileen Barton	
Babette I [Waltz]	W. Hunter (Salford)	
Bedelia	Frank Short (Brimingham)	4th ESTD
Carlton (Progressive)	Ken Fuller (Worsley)	
September	Gerald Bullen (Southport)	
True Love	G. Onyon	
Venetia [Waltz]	Ken Fuller (Worsley)	
Welcome	Terry Drogan (Droylsden)	
Wild Rose	Jack Richardson (Huddersfield)	

Tangos (1957)

Alhambra	W. G. Harrison	
Capri II [Tango]	Ken Fuller (Worsley)	
D'oro [Tango]	Frank Noble and Nora Bray	3rd IDMA
Juan [Tango]	Miss Pauline Collins	
Jupiter	Frank Warren and Vi Clifton	2nd SDF Botham Trophy
L'amour [Tango]	Chas Compton	
La Scala	Eustace Touhey	1st ADA
Magnolia	Raymond Bailey (Macclesfield)	3rd IDMA
Moonlight	Jon Evans	
Pierre [Tango]	George Hague (Stockport)	
Red Moon	Frank Warren and Vi Clifton	1st IDMA (SE)
Senorita [Tango]	————	
Southern Star	Stan and Vi Ross (Watford)	1st NATD
Handley Sheild		
Tango 'M'	Arthur Ives (London)	
Victor	Raymond Bailey (Macclesfield)	4th IDMA
Violetta I [Tango]	Miss Violet Smith (Hove)	
Ysabelle	Kay Ranwell	2nd OTDA Brittain Shield

Foxtrots (1957)

Adele	Adela Roscoe (Nottingham)	
Blues	Ken Fuller	
Diana	G. Shaw (Rotherham)	
Eileen I	Maurice and Eileen Barton	
Eugene I	Mr. and Mrs. A. Thompson (Liverpool)	
Eugene II	Chas. Compton	
Felice	Phyllis Adams (Swindon)	1st BATD Chester Trophy
Hi-Fi	Frank Noble and Nora Bray	1st ESTD
Pearl	Frank Short (Birmingham)	
Roaming	R. T. Almond (Blackpool)	
Sylvan	H. Lockley (Birmingham)	
Unity	John Martin (Edinburgh)	
Windsor	Bill Burge	3rd SDF

Saunters (1957)

Evelene	J. Peake (Bolton)
Memories	Jim and Elsie Preece (Brighton)
Sunset I	Miss Elsie Brook
Sunset II	Capt. A. H. Lemon (Oxford)
Sway	George and Stella Berwick

Two Steps (1957)

Averil	George Fletcher	
Crown	F. Moore	
Fiesta	Joe Stead (Blackpool)	3rd Blackpool
Isle of Man	Elizabeth Clarke	1st ISDC IOM
Marjon	Miss Marjorie Webb (St. Helens)	3rd ADA
Party	John Moore	
Pauletta	Alfred Halford (Preston)	1st NATD
Pickwick	Charles Hales (Ealing)	2nd Dance News

Quicksteps (1957)

Broadway	Edith Farmer
Georgic	Mrs. T. Shaw (Wallasey)
Grosvenor	G. Shaw (Rotherham)
Rock Around	Bill Hall (Stretford)
Winfield	Miss Edith Winfield Taylor

Blues (1957)

Carolina	A. Thompson (Liverpool)	
Island	Bill Wait (Liverpool)	Joint 1st ISDC IOM
Louise	Mrs. Florence Whitefield	2nd ADA
Rock 'n' Roll I	Nancy Clarke and Helena van Gaart	
Rock 'n' Roll II	Alf Kendall (Coventry)	

Miscellaneous (1957)

Albert Glide	Brian Phillips and Pat Stacey (Sevenoaks)	1st SDF Botham Trophy
Crazy Otto Rag (Party)	Alex Moore	
Devon Mazurka	Bryan Wellington (Cardiff)	
Festival Glide	————	
Gay Paree One Step	Nora Bray and Frank Noble	1st Dance News
Gaytime Stroll	Irene Fitton	1st UKA
Glen Garry One Step	Frank Short (Birmingham)	2nd ESTD
Imperial Waltz Quadrille	Jack Crossley	
Liberty Hornpipe	Jock McInnes	2nd NCDTA
Myrvon Gavotte	Myrtle Langton	2nd NATD
Party Samba	Nancy Clarke (Rhyl)	
Regency Gavotte	Jean Bailey (Macclesfield)	
Road to the Isles Schottische II	Jock McInnes	
Scottish Ladbroke	Ralph Ward (London)	
Swinging the Blues	Bill Thornburn	
Wandering Three Step	Bill Botham	

Ann Nixon's Waltz Debut was unusual in having an allemande for the man in the 4th bar. It was an innovation at the time but is common nowadays in Latin-American dances. The Glen Maye Waltz of Jim Brook takes its name from the town and glen in the Isle of Man; it is very popular on the island.

Bob Dale, dancing with Betty Wait, won first prize at the ISDC Douglas Festival with his Rainbow Waltz; it was led off to great applause by Mr. and Mrs. Harry Ashworth at Blackpool and became very popular. Adela Roscoe (1951) and Frank Short (1952) have other old-time Rainbow waltzes.

Different dates are given for the very popular Broadway Quickstep of Edith Farmer but it was certainly featured on the programme for the Manchester MC's ball held at the Locarno Ballroom in Sale on 29th November, 1957.

Bill and Betty Hunter [Babette Waltz (1957)]

Bill and Betty Hunter were founder members of the Manchester MC's Club, Bill being the first President. Their Tudor Quickstep and Picador Tango appear in Bill Botham's 1953 MC's Handbook. Three more of their arrangements are the Bee Bee Quickstep, Gaiety Quickstep and Sapphire Waltz. They celebrated their Golden Wedding in September 1979.

Terry Drogan [Waltz Charmaine (1955), Dreamtime, Empire and Sherwood Foxtrots (1956), Welcome Waltz (1957)]

Terry Drogan of Droylsden arranged more than a dozen dances, the most popular being the Waltz Charmaine (1955) and Iris Foxtrot (1958). He joined the Manchester MC's Club in 1953 and was Chairman for a period. He organised the first MC's ball for the Club at the Princess Ballroom in Chorlton, Manchester which was a great success - this function has continued to the present day. He was President of the FSDI and in 1960 became Chairman of the NASD (National Alliance of Sequence Dancing) formed by the merger of the FSDI with the ASTD (Association of Sequence Dance Teachers). He resigned in 1961 due to ill-health and was succeeded by Wilf Dunn.

PRESENTED IN 1958

Waltzes (Old-Time) (1958)

Camay [Waltz]	Mrs. Patricia Joss (Burnley)	1st Blackpool
Camelia	Arthur and Martine Ives	
Fair Lady	Stan and Vi Ross	BATD
Freesia	Joyce Briggs (Bradford)	1st OBBD Filey
Golden Melody	Frank Noble and Nora Bray	1st ESTD
Honeysuckle Rose	Mme. Black	
Isle of Man	Robert Stewart	ISDC
Lanmoor	Bill Crosbie (Lancaster)	
Linden	Ken Fuller (Worsley)	
London	Will and Kay Ranwell	
Mayflower	Vi Ross (Watford)	1st Dance News Shield
Miramar	Doris Ions	
Regency	Frank Noble and Nora Bray	1st NATD Handley Shield
Roulette	Arnold Taylor	
Saphena	Ann Dixon	3rd Blackpool
Shirley	Will Ranwell	2nd OTDA
Tina	Jack Hayes (Newark)	2nd IDMA
Waltz of the Bells	————	
Winifred [Valse]	Wilf Smith (Birmingham)	
Worral	Stan Ross	BATD

Waltzes (Modern) (1958)

Anniversary	————
Carolina	Ken Fuller (Worsley)
Delight [Waltz]	Syd Black
Dorissa [Waltz]	Ken Fuller (Worsley)
Dutch Spring (Party)	Johnny Arntz
Evening	Rita Pover (St. Helens) 3rd ESTD
Friendship	Joe and Trudy Thompson (Liverpool)
Marcella [Waltz]	E. Rudd (Ulverston)
Marlene [Waltz]	Joe Collier (Clifton, Manchester)
Morecambrian	Bert Hutton (Morecambe)
Sylvia [Waltz]	J. P. Gusman
Whispering I	Terry Drogan (Droylsden)
Willow	Mrs. A. Thompson

Tangos (1958)

Angelus	Ken Fuller (Worsley)	
Del Marina [Tango]	Jeff Chandler (Coventry)	
Fredericka [Tango]	Fred Sellars (Scarborough)	
Glennifer	James A. Wilson (Glasgow)	
Harlequin I	James A. Wilson (Glasgow)	
Isle of Man	Robert and Winifred Abraham	1st ISDC (IOM)
Jeannette [Tango]	Fred Bray Cotten	
Julian	———	
La Ma	Miss Mabel Lovett (Skegness)	
Lavelle [Tango]	Rita Pover (St. Helens)	1st IDMA
Madelaine [Tango]	Ken Fuller (Worsley)	
Majanah I	Raymond Bailey (Macclesfield) (earlier)	
Majanah II	G. Onyon	
Marianne	Ken Fuller (Worsley)	
Mayfair	Barbara Hale (Ealing)	
Mexicana [Tango]	J. Adley (London)	
Monaco	Ken Fuller (Worsley)	
Myrvon (Progressive)	Jack and Myrtle Langton (Dudley)	
Originaire [Tango]	J. W. Johnson	
Ronde II	Michael Gwynne (Bournemouth)	
Rosita I [Tango]	Ken Fuller (Worsley)	
Santa Barbara [Tango]	Lionel Clark (Portsmouth)	3rd ASDT (S)
Sombrero [Tango]	Alfred Halford (St. Helens)	1st DTA
Spanish I	Joe C. Smith	

Two Steps (1958)

Conference	Tony Gallagher	
Elizabeth II	Elsie Brooks (Bradford)	
JP	Reg Penford	ISDC
Martine	Martine and Arthur Ives (Sevenoaks)	2nd ESTD
Premier	Committee of OBBD	
Seaburn	Miss Lilian Harrison (Seaburn)	
Skegness	———	
Social I (Party)	Ken Fuller (Worsley)	
Social II (Party)	James Quinn	
Thistle	I. Mack	
White Rose	Fred and Ada Holmes	

Saunters (1958)

Britannia	Committee of OBBD	OBBD
Catalina	Miss Pat Scott	1st BATD Chester Trophy
Chevalier	Bill Wait (Liverpool)	
Doretta	George Moore	
Evergreen	George Fletcher	
Foxtrot [Saunter]	Lilian Parry	4th ADA
Jaunty	Ivy Fraser (London)	4th IDMA
Lydia	George Gunner	
M	Martine Ives	
Montrose	Iris Kempsell (Edmonton)	1st ISTD
Portchester	Jack Crossley (BBC TV)	
Sentimental I [Saunter]	Ken Fuller (Worsley)	
Springtime	E. V. Wheale	1st OTDA Brittain Shield
Swanmore	Maurice and Eileen Barton	
Therese	Ken Fuller	4th IDMA

Quicksteps (1958)

Brampton	Margaret Dodd (Bexley Heath)	Woolwich DTA
Comet	Frank Warren and Vi Clifton	3rd IDMA (S)
County	Ken Fuller	
Crystal I	Bill Wait (Liverpool)	
David	J. L. Walmsley	
Fair Oak	Maurice Barron	
Harlequin	———	
Julie Ann	Violet Gusman (Portchester)	
Maureen	George Gunner (Croydon)	
Sentimental	Ken Fuller (Worsley)	
Sequence	———	
Susie	A. Lynn	

One Steps (1958)

Columbia	Veronica Moore (Westgate)	
Festival	Frank Noble and Nora Bray	2nd Blackpool
Harlequin	Kathleen M. Wood	2nd IDMA (SE)
Isle of Man	Bob Dale and Rita Pover	1st ISDC (IOM)
Prince of Wales	Jim Williams (Llandudno)	
Recreation	George Dunn	

Blues (1958)

Cafuffule	E. M. C. Mansfield Rhodes (Birmingham)	2nd IDMA (Blackpool)
Priscilla	Joe Collier (Clifton Moor)	
Rock 'n' Roll Rhythm	Nora Capps (Newton Aycliffe)	1st NCDTA
Swinging I	Catherine Betts	
Trudie	Gerald Bullen (Southport)	1st ADA
Vienna	Jack Mercer	

Foxtrots (1958)

Avril I	Sylvester and Ellen Burrows (earlier)	
Avril II	Kay Ranwell	
Delamere	Jo and Kathie Stead (Blackpool)	
Iris	Terry Drogan (Droylsden)	
Jaunty	Ivy Fraser (London)	4th IDMA
Lydia	George Gunner (Croydon)	
Mayley	Jimmie May (Colchester)	
Merry	C. E. Lambert (Barrow)	
Olympic	M. Jennings	
Peke	Lionel Clark (Portsmouth)	
Pennanx	Jack Richardson (Huddersfield)	
Southern	Jack Smith (Portsmouth)	
Susanne	Bob McLean	
Twinkle	L. Lovell (Skegness)	IDMA
Zeta	Doris Westaway	

Miscellaneous (1958)

Alexander Rag	Ken Fuller (Worsley)	
Blackpool Walk	Adela Roscoe (Nottingham)	
Bobette Schottische	Bobby Shields (Bradford)	
Calypso	Jim Williams (Llandudno)	
Cherry Mazurka	Kathleen Ranwell	
Devonaire Gavotte	Bryan Wellington	
Gaiety Mazurka	Anita Dewider	DTA
Lindy Lou Swing	Syd Black (Bishops Stortford)	
Midway [The]	Joe Collier (Clifton, Manchester)	
Northern Parade	Brian Graham	
Palais Swing	Ken Fuller (Worsley)	
Silver Parade	Sidney Owen (Birmingham)	2nd DTA
South American Way (Rumba)	Ken Fuller (Worsley)	
Tea For Two	———	
Trudie Parade	E. Jack	
Verglas (Foxtrot)	———	

The Quest for the Ideal Sequence Leader

(Adapted from Noel Pearce's feature of 1956)

We thought we would leave our regular MC as he put on too many new dances and was always changing the tunes. Not only that but he made newcomers just as welcome as dancers that had been with him for years. Those who went away and came back were treated with friendship - every courtesy was shown to them.

There are lots of dances in our area and we started with Mr. A. Here we were treated like royalty. The MC and his wife split us up time after time to show us the finer points. We like to dance together without too much fuss and this wore us down eventually.

Mr. B was a great stylist with a group of classy, ambitious dancers. He obviously did not think much to dancers of our calibre and left us severely alone.

Mr. C could remember and perform every dance that ever was but his footwork defied description - no-one could learn much by watching him.

Mr. D was orthodox and everything about his dancing session was correct and above reproach. No-one laughed and we had the same feeling as if we had been to a church service.

With Mr. E laughter was the order of the day although we had an uneasy feeling that they were laughing at us but couldn't quite pin it down.

Moving further down the alphabet we found leaders that were too loud and talked too much, others that made announcements that we couldn't hear. Some took an extended interval after each dance, others had started the next dance before we had left the floor.

Weighing it all up, we went back to our original MC who received us with every courtesy. We have learnt that there is no ideal MC - what suits one dancer may not suit another.

Harry and Rose Dabbs - A link with the past

The acid test for dance leaders is can they retain their numbers? When they start a new session somewhere else are dancers knocking on their door? While reliability and standards of performance are important, successful leaders have that extra something that makes their sessions rewarding and enjoyable. Their open-mindedness and concern for others seems to show through - they have a sort of charisma. Harry and Rose Dabbs had these qualities.

Rose Dabbs (née Rosie Johns) started dancing in 1904 when she was 8 years old taking lessons with Fred Moore (father of Alex Moore of ballroom fame). Harry Dabbs took up dancing in his teens being taught by A. J. Latimer and his sister, Marie, in Leytonstone. They married after the First World War and won many old-time competitions in the early 1920's. In 1922 they went into business, retiring to South Benfleet in Essex in 1948. They had done some dancing in the meantime, particularly in the Royal Tottenham ballroom where Freddie Nichols ran old-time dancing for Mecca in the late 1940's. On taking up dancing seriously again after retirement, they found that styles had changed and they took lessons and gained awards with an ISTD coach. In 1952 they started an old-time club which rapidly expanded and aroused interest in surrounding areas. By 1960 they had sessions on five days of the week in various town and villages in the Southend area.

They were first class teachers of old-time and did much to raise the standards of dancing in the clubs. Nevertheless, they were not averse to the modern style and ran mixed programmes including modern dances from the 1950's. They combined high standards of teaching with a great desire to share their knowledge and expertise with others - an example of all that is best in sequence dance leaders.

Their Kingsway Waltz (1961) is a neat arrangement of popular movements which run smoothly into one another. The Telestar Modern Waltz (1962) was arranged by Miss Rose Dabbs.

PRESENTED IN 1959

Waltzes (Old-Time) (1959)

Arene [Waltz]	Arnold Taylor (Bradford)	OBBD Finalist
Bijou	A. Richmond	1st NATD Handley Shield
Chiffon	Jack and Joyce Briggs	
Domino	George and Stella Berwick	
Eirlys	Bobby Howes (Coventry)	1st Rollinson Trophy
Gipsy Princess	Ken Fuller (Worsley)	
Kenley	George Gunner (Croydon)	
St. Omer	R. L. Garrigan (Oxford)	1st ESTD (S)
Wendy	Margarette M. Almond	ADA

Waltzes (Modern) (1959)

Cherie [Waltz]	Ken Fuller (Worsley)	
Christine [Waltz]	Ken Fuller (Worsley)	4th ASTD (S)
Doretta	George and Stella Barwick	
Elaine I [Waltz]	George and Lydia Gunner (Croydon)	
Elise [Waltz]	Jack Richardson (Huddersfield)	
Geneve [Waltz]	Alan Mitchell (Hayling Island)	
Inverness	Terry Drogan (Droylsden)	
Lucerne [Waltz]	Edward Rudd	3rd ASTD
Sincere [Waltz]	A. Shaw (Sheffield)	
Somerville	Jack Jay	
Springtime	Alan Mitchell	
Waverley	Ken Fuller (Worsley)	4th ASTD
Willow Pattern	Anita Singer	3rd DTA

Tangos (1959)

Alysia	Syd Black (Bishops Stortford)	
Anglesea	Rosina Knight (Isle of Wight)	
Black Knight	Frank Warren and Vi Clifton	1st IDMA (SE)
Black Magic	Michael Gwynne	3rd ISTD
Bluebell	Nora Capps	1st NCDTA
Bonita I	Mrs. E. V. Wheale (Middleton, Staffs.)	1st OTDA
Cambria	Terry Drogan (Droylsden)	
Eastoke	Alan Mitchell	1st ASTD Flower Trophy
Florenza	Ken Park (Newcastle)	3rd NCDTA
Harlequin II	Jack and Joyce Briggs	1st UKA
Jealousy [Tango]	Ken Fuller (Worsley)	

Tangos (1959) (continued)

Jose [Tango]	Barry Bush (Coventry)	
Mantilla I [Tango]	Nora Capps (Newton Aycliffe)	3rd OBBD
Marina I [Tango]	Maurice Vallance (Southall)	3rd ISDC IOM
Marina II [Tango]	Syd Black (Bishop's Stortford)	
Mia [Tango]	Ken Fuller (Worsley)	
Michelle [Tango]	Ken Fuller (Worsley)	
Serena [Tango]	Stan Ross (Watford)	2nd OBBD
Supreme [Tango]	Maurice Fletcher and Fay Burrows	1st ISTD
Tyrolean I	Miss Doreen Young (Bristol)	

Saunters (1959)

Annabelle	Harry Greenwood (Bradford)	
Blue Nile	———	Prize Winner
Debonaire [Saunter]	Gerald Bullen (Southport)	SDTA
Promenade II	Phyllis Elston	
Rosemary	R. G. Alderton (Finchley)	
Serene I	T. Livington	
Shadow	Joan Whippey (Reading)	1st Dance News
Windsor	Vic Moore	

Two Steps (1959)

Federation	Ken Fuller (Worsley)	
Pennine	Jack and Joyce Briggs	1st BATD Chester Trophy
Sousa	Syd Walker (Southampton)	
Star	Jimmy Mack (Fulham)	Finalist ISTD
Stella Maris	Mrs. I. Taylor (Blackpool)	1st Blackpool
Tivoli	Frank Short (Birmingham)	2nd ESTD

Quicksteps (1959)

Arizona	John and Ida Hill (Liverpool)	
Avon I	Ken Fuller	
Club	Ken Fuller (Worsley)	1st Woolwich DTA
Dinsdale	Molly Affleck (Sunderland)	2nd NCDTA
Golunio	Peter Sagar	
Granada	Terry Drogan (Droylsden)	

Foxtrots (1959)

Bluebell	Fred and Ivy Bray-Cotten (Brighton)	
Broadway	N. C. Locke	1st BATD
Dream I	Tony Banks	1st ASTD N
Eileen II	Terry Drogan (Droylsden)	
Hillside	George Gunner (Croydon)	
Idaho	Bobby and Eileen Howe (Coventry)	1st IDMA
Karen	Ron Free (High Wycombe)	1st ISTD London
Laurigan	Mr. and Mrs. L. Ratigan (Crewe)	1st ESTD Hayton Trophy
Regnum	Hilda Johnson	2nd ASTD
Snaefell	Robert Stewart (Northampton)	1st ISDC
Venus	J. Jack	
Viceroy (Teaching Dance)	W. T. Owen (Walsall)	

One Steps (1959)

Christine	Pat and Brian Phillips	1st SDF May Botham Trophy
Party	ESTD (Southern Area)	1st ESTD (SE)
Trampoline	Muriel Gladwin (Morecambe)	1st SDF May Botham Trophy

Blues (1959)

Frederika	Fred Dawson (Burnley)	1st Manchester MC's
Park Lane	Leslie Winmill	
Sherrie	Jack Board (London)	

Gavottes (1959)

My Fair Lady	Gwendoline James	
Wedgewood Blue	Frank Noble and Nora Bray	1st OBBD Filey

Miscellaneous (1959)

Bear Step (Party)	Bobby Howe (Coventry)	2nd Springstep Competition
Children's Circle Dance	(Based on Swiss Dance Movements)	
Fredericka Schottische	Mrs. Constance F. Geer (Woolwich)	
Jonida Cha Cha Cha	John and Ida Hill (Liverpool)	
Majong Swing	Marjorie Webb	1st ADA
Marion Glide	Joyce Simmonds	1st UKAPTD
Party Fours	———	
Petite Mazurka	Miss Pat Scott (Bath)	1st BATD Worrall Trophy
Rag Time	Helena Van Gaart	2nd IDMA Blackpool
Saturday Cha Cha Cha	Jack Richardson (Huddersfield)	
Trudie Glide	Ken Fuller	

The Waltz Sincere is an early example of a modern waltz still danced in northern circles today. It starts with 8 bars of a reverse waltz square and includes a whisk, promenade chassé and hesitation change; it is played at 32 bpm.

The Cha-Cha supplement to the 'Melody Maker' of 29th November, 1958 had this to say: "Cha-Cha is sweeping the country. Dozens of records are being released. Established bands are frantically including cha-cha items in their repertoire. The BBC and ITV are featuring it on the air and 'small screen'. And dancers are returning to the dance halls at the call of this exciting rhythm." The Jonida and Saturday Cha Cha Chas are early sequence forms of this dance which has proved a popular addition to the modern repertoire (more than 80 prizewinners between 1975 and 1994).

The calypso is a satirical song extemporised to a syncopated accompaniment; its origins are in Trinidad. The Calypso (1958) is a sequence dance performed to rumba or rock 'n' roll music. It should be danced in loose ballroom hold with the tap steps executed with a forward and outward rolling of the hips and knees.

George and Lydia Gunner [Lydia Saunter (1958), Maureen Quickstep (1958), Lydia Foxtrot (1958)]

The Kenley Waltz takes its name from the Kenley O.T. Dance Club near Croydon where George and Lydia were instructors and MC's. There is also a Lydia Waltz with special music written by one of George's relations.

Will and Kay Ranwell [Honeywell Two Step (1956), London Waltz Shirley Waltz, Cherry Mazurka, Avril Foxtrot (1958)]

Will and Kay of Thornton Heath were MC's with the Streatham and Mitcham and Britannia Clubs. Both the Gunners and the Ranwells were prominent members of the NASD in the South London region and several of their arrangements appear in the following lists; they were on very friendly terms. Will Ranwell was President of OTDA for 6 years.

PRESENTED IN 1960

Waltzes (Old-Time) (1960)

Alster	Ken Fuller (Worsley)	
Belvedere II	Mervyn and Margot Alderman	1st ISDC
Brangwyn	J. Spence (Brighton)	2nd ESTD South
Cherokee	Bobbie Howe (Coventry)	2nd IDMA
Christina	Frank Noble and Nora Bray	1st ESTD Hayton Trophy
Dancers	Michael Gwynne	
Dawn	Joan Wilson (Heanor)	3rd OBBD
Diana	Phyllis Groves	1st DTA
Ellan Vannin	Eva' Swain (Ealing)	
Elysia	Bill and Lily Dormer	1st Woolwich DTA
Engagement	Ken Park	2nd NCDTA
Fairlawn	Arthur Richmond	1st NATD
Fayland	Kay Ranwell	
Grosvenor I	Alfred HAlford	1st DTA
Grosvenor II	Sydney Lynton	IDMA
Julie [Waltz]	Mrs. Constance Geer	
Maytime	Mrs. Glenys Parsons (Cross Keys, Mon.)	
Melody	Frank Noble and Nora Bray	2nd OBBD
Orchid	John W. King (Doncaster)	BATD
Spanish	Len Colvin	

Waltzes (Modern) (1960)

Alexandra	Ken Fuller (Worsley)	
Annette	Ken Fuller (Worsley)	
Candy	Sam Clegg (Lancashire)	
Chi-Co [Waltz]	Lilian Perry (Liverpool)	1st ADA
Homecoming	L. Banks (Ashton-under-Lyme)	
Juliana	Roger Walsh	
Julietta	Roger Walsh	
Margaret	Ken Fuller (Worsley)	
Priory	J. Johnson	
Soas	———	
Star	Terry Drogan (Droylsden)	
Starlight I	Ken Fuller (Worsley)	
Superbe [Waltz]	Norman Knowles (Denton)	

Tangos (1960)

Autumn	Ken Fuller (Worsley)	
Lilani	Vera Matthews (Cardiff)	1st IDMA
Minerva	Frank Short (Birmingham)	1st ESTD
Riverside [Tango]	Robert Styles (High Wycombe)	1st IDMA
Rosita II [Tango]	Frank Noble and Nora Bray (Huddersfield)	2nd Blackpool
Sebastian II	Stan Ross (Watford)	1st OBBD
Silverside	R. Styles (High Wycombe)	1st IDMA (SE)
Sweet Afton	Jack Crossley	
Willows	Mrs. M. Bryant (St. Helens)	1st UKAPTD
Windsor II	J. E. Toulney	ISTD
Zetland	John Borthwick	

Foxtrots (1960)

Amanda	George Griffiths (Woking)	2nd DTA
Colindor	Colin McLachlan (London)	
Gloria	———	
Jeffrey	George Gunner (Croydon)	1st NASD
Lucinda	Bill and Betty Elsdon (London)	1st IDMA (SE)
Millbrook	Freddie and Mary Wilkins (Edmonton)	1st Dance News Trophy
Sapphire	W. C. Hunter (Worsley)	

Two Steps (1960)

Edinburgh	Barbara Hale (Ealing)	1st ISTD (London)
Lindy Lou	Capt. A. H. Lemon (Oxford)	1st OTDA
Newton	Tom Bryant (St. Helens)	1st UKAPTD
Prince	Jimmie Mack	2nd ISTD London
Zig Zag	Cecil Rualt	

Blues (1960)

Adrian	George Gunner (Croydon)	
Deep River	Fred Rovery (Oxford)	1st ESTD (S)
Piccadilly	Joe Collier (Bolton)	
St. Helens	Frank Warren and Vi Clifton	
Southlands	Robert Stewart	2nd ISDC (IOM)

Quicksteps (1960)

Brittania I	Ken Fuller (Worsley)
Elevera	Miss V. Lund (Calgate)
Piccadilly	Miss D. Stockbridge (Manchester)

Saunters (1960)

Evening	Ken Fuller (Worsley)	2nd NASD
Royal Wedding I	Molly Affleck (Sunderland)	3rd NCTDA
Ruby	A. Thompson (Liverpool)	
Sunnyside	Miss Norma Young	1st BATD Chester Trophy

Miscellaneous (1960)

Aba Daba	Nora Bray and Frank Noble (Huddersfield)	1st Blackpool
Anglia Glide	Albert Lambourne	1st SDF Botham Trophy
Bayfield Mazurka	———	
Fiesta	Audrey Broome (Brigg)	
Happy Cha Cha Cha	Ken Fuller (Worsley)	
Honey Mazurka	Miss Ivy Fraser (London)	3rd IDMA
La Belle Suzanne	Fred and Jess Burger	
Marlborough Gavotte	Mr. and Mrs. Abraham	2nd ISDC
Party Twist	Ken Fuller (Worsley)	
Shiralee Gavotte	Eric and Phyllis Bolton (Nelson)	
Silver Fox	Bill Wait (Liverpool)	3rd ISDC (IOM)
Tower Swing	Ken Fuller (Worsley)	
Westoe Parade	Nora Capps	1st NCDTA

The Royal Wedding Saunter commemorates the wedding of Princess Margaret and Mr. A. Armstrong Jones on 6th May, 1960. In 1978 Ken Park arranged an old-time Golden Wedding Waltz specially for Molly Affleck (1st Prize NCDTA). She had a Silver Wedding Waltz in 1953 (2nd NCDTA). Her other dances include the Sapphire Blues (1954), Gardenia Waltz (1955) and Dinsdale Quickstep (1959).

John and Ida Hill [Golden Festival Tango (1954), Tango Barcelona (1955), Lindy Lou Swing (1958), Arizona Quickstep (1959)]

The Hills of Liverpool were MC's at the Tower Ballroom in New Brighton just across the Mersey; their programmes were noted for their modern sequence content. They were members of the Manchester MC's Club and the Secretary, Ken Fuller, wrote the Tower Swing (1960) for them. Although swings are classed as old-time dances very few were arranged before 1960.

PRESENTED IN 1961

Waltzes (Old-Time) (1961)

Edlena	Albert Ford (Dukinfield)	
Juroy	Roy Brittle	2nd ISDC IOM
Kingsway	Harry and Rose Dabbs (Hadleigh)	
Marguerite [Waltz]	Margo Alderman	4th IDMA
Mavona	Ken Park (Newcastle)	2nd NCDTA
Romany	Will Ranwell	1st OTDA
Rosewood	Frank Warren and Vi Clifton (London)	2nd IDMA
True Love	Mr. G. Onyon (Hertford)	
Venus	Bill Clark (Portsmouth)	
Weekend	Jean Stokes and Mr. Berry (Eltham)	1st Woolwich DTA
Worrall	Phyllis Adams (Swindon)	1st BATD Worrall Trophy

Waltzes (Modern) (1961)

Quorn	Jim Long (Leicester)	
Riley	Jacqueline Jay (London)	
Savoy [Waltz]	Jon Evans	1st UKAPTD
Serenade [Waltz]	Mrs. Ann Beardsworth (Accrington)	
Silver	Thelma Caddy	
Sorrento [Waltz]	Ken Fuller (Worsley)	
Summertime	Thomas Brooke	
Suzanne	H. Lawton (Newcastle-under-Lyme)	2nd NASD Flower Trophy

Saunters (1961)

Brooklyn	Raymond Capps	1st NCDTA
Dunnwood	George Gunner (Croydon)	Jnt. 1st OTDA
Ilkley Moor	George Mott and Hilda Cowling	
Marina	Arthur Lightfoot (Leeds)	1st ISDC IOM
Progressive	Sylvia and Holland Brockbank (Bournemouth)	1st BATD Chester Trophy
Revé [Saunter]	Rita Pover (London)	1st OBBD Filey

Tangos (1961)

Bell	Mr. and Mrs. Arthur Dunn (Portsmouth)	
Isola	L. A. Clark	
Layton	Diane Winslade	
Lilac	Ken Fuller (Worsley)	
Moderna [Tango]	Kay Ranwell	Joint 2nd OTDA
Olympic	Alan and Brenda Holt (Leigh)	
Raymonde [Tango]	Joan Stokes (Eltham)	3rd Woolwich DTA

Tangos (1961) (continued)

Rosanna	Ken Fuller (Worsley)	1st NASD Flower Trophy
Serida [Tango]	Rita Pover (London)	1st Dance News
Trevan	Trevor J. Downe	
Twilight	Dorothy Wilson and Clifford Potts	1st ESTD
Whispering	Ken Fuller (Worsley)	

Two Steps (1961)

Howard	Maurice Tait (Nottingham)	
Kennan	———	
Kentucky	———	
Southern	Arthur Ives	1st ESTD
Victoria	Mrs. Betty Elsdon (North London)	1st Blackpool
		Bickerstaffe Shield

Foxtrots (1961)

Danuta	Robert Stewart	NATD Handley Shield
Flirtation	L. C. Lark	
Franfield	F. W. Wheale (Tamworth)	
Glad Rag	Miss D. Jennings	2nd Woolwich DTA
Gwenneth	Ken Fuller (Worsley)	
Locarno	Joe Collier (Bolton)	
Kingsmoor	George Carter	1st SDF Botham Trophy
Manhattan	Ken Fuller (Worsley)	
Mitzi	J. Johnson (Colchester)	

Cha Cha Cha (1961)

Barn Dance	W. N. Baker (Manchester)	
Cheery	Harry Greenwood	
Jacqueline	Laurie Ratigan (Crewe)	1ST DTA London

Quicksteps (1961)

Bluebell	Ken Fuller (Worsley)
Crescent	Ken Fuller (Worsley)
Dalston	Jim Dalton (Todmorden)
Dena	Ken Fuller (Worsley)
Elizabeth	———
Glamis	———
Jovi	George Gunner (Croydon)
Pauletta I (Party)	Molly Affleck (Sunderland)

95

Miscellaneous (1961)

Californians	R. Bailly	IDMA
Classic Gavotte	Maurice Tait (Nottingham)	1st ISTD
Continental [Rumba]	Alan and Brenda Holt (Leigh)	
Cotswold Cotillon	J. F. Hanglin (Broadway, Worcs.)	DTA
El Paso	Alan and Brenda Holt (Leigh)	
Hamilton Glide	Martine Ives	
Jasmine Gavotte	G. Onyon (Hereford)	1st DTA
Miranda [Samba]	Jim Brennan (Warrington)	
Normansie (Foxtrot)	George Gunner (Croydon)	3rd NASD Flower Trophy
Plantation Blues	E. Lockwood (Huddersfield)	
Riversdale Blues	John Gould	3rd ISDC IOM
South West One Step	Frank Warren and Vi Clifton	Joint 2nd IDMA (SE)
Um-Pah Parade (Novelty)	Laurence Ratigan (Crewe)	

The Dunnwood Saunter is named after Wilf Dunn (President of NASD in 1961) and Wilf Wood of Ryde in the Isle of Wight. Wilf and Jessie Wood were MC's for many years at the Trouville Hotel in Sandown. The Saunter has 4 sections each starting with 2 forward walks.

The Cotswold Cotillon has figures from the Brittania Saunter, Latchford Schottische, Military, Boston and Premier Two Steps, Eva and Naval Three Steps, La Mascotte and the Gainsborough Glide. Other modern square dances are the Queen's Quadrilles (1953) and Imperial Waltz Quadrilles (1957) (512 bars) by Jack Crossley and the Tango Quadrilles. The Lancashire Square Dance (1952) and Princess Progressive Square Dance (1952) have the dancers in two circles with man facing and lady backing to the wall; they have much shorter sequences of 24 and 48 bars respectively.

Rita Pover

Rita Pover has been a most successful arranger of popular and championship dances. Her Tango Serida (1961) is a well-known old-time tango sometimes used as a progressive dance. Dancing with Bob Dale at the ISDC Douglas Festival of 1958 she won the One Step Award with the Isle of Man One Step. Her Saunter Rêve (1961), Tango Victoria (1963) and Regis Waltz (1964) are Official Board championship dances; some dozen of her dances appear in the lists from 1956 to 1969.

Holland Brockbank (1913 - 1993)

[Royal Saunter (1953), Progressive Saunter (1961)]

Holland Brockbank was a Manchester man who made a great contribution to the development of sequence dancing. He was a gentleman in the best sense of the word, a fine dancer and a man of great courage and persistence. He was the only son of Thomas Holland Brockbank who died when Holland was only 12. An attack of snow blindness when on holiday in Switzerland in his twenties impaired his vision and he changed from his career in accountancy to ballroom dancing becoming in time a Fellow and Examiner for BATD and ISTD. While serving with the fire service during the war he met and married Sylvia Pratt who ran her own school of dancing at the Bournemouth Pavilion. Holland and Sylvia were MC's for a time on the radio programme 'Those Were The Days' and did much to popularise sequence dancing. Further ill-health restricted his dancing however and he joined Michael Gwynne in what later became the Brockbank-Lane Script Service.

Percy Lane (1913-1988)

Percy Lane and Holland Brockbank met and became friends while serving on the Fire Service in the Weymouth area during World War II (Sylvia Pratt was on the switchboard). Percy was a great organiser of social events and ran a small dance band. He was persuaded to take up dancing and dance teaching and ran a thriving dance school in Weymouth. Two of his dances are the Duet (Cha Cha) (1973) and Tiara Tango.

Ron Lane (1947-)

Ron Lane is the only child of Percy and Marjorie Lane. He gained his first BATD old-time medal at the age of 5 being taught by Holland Brockbank. He took up ballroom and Latin dancing and had some successes in amateur competitions. He worked for 23 years in the Ministry of Defence leaving to join his father in the Brockbank-Lane Script Service. Some of his recent successes (dancing with Audrey Bromage) are the Tuscany Tango (1991), Sahara Foxtrot (1991), Renaissance Rumba (1992) and Miami Rumba (1993).

PRESENTED IN 1962

Waltzes (Old-Time) (1962)

Adela [Waltz]	Joan Wilson	
Bobette	Betty Dyce (Loughton)	
Bonsoir	G. H. Beale (Middlesborough)	
Celeste [Waltz]	Marjorie Webb (Doncaster)	1st BATD Worral Trophy
Delight [Waltz]	Maurice Tait and Pauline Pritchard	2nd OBBD
Elite	Lewis and Joan Wilson (Heanor)	2nd Blackpool
Evergreen	Betty Elsdon (London)	1st IDMA
Jeremy	Laurence Ratigan (Crewe)	
Mona Isle	Irene Taylor (Blackpool)	3rd ISDC IOM
Springfield	Peggy Spencer (Newcastle-upon-Tyne)	1st NCDTA
Yvette [Waltz]	John King (Doncaster)	1st ADA

Waltzes (Modern) (1962)

Alanric	Ted Emery and Sylvia Last	1st SDF Botham Trophy
Doreen	Albert Ford (Dukinfield)	2nd NASD North
Dorice [Waltz]	Mr. and Mrs. Kirkby (Millom)	
Eileen [Waltz]	Ken Fuller (Worsley)	
Janette	Michael Gwynne	
Josephine [Waltz]	Len Shearn (Bristol)	1st ADA
Lindley	Mr. and Mrs. Rothwell (Nelson)	
Souvenir [Waltz]	Ken Fuller (Worsley)	
Telstar	Committee of BATD	
Telestar	Miss Rose Dabbs (Hadleigh, Essex)	

Quicksteps (1962)

Aztec	Michael Gwynne	
Helena	Lewis and Joan Wilson (Heanor)	1st Blackpool Bickerstaffe Shield
Kelsus	Charles and Dorothy Blundell	
Kingston	Ken Fuller	1st NASD Pennine Trophy
Lulu	Harry Greenwood (Bradford)	
Mulvany	Diana Winslade (Thornton Heath)	1st OTDA
Tipsy (Novelty)	———	

Two Steps (1962)

Adelaide	Mrs. Glenys Parsons (Cross Keys, Mon.)	3rd Blackpool
Gazelle	S. Hooker	1st ISTD
Rialto	David Rollinson	1st OBBD Filey
Wardwick	Joan and Lewis Wilson	1st NATD Handley Shield

Tangos (1962)

Alassio	M. Gwynne	
Capri III [Tango]	Roy Brittle (Newport, Mon.)	2nd ISDC IOM
Fiesta II	Eva Swain (Acton)	
Juroy	Roy Brittle (Newport, Mon.)	
Michaelmas	Constance Geer (London)	
Telstar	David Stead (Blackpool)	

Saunters (1962)

Pauline [Saunter]	Ken Fuller (Worsley)	
Reg 'n' M [Saunter]	I. Johnson (Chichester)	
Seashore	Joyce Simonds	1st UKAPTD
Serene II	Irene Norris (London)	1st ISTD (London)

Cha Cha Chas (1962)

L.A.	———
Margarite [Cha Cha]	J. Collier (Bolton)
Warrington	Jim Brennan (Warrington)

Swings (1962)

Jim Jam Jive (Fun Dance)	Ronald Timmins (London and Bournemouth)	
Midnight	Joyce Simmonds (Rhyl)	1st UKAPTD
New Madison	Bill and Doris Traill	1st Woolwich DTA
Startime	John King (Doncaster)	1st BATD Chester Trophy
Sunshine	Ken Fuller (Worsley)	3rd NASD

Miscellaneous (1962)

Azalea Foxtrot	Jacqueline Jay	
Bambi Blues	David Rollinson and Barbara Heathcote	1st Dance News Trophy
Blues Twist	Ken Fuller (Worsley)	
Club Madison	Mr. and Mrs. Ford (Dukinfield)	
Hyacinth Blues	Molly Affleck (Sunderland)	
January Foxtrot	M. Berry (Welling)	1st IDMA
Oliver Twist (Novelty)	Eddy Ghys (Chelsea)	
Oriental Mazurka	———	
Progressive Waltz Glide	Miss Eva Swain (London)	
September Glide	Robert Stewart (Northampton)	1st ISDC IOM
Yates A Four Step	Dorothy Higgins (Worcester)	1st OTDA Brittain Shield

Sequence Dancing in Scotland

Old-time sequence dancing has always been popular in Scotland since it has some affinity with Scottish dancing and seems to suit the national temperament. 'Let's have a Ceilidh' (The Essential Guide to Scottish Dancing) written by Robbie Shepherd in 1992 gives scripts and music for 20 dances - at least half of these would not be out of place in any old-time session.

Ballroom dancing has also been very popular in Scotland - the Scottish Dance Teachers' Alliance was formed in 1934. An excellent account of the history of ballroom dancing is 'Oh, How we Danced' by Elizabeth Casciani *(Mercat Press, 1994)*. This contains an excellent account of the history of old-time dancing in Scotland. There are photographs and quotations from books and newspapers; references are made to Charles Wood, the Warren family and the dancing schools in Glasgow, Edinburgh and elsewhere.

The Scottish MC's Dancing Association (SMCDA) formed by sequence dancers was established in 1932 well before the old-time revival. This body has run dancing competitions for more than 40 years. Open Amateur Modern Sequence Competitions in accordance with Offical Board rulings were run at the Albert Ballroom in Glasgow in 1966 and at Singer's Hall in Clydebank in 1968. Activities of this kind helped to bring about recognition of modern sequence dancing by the ballroom associations. Billy Smith who compiled their book of dances in the 1950's was President in 1962.

The Glasgow and District Dancing Association (GDDA) was formed by James Wilson following meetings in the Kelvingrove Labour Party Rooms in Glasgow. In 1957 there were 100 members (all MC's) with Matthew Gaitens as President and Mrs. R. M. Rennie as Secretary. It ran dances and outings for members and organised a Scottish Open Amateur Old Time Dancing Championship. Bert Finlay of Kirkcaldy was the dance instructor of the club in the 1960's. Many of the leading sequence dancers in Scotland were members of both SMCDA and GDDA.

Dancing and the BBC

Modern dance music was played on radio mainly for entertainment from 1923 onwards by Henry Hall, Jack Payne, Jack Hylton, Ambrose and others. In 1936 Victor Silvester produced his strict tempo records and gave dancing lessons with his orchestra in 1939. The BBC TV Dancing Club started in 1948 (Roll up the Carpet and Dance). The Dance Club Trophy competitions judged by viewers started in 1949; Victor Silvester gave dancing instruction from 1951 onwards (see page 45).

The broadcasting of old-time dance music started on Midland Region with Freddie Merrin and his Commanders in 1932. His live recording of dance music from Nottingham Palais de Dance was changed from Saturday to Wednesday which was old-time night with Adela Roscoe and Freddie Fitzgerald as MC's. Public reaction was so favourable that old-time was soon transmitted from other areas. In 1942 the BBC engaged Harry Davidson and his orchestra for 'Those Were the Days'.

A typical broadcast from a studio in the Criterion Restaurant, London would be along the following lines. After practising the chorus song the red light would glow and Freddie Grisewood would announce the first dance; Harry Davidson would raise his baton and the invited guests would take their partners for the first sequence. Dancing would continue for 45 minutes with hardly any intervals between the dances. To be present at one of these sessions was a memorable experience and a chance to meet with some of the famous personalities of the dancing world. Sydney Thompson's programme featuring old-time dancing, called 'Take Your Partners' started in 1954 and by 1956 there were dancing programmes on both BBC and ITV.

Dance teachers fortunate enough to appear on these programmes not only became famous but also had considerable freedom in choosing which of the older sequence dances to revive. Some produced dance books and lists of scripts, others formed bands and record companies. Prominent among these were A. J. Latimer, Sydney Thompson, Charles Crathorn, Cecil Rualt and Holland Brockbank.

Cecil Rualt [Zig-Zag Two Step (1960)]

Cecil Rualt was Co-principal of the Humphries School of Dancing in the 1960's and a member of the Old-Time Advisory Committee of the Official Board. She was a fellow examiner and Chairman of the Victorian and Sequence Dance Branch (Old Time) of the Official Board. Two of her books are:-

'Popular Old Time and Sequence Dances', Cecil Rualt, Humphries School of Dancing, 1952
'Old Time Dancing', Cecil Rualt, Frederick Muller, 1964

Her partner, Norah Galloway, wrote the section on old-time dancing in *'The Complete Ballroom Dancer', ed. Leonard Scrivener, Evans Bros., London, 1957*

Sydney Thompson [A Waltz for the Queen (1953)]

Sydney Thompson with his wife, Mary, and orchestra were very prominent in the old-time revival following the appearance of 'Take Your Partners'. He thought that the introduction of too many new dances in the modern style encouraged teachers to teach 'dances' but not 'dancing'. For many years he ran a company based in Pinner providing music for sequence and ballroom dancers.

Two of his books are:-

'Theory and Practice of Old Time Dancing', 1950
'Old Time Dance Book', Sydney Thompson, Burke, 1956

Charles Crathorn

Charles Crathorn was MC for a time with the Harry Davidson Orchestra in 'Those Were The Days' after A. J. Latimer. He toured the country with the orchestra and did much to promote the development of sequence dancing.

Scripts of some of the dances made popular by broadcasting appear in his book *'Old Time Dancing', Arco Publications, 1963.*

PRESENTED IN 1963

Waltzes (Old-Time) (1963)

Alexandra	Tom and May Bryant (St. Helens)	1st UKAPTD
Angella	Bill Wait (Liverpool)	1st ADA
Anniversary	——	
Davian	Gillian Stead (Blackpool)	1st OBBD Filey
Debonaire [Waltz]	Miss Irene Norris	1st BATD Worrall Trophy
Starlight	Ken Fuller	
Zephyr	L. V. Genders (Birmingham)	

Waltzes (Modern) (1963)

Autumn	Arthur Shaw	
Barrita [Waltz]	Fred and Doris Kirkby	3rd NASD North
Frandor	F. Lloyd	2nd ISDC IOM
Loraine [Waltz]	Ken Fuller (Worsley)	
Maida	Elsie Morgan (St. Helens)	
Parmela	Albert Ford (Dukinfield)	
Progress	A. Thompson (Liverpool)	
Ramona [Waltz]	Ken Fuller (Worsley)	
Regent	J. Dowling (Southport)	
Rose Lane	Mrs. Ann Beardsworth (Accrington)	1st NASD Pennine Troply
Wyoming II	Ken Fuller (Worsley)	

Tangos (1963)

Albany	Frank Short (Birmingham)	1st DTA
Collette [Tango]	Ken Fuller (Worsley)	
Countessa [Tango]	Jack Huddle	1st SDF Botham Trophy
Golden II	John Drinkwater (Chadwell Heath)	2nd OBBD
Marina III [Tango]	Joan and Lewis Wilson (Heanor)	
Red Rose	Ken Fuller (Worsley)	
Roulette [Tango]	Elsie and Jack Richardson	
Tahiti [Tango]	Ken Park (Shiremoor)	1st NCDTA
Tina	Jack Crossley (Forest Gate, London)	1st ISTD
Tip Toe	Jeff and Irene Robinson (Atherton)	
Toreador	Irene Norris	1st BATD
Victoria [Tango]	Rita Pover (London)	1st ISTD

Saunters (1963)

Butterfly	Leslie and Mamie Lovalt (Poole)	
Eileen [Saunter]	Dorothy Casey (Newcastle-upon-Tyne)	2nd NCDTA
Royal Wedding II	Dorothy Higgins	
Samantha	Mary Wilkins (London)	1st NATD Handley Shield
Saunter 63	Eva Swain (London)	
Sherwood	Mrs. Joan Wilson (Heanor)	1st Blackpool
Silver II	Guy Higgins (Worcester)	1st OTDA

Quicksteps (1963)

Avon II	———
Carlton I	Ken Fuller
Festival	Jack Smith (Portsmouth)
Hi-Fi	Albert Ford (Dukinfield)
Holiday	Mrs. Constance Geer (London)
Jollity	Jack Smith (Portsmouth)
Jovial	Jack Smith (Portsmouth)
Regent	Jack Dowling (Southport)

Gavottes (1963)

Empire	Bill Elsdon	IDMA
Ena	Lewis and Joan Wilson	2nd OBBD
Marina	Ken and Glenys Parsons (Cross Keys)	1st ISDC IOM

Blues (1963)

Bee Bee	Laura Ray (Minehead)	
Madison	Mrs. Rickey Cunningham	
Richmond	R. Stewart (Northampton)	3rd ISTD IOM

Swings (1963)

Madison	Ken Fuller (Worsley)
Savoy	———
Tio Pepe	Marjorie Webb (Doncaster)

Miscellaneous (1963)

Bossa Lou (Bossa Nova)	Lewis D. Wilson (Heanor)	
Charina (Cha Cha Cha)	Frank Short (Birmingham)	
Eccles Two Step	Mrs. Peggy Dexter (Newcastle-upon-Tyne)	3rd NCDTA
Festival Parade	———	
Franciscan Sway	Tony Eato and Tina Morgan	1st Dance News Slough
Handel's Quadrille	Mr. Handel	

Miscellaneous (1963) (continued)

Limbo Rumba	H. Greenwood (Bradford)	
Looee Cha Cha	Louie Wilkinson	1st UKAPTD
Madison Parade	Ken Fuller (Worsley)	
Marina Foxtrot	A. Thompson (Liverpool)	
Ragtime Roll	————	
Somerset Stroll	Miss Laura Bray/Mr. Bernard Gale (Minehead)	1st DTA (W)

Lewis and Joan Wilson [Adela Waltz (1962), Elite Waltz (1962), Helena Quickstep (1962), Wardwick Two Step (1962), Sherwood Saunter (1963), Ena Gavotte (1963), Bossa Lou (1963)]

The Wilsons were one of the most successful sequence dancing pairs of all time. They had prize-winning awards covering a wide range of dances as can be seen from the lists from 1962 into the 80's. They were excellent teachers, good demonstrators and Carl Alan award winners. They were very popular demonstrators at the big annual festivals of the Yorkshire Sequence Dance Federation.

Their Bossa Lou is one of the few examples of a sequence bossa nova. This is a dance from Brazil (1958-1960) which has elements of the samba and rumba. It is danced with a twisting body action without rise or fall. Although sequence dancers seem to enjoy it the style has never really caught on. Other sequence bossa novas are the Broadway Bossa Nova (1969), Bossa Nova Blues (1972), Bossa Nova '87 (1987) and the Bella Bossa Nova (1992).

The Stead Family

Joe and Kathy Stead of Blackpool were British Amateur O/T Champions in 1947, 1948 and 1949. Some half dozen of their sequence dances appear in the lists between the Royal Two Step (1952) and Fiesta Two Step (1957). David and Gillian Stead were British Old Time Professional Champions in 1967. About 10 of their dances appear in the lists between 1953 and 1966.

PRESENTED IN 1964

Waltzes (Old-Time) (1964)

April	Frank Noble and Nora Bray	BATD
Autumn I	D. Stead	3rd Blackpool
Autumn II	Nancy Clarke (Rhyl)	
Cambrian	K. Holmes and M. Howarth	1st ADA
Glen Helen	Ken and Glenys Parsons (Cross Keys)	3rd ISDC IOM
Regis	Rita Pover	1st OBBD Filey
Sandford	Bill Wait (Liverpool)	1st ADA
Sapphire	Lewis and Joan Wilson (Heanor)	2nd NATD
Willow	Ken Park	NCDTA

Waltzes (Modern) (1964)

Celebration	J. and E. Richardson	3rd NASD Yorks.
Chandelier	E. and J. Richardson	
Charisse [Waltz]	J. Simmonds (West Bromwich)	
Charming [Waltz]	Jack Such	
Diane II [Waltz]	Betty Baker (Manchester)	
Janine [Waltz]	Ken Fuller (Worsley)	
L'Aimant [Waltz]	Fred and Doris Kirkby	NASD (NA)
Rosemary	S. Powell (Woodley)	
Spire	W. Rhodes (Bakewell)	
Whispering II	Ken Fuller (Worsley)	
Woodside	J. Fanning	1st ADA (Scotland)

Foxtrots (1964)

Caravelle	Bernard and Vera Proctor (Calmore)	3rd DTA (S)
Harmony I	Albert and Ellen Ford (Dukinfield)	
Highcroft	C. A. Hopworth (Batley)	2nd NASD Yorks.
Indiana	Irene Norris	1st BATD
Kathleen	Ken Fuller (Worsley)	
Parisienne	Kitty Moore (Bexley Heath)	3rd NATD
Pee Gee	Mr. and Mrs. A. R. Street	2nd DTA (S)
Tina	D. Williams	

Tangos (1964)

Alemeda [Tango]	Kathleen Volke	2nd ISDC IOM
Del Mar	Frank Sage (New Malden)	1st UKAPTD
Fiesta III	John Bridges	
Lloret	Gillian Stead (Blackpool)	3rd OBBD

Tangos (1964) (continued)

Majorca [Tango]	Frank Short (Birmingham)	2nd DTA
Springtime	Mrs. B. Shuttleworth (Blackpool)	3rd NASD North
Tarragona	A. H. Mitchell (Hayling)	1st SDTA Anne Marie Cup
Valencia I [Tango]	A. Thompson (Liverpool)	3rd NASD North

Quicksteps (1964)

Beverley I	Mr. W. Donson (Halifax)	3rd NASD North
Beverley II	L. Morton	
Claremont	Ken Fuller (Worsley)	2nd NASD North

Blues (1964)

Camelot	Will Richardson (London)	1st SDF Botham Trophy
Dolly	Robert Stewart	1st ISDC IOM
Merseyside	Jack Dowling (Southport)	

Saunters (1964)

Elite [Saunter]	Fred and Doris Kirkby (Millom)	1st NASD Pennine Trophy
Kayjon	Kathleen Volke (Staines)	1st ISTD (S)
Maldor	Mr. A. Folies (Newcastle)	2nd NCDTA
Marlessa	Peggy Dexter (Newcastle-upon-Tyne)	3rd NCDTA
Santana [Saunter]	Raymond Bailey (Macclesfield)	1st IDMA
Savannah	Fred Holmes (Sheffield)	1st DTA
Summertime	Robert Stewart	1st ISTD

Two Steps (1964)

Casino	Alf and Kitty Moore	1st NATD
Highland II	W. Stocks	
Tiara	Mrs. Joan Wilson (Heanor)	2nd Blackpool

Miscellaneous (1964)

Black Domino	Frank Short (Birmingham)	
Camelot	Will Richardson	1st SDF
Dolly Weaver	Lewis Wilson (Heanor)	1st Blackpool
Dutch Samba	Jacqier Alphenaar	UKAPTD
Empress Schottische	Gillian Stead (Blackpool)	4th Blackpool
Grosvenor Glide	Bill and Betty Elsdon	1st Dance News Slough
Jo-Ella Sway	John Dowling and Joan Collings	2nd IDMA
Jovial One Step	Bill Brewster	
Jubilee Jinks (Party)	Jack Drinkwater (Chadwell Heath)	1st Southend-on-Sea
Lincoln Swing	E. J. Pestell	1st OTDA Jack Smith Shield
Paso Madrid	Jim Brennan (Warrington)	
Royal (Royale) [Rumba]	Nancy Clarke (Rhyl)	

PRESENTED IN 1965

Waltzes (Old-Time) (1965)

Careth	Gillian Stead (Blackpool)	1st Blackpool
Cherell	Brenda Belcher	3rd DTA
Givendale	Maud Berry	1st IDMA
Northern Star	Gilbert Daniels (South Shields)	1st NCDTA
Queens	Mrs. M. Parr (Warrington)	1st UKAPTD
Silverdor	Colin McLachlan (London)	2nd SDF
Sorrentino [Waltz]	Miss Nora Carter	3rd ISDC (IOM)
Springtime II	Bill Traill	1st BATD
Virene	Vicki Wheale	OTDA Brittain Shield

Waltzes (Modern) (1965)

Carolyn (Progressive)	Jack Crossley (Forest Gate)	
Elaine II [Waltz]	Dennis and Joan Rothwell (Nelson)	1st NASD (N)
Forget Me Not	J. Collier (Bolton)	
Greensleeves	———	
Harwinn	Harry and Winnie Bate (Irlam)	
Idaho	John Borthwick	
Joanette	Ken Fuller (Worsley)	
Kildare	Florence Newbegin (Newcastle-upon-Tyne)	2nd NCDTA
Linden	Ken Fuller (Worsley)	
Maytime	Ken Fuller (Worsley)	
Novella	George Mott and Hilda Cowling	2nd NASD Yorks.
Siesta [Waltz]	W. Taylor	1st NASD Yorks.
Silverdor	Colin McLachlan (London)	2nd SDF (London)
Sylvellen	Sylvester Burrows (Haydock)	1st Blackpool
Topaz	Lewis and Joan Wilson (Heanor)	
Wentworth	Ken Fuller (Worsley)	
Windsor I	Bill Wait (Liverpool)	1st ADA
Woodlands	Harold Weston (Brixton)	
Yvonne	Ken Fuller (Worsley)	

Saunters (1965)

Autumn I	Michael Barry (Welling, Kent)	1st Woolwich DTA
Benson	A. Mills (Smethwick)	
Clarendon II	W. Donson	3rd NASD Yorks.
Sing-a-long	E. J. Pestell	2nd ADA
Shenandoah	W. Donson	

Tangos (1965)

Bermuda	——	
Canasta [Tango]	J. E. Little (Enfield)	1st ISTD
Dawn	Lewis and Joan Wilson (Heanor)	1st OBBD Filey
Dorian	Doris Johnstone	DTA
Encano [Tango]	Jack and Elsie Richardson (Huddersfield)	
Florida [Tango]	B. Shuttleworth	
Guitar	David and Gillian Stead	1st DTA
Isabella	Ken Fuller (Worsley)	
Lynwell	Mr. and Mrs. Goddard	
Malouine	Norman Bowley (Chingford)	1st OTDA Brittain Shield
Maytime	Ken Fuller (Worsley)	
Roseleigh	George Mott and Hilda Cowling	1st NASD
Sabena [Tango]	Bill and Vi Gage	2nd SDF London
Starcross	W. Richardson (London)	3rd SDF
Tango 65	David Stead (Blackpool)	2nd Blackpool
Troubador	Ken Fuller (Worsley)	
Violetta II [Tango]	Lewis and Joan Wilson (Heanor)	NATD
Wyeland	W. T. Hope (Hereford)	1st OTDA

Foxtrots (1965)

Anita	Ben Shuttleworth	
Bermuda	Frank Short (Birmingham)	1st DTA Mid.
Chiltern	F. Westley (Aylesbury)	
Emerald	J. and E. Richardson (Huddersfield)	
Fantail	Bob Houghton (London)	Blackpool (Merit)
Malouine	Norman and Elsie Bowley (Chingford)	1st OTDA Brittain Shield
Maxie	David Bray	
Oasis	Wilf Wood (Isle of Wight)	
Piccadilly	Frank Short (Birmingham)	
Royston	E. V. Wheale	1st OTDA
Vilia	J. and E. Richardson (Huddersfield)	

Blues (1965)

Beverley	Ken Fuller (Worsley)	
Blue Lady	Rose Hamill (North Shields)	3rd NCDTA
Martino	D. Jennings (Eltham)	Joint 2nd Woolwich DTA
Syland	Holland Brockbank and Miss Sylvia Pratt	BATD

Quicksteps (1965)

Cairoli	Lewis and Joan Wilson (Heanor)	2nd Blackpool
Cameron	Ken Fuller (Worsley)	
Caron	Clare Smith	1st SDF Botham Trophy
Clover	Ken Fuller (Worsley)	
Dale	Cliff Marks	
Denry	Rene Buckley (Manchester)	
Jubilee	Albert Ford (Dukinfield)	
Kentucky	Ken Fuller (Worsley)	
Pauletta II	Ken Fuller (Worsley)	
Waverley	Ken Fuller (Worsley)	2nd NASD North

Swings (1965)

Melody	Mrs. Iris Kempsell (Edmonton)	1st ISTD
Sefton	Ken Fuller	
Viennese I	Jim Brennan	3rd ADA

Miscellaneous (1965)

County Gavotte	Sam and Irene Faultley (Barking)	1st Dance News
Dorian Two Step	Doris Johnstone	4th DTA
Doris Cha Cha Cha	Ken Fuller (Worsley)	
Frisco Four Step	A. Hill	1st NATD
Ivory Rag	Ken Fuller (Worsley)	
Kaymar Sway	Lewis and Joan Wilson (Heanor)	1st ISDC IOM
Lynton Stroll	Bill Traill (Maidstone)	1st Woolwich DTA
Phillipa Mazurka	Vickie Marsden	1st OTDA Elizabeth Cup
Rio Rumba	Jim Brennan (Warrington)	
Rosita Cha Cha	Jim Brennan (Warrington)	1st UKAPTD
Sapphire Samba	Jim Brennan (Warrington)	
Tiddley Jinks	Ken Fuller (Worsley)	

Jim Brennan [Samba Miranda (1961), Warrington Cha Cha Cha (1962)]

Jim Brennan of Warrington has a flair for arranging Latin American and party dances. His arrangements include the Paso Madrid (1964), Rosita Cha Cha Cha (1965) and Sapphire Samba (1965) which are OBBD championship dances; his Didi Town Parade appears in Nancy Clarke's 'Party Dances' (this gives 1950 for the date of his Samba Miranda).

Old-Time and Modern Sequence Dancing

Since the introduction of 'modern' dances based on a walking action there have been problems for committed old-time leaders who place great value on the music, techniques and dances of the past with the formality, politeness and consideration for others inherent in the style. If they include only old-time dances they may be thought not to be moving with the times and lose clients - if they introduce dances like the quickstep and foxtrot, how far should they go?

The figures below show that this problem has got worse over the years with old-time dances being replaced by modern forms.

Numbers of New Sequence Dances

		1955	1965
Old-Time	Old Time Waltz	14	9
	Two Step	11	1
	Gavotte	2	0
Modern	Modern Waltz	7	19
	Quickstep	2	10
	Foxtrot	1	11

The preservation of the 'purity' of old-time values is a still major preoccupation of old-time enthusiasts. Dances arranged after 1958 are regarded with some suspicion even if they are two steps or gavottes and arguments still appear in the press as to whether dances such as the Mayfair Quickstep and Melody Foxtrot are old-time or modern.

The 1975 ruling of the Official Board for new official modern sequence dances has meant that one third of the new dances are now Latin-American dances like the rumba, cha cha cha and jive; this has further accentuated the differences. Allocating one third to old-time dances has, however, had an effect in promoting dances in the old-time style which might otherwise have disappeared from the modern sequence repertoire.

PRESENTED IN 1966

Waltzes (Old-Time) (1966)

Alaine	Alan Hancock (Shiremoor)	OBBD Finalist
Edelweiss II	M. Berry	2nd Blackpool
Estella	E. J. Pestell	
Hazel	Michael Berry and Iris Maynard (Welling)	2nd Blackpool
Lorraine [Waltz]	Jacqueline E. Gipson	1st BATD Worral Trophy
Mysetta	Kay Ranwell	1st OTDA Brittain Shield
Priory	B. N. Chapman (Bradford)	

Waltzes (Modern) (1966)

Alback	Jack Jay	
Crinoline	———	
Empress	Lewis and Joan Wilson (Heanor)	1st Blackpool
Etelle [Waltz]	Rodney and Nellie Hargreaves (Accrington)	1st NASD North
Lanodale	Ken Fuller (Worsley)	
Laura I	Ken Park	3rd Blackpool
Laura II	George McAllister	2nd ADA Scotland
Marianne [Waltz]	Jim Dalton (Oldham)	
Marigold	J. and E. Richardson (Huddersfield)	
Maybelene	John Drinkwater (Forest Gate, London)	1st UKAPTD
Michelle [Waltz]	Ken Fuller (Worsley)	
Monterey	Joe Collier (Bolton)	3rd NASD North
Parisienne	Mrs. Gillian Stead (Blackpool)	4th Blackpool
Tulip	H. Thornhill (Pendleton)	3rd NASD North

Tangos (1966)

Brazil [Tango]	Frank Short (Birmingham)	
Fiesta IV	Ken Park	1st NCDTA
Janeen	Jeff Robinson (Tyldlesley)	
Leonora [Tango]	Marjorie French (Rothwell, Northants.)	2nd IDMA
Paraguay	B. Ranwell	1st OTDA
Rosella I	Miss Nora Capps	Finalist OBBD
Sabena	———	
Valencia II [Tango]	Will Richardson (Forestgate)	1st SDF Botham Trophy

Saunters (1966)

Granchester	Rita Pover	OBBD
Liesl	Paul and Cherry Nicholls	1st DTA
Shanakeill	Lewis and Joan Wilson (Heanor)	2nd IDMA
Sharandon	W. Donson (Halifax)	3rd NASD
Solwin	Lewis and Joan Wilson (Heanor)	1st Blackpool
Supreme [Saunter]	Roger N. Willis	1st BATD Chester Trophy

Quicksteps (1966)

Bluebird	Jim Brennan (Warrington)	
Congress	Mrs. Betty Dyce (Loughton)	1st IDMA
Derby	Bill Wait (Liverpool)	
Diddy	Lewis Wilson (Heanor)	3rd Blackpool
Empire	Steve White (Wath-on-Dearne)	
Omega	J. and E. Richardson (Huddersfield)	
Ukandoit	Harry Greenwood (Bradford)	
Victoria	Ken Fuller (Worsley)	

Foxtrots (1966)

Adriana	Rita Pover (Forest Gate)	Blackpool Finalist
Aud En El	Mr. and Mrs. N. E. Pickering (Birmingham)	
Dale	Cliff Marks	
Flamingo	Jim Brennan	3rd DTA
Mardale	J. Collier (Bolton)	2nd NASD North
Martin	W. Donson	3rd NASD Yorks
Venetian	Kitty Moor	1st NATD

Two Steps (1966)

Balmoral	Tony Dyer (Wombwell)	1st Dance News
Clynol	Derek Tonks	4th Blackpool
Peterton	Phyllis Hetherington	NCDTA
Reylock	Marilyn Colyer (Rainham)	3rd ISDC IOM

Miscellaneous (1966)

Chelsea Glide	Brenda Belcher (Pontypool)	4th DTA
Chiki Cha Cha Cha	Ken Park	2nd Blackpool
Fiona's Polka (novelty dance)	Mr. N. Johnston (Carlisle)	
Guernsey Glide	Ken Fuller (Worsley)	
Rainbow Blues	Jim Brennan (Warrington)	2nd ADA
Sunshine Stroll	Ted Burroughs	1st ISTD
Trixie Swing	Lewis and Joan Wilson (Heanor)	1st ISDC IOM
Westbury Blues	Sam and Irene Faultley (London)	1st ISTD (SE)

Sequence Dancing and the Ballroom Associations

By the middle 1960's modern sequence dancing had become so popular that the ballroom associations decided to give it more attention. Headlines in 'Dance World' for 1965 were "Sequence Storm Brewing" (1st July) and "Challenge of Modern Sequence" (8th July). Walter Whitman was the feature writer and there were many letters from correspondents. The Official Board made arrangements to form a committee to look into defining the style and consider the production of a booklet of dances for teaching and competition purposes. Although the ADA had set up a modern sequence branch in 1960 this type of dancing had been largely ignored by the other associations and there was much misunderstanding. Then (as now) it was held in low esteem by the ballroom dancers. A. H. Franks (1940-1945): "Sequence dancing has really no place in the art of ballroom dancing and such dances are regarded as novelties." Victor Silvester (1950): "Sequence dancing is very easily learned ... ideal for the absolute beginner." Dance News headline for 10th June, 1965 "Modern Sequence Dancing is Conga, Lambeth Walk ... ."

These were early days for modern sequence dancing and there was often much heat but little light in the discussions - even today there is still controversy. Misunderstandings arise in part from the use of the term 'modern' in several different senses but a more important factor is a fundamental difference in approach between ballroom and sequence dancers - this is examined in more detail in Chapter 5. Committed ballroom dancers tend to see dancing as an art-form practised by a trained elite - they are much concerned with technique, qualifications and competitions. Sequence dancers in contrast see their dancing as a pleasant pastime for people who like to meet together several times per week to go round in time to the music. These groups rarely mix together and that is a recipe for lack of understanding.

In the summer of 1965 however the subject began to be tackled in real earnest. The Official Board Committee under the chairmanship of Keith Jones held a lengthy meeting which produced the following recommendations:-

1. That Modern Sequence Dancing be defined as a sequence based on the Modern or Latin-American syllabi of teachers' organisations who are corporate members of the Board.

2. That competitions in Modern Sequence Dancing be recognised and encouraged, but these competitions be not granted championship status.

3. That a list of dances be created for competition work, and that when this list is compiled consideration be given to recommended dances submitted by the corporate members of the Board.

4. That competitions in modern sequence dancing be judged by persons who have reached their 21st birthday and who currently hold at least the degree of associateship (by examination) in either the Modern, Latin-American or Old Time branches in an examining body represented on the Board.

5. That a new classification of dancing, Modern Sequence Dancing, be incorporated into the Official Board Rules.

Some of the modern sequence dancers were not altogether happy with what might be regarded as a 'takeover' by the Official Board. A letter in the 'Dance News' of 1st July, 1965 has the passage, "these so-called investigating committees are on the cash in, they will try and take over our 'Modern Sequence'. 'Technique' and medal tests and professional exams (will be introduced). The consequence will then be the same as what has happened in the past to Modern Ballroom and Latin American dancing - over-techniqued, showy, a trend of dancing for the experts and competition dancers. In simple words, 'They will kill it'."

Fortunately, modern sequence dancing has been too sturdy a plant for this to happen; since 1975 it has had a stable, balanced structure satisfactory to most.

PRESENTED IN 1967

Waltzes (Old-Time) (1967)

Adelaide	Lewis and Joan Wilson	1st OBBD
Alison	Jim and Phyllis Goland (Sheffield)	1st OTDA Brittania Shield
Corsair	Keith and Margaret Holmes	1st ADTA
Granethel	Ken Fuller (Worsley)	
Midland	George and Stella Berwick	
Minerva	Edgar Holroyd	1st IDMA
Wulfruna	Derek Tonks (Wolverhampton)	OBBD Finalist

Waltzes (Modern) (1967)

Caravelle	Iris Maynard	IDTA
Casino	Terry Drogan (Droylsden)	
Charmaine II [Waltz]	Clarry Clarke	IDMA
Dream	Robert Stewart (Northampton)	1st NATD
English Rose	W. Richardson (Forest Gate)	3rd NASD
International	Frank Lister	3rd OBBD
Kentucky	Ken Fuller (Worsley)	
Linda	Fred and Phyllis Taylor (Huddersfield)	1st NASD North
Melodrene	Derek Tonks	2nd Blackpool
Moonlight	Arthur Lightfoot	2nd Blackpool
Selby	Mr. and Mrs. Neil (Stretford)	2nd NASD North
Vienna	Robert Stewart	ISTD
Viscount	Freddie Wilkins (Edmonton)	
Wayne	Phyllis Adams (Worral Trophy)	BATD
Winifred	Frank Short (Birmingham)	

Tangos (1967)

Annalita [Tango]	May Botham (Wythenshawe)	
El Cid	Ken Park (Shiremoor)	1st Blackpool Mod.
Katrina	Jim Brennan	ADA
La Cumparsita	Ken Fuller (Worsley)	
Madelena [Tango]	Ken Fuller (Worsley)	
Manyana	Lewis and Joan Wilson (Heanor)	1st Blackpool O/T
Marisa	Ken Fuller (Worsley)	1st NASD North
San Rico	J. and E. Richardson (Huddersfield)	
Toledo II	Tony and Denise Dyer	2nd ISDC
Trident	Betty Baker (Manchester)	
Windsor III	John Borthwick (Manchester)	

Foxtrots (1967)

Alana	Lewis and Joan Wilson (Heanor)	3rd Blackpool Mod.
Albertine	Edward Rudd (Ulverston)	
Ashfield	Mrs. Ida Hill (Ashton-in-Makerfield)	
Broadwell	——	
Dunrich	Mrs. V. Wheale (Tamworth)	1st OTDA Jack Smith
Shield	——	
Embassy	Ken Fuller (Worsley)	
Gaynor	J. E. Garrad (Skegness)	
Glynlee	J. Hutchinson	
Hillary	Harry and Winnie Bate (Irlam)	3rd NASD North
Melanie	Mrs. Irene Watling (Erith)	1st Woolwich DTA
Millward	Terry Drogan (Droylsden)	
Rainbow	Albert Lambourne	1st SDF Botham Trophy
Winter	——	

Quicksteps (1967)

Cresta	J. McElvey	
Happy Feet	Alex Moore	
Kevin	Sylvie and David Last	2nd SDF London
Ruby	Albert Ford (Dukinfield)	
Universal	Jacqui Gipson (Forest Gate)	1st OBBD

Sways (1967)

Aron	Robert Stewart (Northampton)	1st ISDC
Margerita	Brian and Christina Yarnold	Dance News
Panama	Sam and Irene Faultley	1st ISTD
Silver	Jaqueline Gipson	2nd DTA
Whisky	Joy Ralph	

Saunters (1967)

Blueberry	Ken Fuller (Worsley)	
Dakota	Edgar Holroyd	2nd OBBD
Millicent	Frank and Milly Lee (Southsea)	
Natalie	Ken Fuller (Worsley)	
Sky Blue	Ken Park	NCDTA
Yucatan	Bill Traill (Maidstone)	BATD

Two Steps (1967)

Gay Step	Ken Park (Shiremoor)	4th Blackpool
Lynx	G. Higgins (Worcester)	1st OTDA
McNamara's	Ken Fuller (Worsley)	

Miscellaneous (1967)

12th Street Rag	Ken Fuller (Worsley)	
Amor Samba	E. Whinfield	NCDTA
Cameo Gavotte	Jean Sage	1st UKAPTD
Cat Step	————	
Regal Gavotte	Maurice Tait (Nottingham)	1st NATD
Roban Stroll	W. Donson (Yorks.)	
Social Swing (Novelty)	Ken Fuller (Worsley)	
Somerset Swing	Ted Burroughs	3rd ISDC IOM
Victory Cha Cha	Ken Park (Newcastle-upon-Tyne)	NCDTA Finalist

George F. Mott (1911-1993)

George Mott was one of the founding fathers of modern sequence dancing. He was a man of many talents with great energy and vision. Born in London, he moved to the Bradford area marrying his wife Jessie in 1935 and raising 5 sons and a daughter. He was a keen cyclist, swimmer and amateur musician and later on became an authority on dancing, being made a life member of the IDTA. Trained originally as a woodworking machinist, he eventually joined his eldest son, Derek Arnold (Mott), in a music business as partner and technical adviser. Music for sequence dancing was in short supply at that time and father and son decided to produce their own records. At its height Astron Music had some 100 titles and still retains the copyrights; Northern Dance Services of Shipley is still one of the main suppliers of scripts and music for sequence dancing.

Originally an old-time dancer, George adapted readily to the modern style. He formed the Wharfedale School of Dancing in Otley which produced many excellent dancers and he ran many dances in the surrounding areas. His Yorkshire Sequence Dance Federation (YSDF) formed in 1967 still holds its large annual festival in Bridlington. Some of his dances (with his partner, Hilda Cowling) are the Ilkley Moor Saunter (1961), Roseleigh Tango (1965), Yellow Bird Tango (1970) and Rumba Carioca, Novella Waltz (1965).

Modern Sequence Championship Dances

Following the deliberations of the Official Board Committee in Modern Sequence Dancing in 1965, a handbook was produced in May 1966. This contained 23 dances including 3 'Manchester' dances - the Cha Cha Margarite (Joe Collier), and the Kingston Quickstep and Red Rose Tango (Ken Fuller); these were omitted from the next issue. The championship dances for 1995 are given for comparison.

	1966	**1995**
Waltzes	Woodside (1964), Magenta (1951) Sylvellen (1965), Patricia (1954)	Woodside (1964), Engagement (1969), Caravelle (1967), Helenbrooke (1979) Rayen (1979)
Tangos	Victoria (1963), Scintilla (1955) Red Rose (1963), Trelawney (1954) Madrid (1954)	Victoria (1963), El Cid (1967) Tarquilla (1978)
Quicksteps	Mayfair (1956), Helena (1962) Kingston (1962), Derby (1966) Broadway (1957)	Eivona (1974), Quando (1979) Universal (1967
Foxtrots	Idaho (1959), Millbrook (1960)	Claringo (1973), Benita (1974) Glenroy (1976), Rosslyn (1973)
Sambas	Sapphire (1965), Dutch (1964)	Sapphire (1965), Katrina (1972) Shadow (1980)
Paso Dobles	Paso Madrid (1964)	Paso Madrid (1964), Paso Deena (1974)
Cha Cha Chas	Rosita (1965), Jacqueline (1961) Margarite (1962)	Rosita (1965), Sally Ann (1973) Tutti-Frutti (1974)
Rumbas	—	One (1971), Bianco (1977) Blue Mosque (1979), Caribbean (1976) Marquesa (1973)
Jives	—	Jupiter (1973), Jubilee (1977), Justa (1975)
Blues	Bambi (1962)	—

PRESENTED IN 1968

Waltzes (Old-Time) (1968)

Chester	———	
Days That Were	Sylvia and Holland Brockbank	
Gossamer	Maurice Tait and Pauline Pritchard	1st NATD
Malvern	Pat and Florrie Sherman	Joint 1st OTDA
Memoir	Ken Park (Newcastle)	2nd NCDTA
Opal	Alf and Kitty Moore	1st ISTD
Osborne	Mr. and Mrs. J. Aldren (Wirral)	3rd IDTA
Susanne [Waltz]	Bill Traill (Maidstone)	1st BATD

Waltzes (Modern) (1968)

Babette II [Waltz]	Arthur Lightfoot (Leeds)	3rd OBBD
Blue Lady	Miss Marjorie Atkinson (Leeds)	
Blue Moon	Frank Lee (Southsea)	3rd SDTA
Columbine [Waltz]	Ken Fuller (Worsley)	
Fernside	J. and E. Richardson (Huddersfield)	
Harmony I	Elizabeth French (London)	3rd IDTA
Hawthorns	J. Simmonds (West Bromwich)	
Isobel [Waltz]	Ken Fuller (Worsley)	
Jasmine	Ken Fuller (Worsley)	
Louise [Waltz]	Arthur Osborne (Thornton Clevelys)	1st NASD North
Lullaby II	Harry Greenwood (Bradford)	3rd NASD Yorks.
Marie II [Waltz]	Arthur Lightfoot	OBBD
Riverside	Philip Grooms	
Royale [Waltz]	Gilbert and Margaret Smithies	2nd NASD

Tangos (1968)

Castella	Edward and Moira Winfield	NCDTA
Del Sol [Tango]	Pauline Pritchard	
Delilah [Tango]	Ken Fuller (Worsley)	
Diablo [Tango]	Maurice Tait (Nottingham)	1st NATD
El Paseo	G. E. Nessling	OTDA (NW)
Gaytime	John and Irene Fitton	1st ADA
Marella [Tango]	Jack Crossley (London)	1st OBBD
Moonstone	Bill Traill (Maidstone)	1st BATD
Rio II	Ken Fuller (Worsley)	
Rocola [Tango]	Lewis and Joan Wilson (Heanor)	1st Blackpool
Romero II [Tango]	W. Lancaster (Leeds)	
Seville I	Arthur Lightfoot	2nd BATD

Tangos (1968) (continued)

Stewart	Robert Stewart	1st Dance News Trophy
Tanya [Tango]	Ken Fuller (Worsley)	
Theresa	Tony and Denis Dyer (Wombwell)	1st IDTA

Quicksteps (1968)

Clarissa	W. J. Smith	2nd SDF London
Clifton	Ken Fuller (Worsley)	
Concorde	Ken Fuller (Worsley)	
Conway	Jack Crossley	2nd OBBD
Hilton I	Derek Tonks and Beryl Bates	IDTA Mid.
Katie	Harry and Winnie Bate (Irlam)	1st NASD Pennine Trophy
Koala	Iris Kempsell	ISTD
M. T.	W. Donson	
Myric	Ken Fuller (Worsley)	
Olympic	Lewis and Joan Wilson (Heanor)	1st Blackpool
Twinkle	Harry Jackson	1st ISTD (SE)

Blues (1968)

Belinda	John Hunter	3rd NASD North
Mercia	Ray and Renee Hemming (Pershore)	1st OTDA
Plemont	William Harvey	3rd ISDC
Rossmore	Jeff Aldren	2nd Blackpool
Valentine	Arthur Osborne (Cleveleys)	3rd NASD

Saunters (1968)

Aviemore	Robert C. W. Stewart	1st UKAPTD
Bewitched	Ken Park	4th Blackpool
Lynton	Miss Iris Follis (Newcastle-upon-Tyne)	3rd NCDTA
Martine [Saunter]	David Bullen	2nd ADA
Romantique	———	
Suzanne [Saunter]	Tony and Denise Dyer	2nd ISDC
Wilton	Raymond Williams	2nd IDTA

Two Steps (1968)

Cavalier	Maurice Tait (Nottingham)	
Dot's	Bill Wait (Liverpool)	1st ADA
Paris	Sylvia and Holland Brockbank	

Foxtrots (1968)

Blue Moon	Jack Richardson (Huddersfield)	
Celebration	Tony and Denise Dyer (Wombwell)	4th IDTA
Delphine	Cliff and Gwen Abbott	2nd NASD Yorks.
Denholme	Lloyd Holmes (Rochdale)	
Honey	Ken Fuller (Worsley)	
Jacqueline	Ken Fuller (Worsley)	2nd NASD North
La Renda	Colin and Doris McLachlan	3rd SDF (London)

Miscellaneous (1968)

Aggi Samba	Vivien Carrie	OBBD
April Sway	Lionel and Pat Topp (Southampton)	1st DTA
Ascot Glide	Frank Short (Birmingham)	2nd IDTA (Midland)
Cokernut Hop	Ken Fuller (Worsley)	
Easter Parade	Ken Fuller (Worsley)	
Jade Gavotte	Peter Sharp (London)	Joint 2nd OBBD
Kenton Cha Cha Cha	Ken Holden	2nd IDTA
Lorrain Rumba	Jim Brennan	1st UKAPTD
Marguerite [Rumba]	Bob and Margaret More	1st IDTA
Marian Stroll	Lewis and Joan Wilson (Heanor)	1st UKAPTD
Mini Step	Ken Fuller (Worsley)	
Royale [Schottische]	Eric Holden (Leicester)	1st IDTA
Sapphire Sway	———	
Silverdale Glide	Will Richardson	1st SDF Botham Trophy
Starlight Stroll I	Mrs. Elaine Sharp (Padiham)	1st IDTA (N)

Tony and Denise Dyer (Wombwell)

With almost 30 dances in the lists between 1967 and 1980 this couple form a bridge between the old and the new. Apart from saunters their arrangements were mainly modern and Latin-American.

Derek Tonks and Beryl Bates (Wolverhampton)

Derek and Beryl have almost the same number of successes as the Dyers over the same period - they were great rivals. Their Waltz Daniela (1976) (the chassé waltz) is a great favourite; the Benita Foxtrot (1974) is an OBBD championship dance. Derek Tonks is a director of IDTA and a writer on sequence affairs. Both Derek and Beryl are examiners for IDTA.

Walter Whitman

Walter Whitman was one of the greatest authorities on old-time dancing being sometimes referred to as 'Mr. Old-Time Dancing'. He had considerable journalistic ability and wrote for 'Dance News' and other periodicals; he was noted for his quirky, straightfaced humour. His health failed towards the end and he died in 1969. He is commemorated by the old-time Whitman Waltz of Stan Ross - a prize winner in the Isle of Man in 1969. Two of his books are:

'Modern Dancing', Walter Whitman, Collins, 1963
'The Complete Old Time Dancer', Walter Whitman and Victor Silvester, Herbert Jenkins, 1967

Alex Moore

Alex Moore was a championship dancer and a first-class teacher. He was President of ISTD and Honorary President of the International Council of Ballroom Dancing. Some of his 16 - bar sequences designed for teaching purposes were given names - e.g. the Happy Feet Quickstep (1967). He changed the name of his River Tango (1969) from Guitar Tango to avoid confusion with David and Gillian Stead's 1965 tango of the same name. In his monthly letter service in 1965 he wrote "Modern sequence dancing is here to stay, possibly for a very long time. The Official Board is about to standardise a number of these dances so that the same ones are taught throughout the country. My advice to teachers is to give it a try." He had a keen analytical mind and a good literary style. His books include:-

'Ballroom Dancing', various editions 1936-1992
'Popular Variations', Alex Moore School of Dancing (1954-1989)
'The Revised Technique', ISTD (1948-1993)

Nancy Clarke (Rhyl)

The Sherrie Saunter (1949), American Quickstep (1952) and Tipsy Two (1952) were early successes; her Rumba Royal (1964) has always been popular. She produced a book of Party Dances for the IDTA in November 1970 - she was President of this organisation in 1994 and Chairman of the Sequence Advisory Commmittee.

PRESENTED IN 1969

Waltzes (Old-Time) (1969)

Apollo	Bill Smith	1st SDF Blundell Trophy
Glengarry	Margo Alderman	1st UKAPTD
Golden Wedding	J. M. Hutchinson (Farnworth)	
Malina [Waltz]	Jess and Fred Morgan (London)	
St. Albans	Tom and Eva Bray	1st ISDC IOM
Wearside	Lottie Whitfield	1st BATD Worral Trophy
Whitman	Stan Ross (Worthing)	IOM

Waltzes (Modern) (1969)

Alicia [Waltz]	Harry and Winnie Bate (Irlam)	
Alpha	Marjorie and Howard Holloway	OBBD
Beverley	Mr. Perfect	
Cavendish	J. Borthwick	
D'Laine	W. Schofield	
Davidian	Colin McLachlan (London)	1st SDF Botham Trophy
Engagement	Ken Park (Newcastle)	1st Blackpool
Harlequin	Ellis Pott	
Magnolia	Jim Dalton	
Pennine	Arthur Osborne (Thornton Clevelys)	1st NASD North
Prince Charles	Harry and Elizabeth Wells (Leyton)	2nd IDTA
Roulette [Waltz]	Lewis and Joan Wilson (Heanor)	1st OBBD
Sandra	Henry Taylor (Partington)	
Tammy	Ken Fuller (Worsley)	
Voice in the Night	George F. Mott (Shipley)	Silver Dollar Company
Waltz of the Moon	James Cheetham	
Waltz of the Valley	Bill and Maud Stevenson	1st ADA Mid.
Westvale	Alf Thompson (Liverpool)	
Yvette	A. Ford	

Tangos (1969)

Apollo [Tango]	Ken Fuller (Worsley)	
Balalaika	John and Irene Fitton (Southport)	1st ADA
Blue III [Tango]	Ken Fuller (Worsley)	
Golden Wedding	Sidney Walker (Southampton)	2nd Torquay
Granero [Tango]	Derek Tonks and Beryl Bates	2nd IDTA
Planet	Joan and Lewis Wilson (Heanor)	4th Blackpool
Prince of Wales II	Harry Wells (Leyton)	1st Dance News

Tangos (1969) (continued)

River (Guitar)	Alex Moore	
Rosarie	J. and E. Richardson	
Rovero	Lawrence Norton	IDTA London
Spanish II	Glyn and Anne Watkins	Blackpool
Tivoli	Frank Short (Birmingham)	3rd SDTA
Tyrolean II	Frank and Milly Lee (Southsea)	1st DTA

Quicksteps (1969)

Beryldene	Derek Tonks and Beryl Bates	1st IDMA (Mid.)
Cabaret	Betty Baker (Withington)	
Delwood	Jim Dalton	
Holyrood	Edgar and Doris Holroyd	1st UKAPTD
Houghton	R. C. Bone	
Kimberley	Bill Traill (Maidstone)	1st BATD
Marji	Jim Dalton	
Roylat	Mary and Henry Taylor	4th NASD North

Foxtrots (1969)

Fawley	Freddie Wilkins (Edmonton)	ADA
Glenavon	Derek Tonks and Beryl Bates	4th Blackpool
Jameson	Jim Hutchinson (Farnworth)	
Sefton	Arranged by ADA	
Sunbeam	Mr. and Mrs. Smithies (Accrington)	3rd NASD North
Zambra	J. and E. Richardson	
Zeeta	Miss J. Richards (London)	3rd IDTA

Saunters (1969)

Ennerdale	Alf and Kitty Moore	NATD
Kelly's	Ken Fuller (Worsley)	
Regency	Rita Pover	1st OBBD
Serenade II [Saunter]	Ken Park	NCDTA
Silhouette	Miss Florence Proctor (Bedlington)	3rd NCDTA
Woodside	Ken Fuller (Worsley)	

Swings (1969)

Cabaret	Frank Short (Birmingham)	1st IDTA
Cuban	————	
Happytime	James Cheetham	
Londinium	Ray Hemming	1st OTDA
Ragtime	Jeff and Muriel Aldren (Eastham)	1st Blackpool
Saturday	Lewis and Joan Wilson	1st BATD

125

Blues (1969)

Drift	————	1st OTDA
Kentucky	Sam and Irene Faultley	1st ISTD
Woodland	Tony and Denis Dyer	Blackpool

Miscellaneous (1969)

Autumn Stroll	Derek Tonks and Beryl Bates	2nd Blackpool
Broadway Bossa Nova	J. M. Ogden (Leicester)	IDTA
Broadway Stroll	Doris Westaway	
Carousel Cha Cha Cha	Lewis and Joan Wilson (Heanor)	3rd Blackpool
Cavendish Glide (Progressive)	Mrs. Doris Olivant and Miss Margarite Carter	1st ISTD
Erimus	John Cox (Middlesborough)	
Jackpot Jinx (Novelty)	Lewis Wilson	1st ISDC IOM
London Stroll	Harry Wells (Leyton)	1st IDTA
Rock Jive (Barn Dance)	————	
Shaftesbury Sway	Mrs. Iris Follos (Gateshead)	2nd NCDTA

The scripts of the Saturday Swing (1969), Jackpot Jinx (1969) and the Hip Over by the Wilson's appear in Nancy Clarke's Party Dances.

Derek Arnold (North Star Publishers)

Derek Arnold of Otley is the eldest son of the late George Mott. After considerable experience in the entertainment field he set up a record shop and became a specialist in dance records. With his father as technical adviser he started to produce his own records (Ariston Music). Many of these records were sold through Northern Dance Services and Derek eventually set up the magazine 'Dance Monthly' in March 1972 to advertise the music and provide information for sequence dancers; in 1989 the title was changed to 'Sequence Dancing World'. This magazine is sent to subscribers to the regular script service for new dances. It is the only journal devoted to the interests of social sequence dancers and contains many articles of interest, letters and details of forthcoming events. North Star Publishers also advertise collections of dance scripts and other books on sequence dancing. In his time Derek Arnold has run old-time and modern sequence dancing festivals, inventive dance competitions and dancing holidays. He is a 'live wire' and his magazine provides a most useful forum for discussion of all aspects of the modern and old-time style.

The Voice in the Night Waltz came into being as the result of a novelty competition sponsored by Silver Dollar Records Ltd. George Mott was asked to arrange 10 bars of a modern sequence waltz with five alternative 6-bar endings. Competitors were asked to forecast how the panel of judges would place these alternatives in order of attractiveness and also add up to 12 words stating why they liked ballroom dancing. First prize was a colour TV with three other prizes for the runners-up.

The moving force behind Silver Dollar was Ernest Wilson - at one time pianist with Victor Sylvester. His flowery individual style supported by bass and drums made the group one of the most successful recording combinations of the 60's and early 70's. The music was well suited to sequence dancing and sing-a-long and Northern Dance Services hold the rights to many of his recordings.

Ken Park [Engagement (O/T) Waltz (1960), Engagement (Mod) Waltz (1969), Serenade Saunter (1969)]

Ken Park of Newcastle (with help from his wife, Elaine) has been a most prolific and successful arranger of sequence dances. The lists contain more than 40 of his dances from 1960 to the early 1980's - many being prize-winners in NCDTA competitions. The Engagement (Mod) Waltz (1969), Aquarius Rumba (1970) and Rumba Casanova (1975) are favourites with the general run of sequence dancers. His Tango El Cid (1967), Engagement Waltz (1969) and Tango Tarquilla (1978) are OBBD championship dances.

Harry Greenwood [Lullaby Waltz (1968)]

Harry Greenwood of Bradford was a member of BATD, IDMA and NASD. Trained in old-time dancing he began to teach the modern style in 1954. With his partner, Mrs. Paton, he arranged the first Old Time New Year's Ball at the Mecca Locarno in Bradford in 1962. Some of his dances are the Hazel Gavotte (with T. Edney) (1952), the Cheery Cha Cha Cha (1961), Lulu Quickstep (1962), Limbo Rumba (1963) and Ukandoit Quickstep (1966).

PRESENTED IN 1970

Waltzes (Old-Time) (1970)

Azalia	Betty Baker	
Christian	Anthony Harley	2nd Blackpool
Dominique	Doris Traill	BATD
Embassy II	Phillip Cockram	UKAPTD
World Cup	John and Vi Clifton (London)	1st SDF

Waltzes (Modern) (1970)

Amber	Harry Bates (Kingston-upon-Hull)	
Annabelle [Waltz]	Ken Fuller and Betty Baker	
Houghton	R. C. Bone (Thorne)	
Jasmin	H. Jay (Worthing)	1st SDTA
Moulin Rouge [Waltz]	David Bullen	1st ADA
Nocturne	Margaret Donald (Glasgow)	1st BATD
Ozette	Derek Tonks and Beryl Bates	IDTA Mid.
Ronet	Lloyd Holmes (Rochdale)	
Square	Gilbert Daniels	NCDTA
Stardust	Margaret Smithies (Accrington)	1st NASD
Wallington	Miss Iris Loraine (Wallington)	

Tangos (1970)

Arrogar	Derek Tonks and Beryl Bates	2nd IDTA Mid.
Campari	Ken and Elaine Park (Newcastle)	2nd ISDC IOM
Continental [Tango]	G. Walton (Bredbury)	3rd NASD North
Espana [Tango]	Ken Fuller (Worsley)	
Geraldine	Mr. and Mrs. E. McNeil (Stretford)	2nd NASD North
Kensway	Ken Park	1st NCDTA
Mexican	John Holloway (Bradford)	
Myensa [Tango]	Mary and Henry Taylor	
Suhali [Tango]	Joan and Lewis Wilson (Heanor)	1st IDTA
Solair [Tango]	Robert Stewart (Northampton)	1st OBBD
Torro	Don and Joy Ralph	1st ADA
Yellow Bird	George Mott (Shipley)	
Yvonne	Yvonne and Roger Cockery	Woolwich DTA

Swings (1970)

International	Theo and Doreen Ball	IDTA (SE)
Mexican	Brian and Christine Yarnold	1st Dance News
Party	Ken Fuller (Worsley)	

Quicksteps (1970)

Annette	Ted and Ruth Emery	2nd SDF London
Apollo	Arthur Lightfoot (Leeds)	1st Blackpool
Coral	E. and J. Richardson (Huddersfield)	
Delight	Ken Akrill	1st IDTA
S.B.	Sylvia and Holland Brockbank	3rd BATD
Seventy	Peter Varley	1st OBBD
Virginia	Iris Kempsell (London)	1st ISTD

Saunters (1970)

Anya	Marjorie and Tony Radmore	1st IDTA
Carolina	Tony Dyer (Barnsley)	1st Blackpool
Concorde	Alf and Peggy Hoskings	1st SDF Botham Trophy
Dafny	Joan Daft	
Esseldo	Jim Hutchinson	4th NASD North
Jozan	Joan and Lewis Wilson	1st ISDC IOM
Marelda	Ralph and Winnie Cox (Bramley)	1st IDTA (NE)

Foxtrots (1970)

Blue Star	J. and E. Richardson (Huddersfield)	
Delwood	Jim Dalton	
Filey	Fred Dawson	
Long Lea	Joan and Lewis Wilson	1st OBBD
Twilight	Harry Wells (London)	1st IDTA (SE)
Wandering Star	J. and E. Richardson (Huddersfield)	

Miscellaneous (1970)

Aquarius [Rumba]	Ken Park	NCDTA
Ballerina Gavotte	Frank and Millie Lee (Southsea)	
Burlington Cha Cha Cha	Kit Hastings	
Capri Cha Cha Cha	Yvonne Stanley and Maurice Tait	NATD
Eastham Blues	Mr. and Mrs. J. Aldren (Cheshire)	1st IDTA (NW)
Guadalajare Gavotte	Mr. and Mrs. Bill Traill (Maidstone)	1st BATD
Holiday Parade	Jeff and Muriel Aldren (Eastham)	3rd ISDC IOM
Leofric Gavotte	Alan Grassby and Estelle Grosvenor	1st ISTD
Peppermint Jive	Audrey Frew	1st OBBD
Rainbow Cha Cha	Jean and Graham Tuckfield	
Shadow Stroll	Yvonne and Roger Corkery	Woolwich DTA
Siesta Stroll	Yvonne Stanley	NATD
Sombrero [Samba]	R. Buckley (Manchester)	

Too Many New Dances

Modern sequence dancers often complain that they spend time mastering new dances which soon go out of fashion. Others consider that some of the newer dances are not as good as the old; some feel that there are more dances to learn than there used to be. There is some truth here but also an element of myth as is common when knowledge is passed on largely by word of mouth. It could be argued that new dances are the life-blood of the modern sequence dancing movement. Certainly attendances rise when the new dances appear - dancers would not come out dancing several nights per week for a fixed programme.

It is, perhaps, not the number of new dances which is most important but the degree of uniformity over the country. Dancers like to feel that if they move about or go on holiday they will find dancing sessions with programmes consisting largely of sequences within their repertoire. Since 1975 there has been an agreed list of new official dances which has largely resolved this problem - if dancers can perform these competently all should be well. Whether 45 per year (roughly a new dance every week) is too many depends on the dancer's enthusiasm. It is not enough for really keen dancers but too great a load for dancers wishing to go out once a week or for good dancers with declining health. The number of new dances to be learned is possibly less than in the past. Certainly in the north it was the practice to learn the unofficial (Manchester) dances as well as the official prizewinners; some hundreds of these dances written since 1975 have been excluded from the lists.

"We're going out sequence dancing as we've done for many a year -
It seems to have taken ages for new dances to appear.
We've mastered all the 'oldies' and when we take the floor -
We don't want less new dances we want more and more and more!
We like the little easy ones that give our brains a rest -
But those with all the tricky steps we really like the best!"

Ken Fuller (Worsley, Manchester)

Discussion of too many new dances leads us naturally to consider 'Mr. Sequence' himself. Assiduous readers of the list will note many new dances arranged by Ken Fuller of Worsley. These represent only a fraction of his vast output of more than 300 sequence dances of high quality. Of late, his modesty has compelled him to use a variety of pen-names such as John Brookes, Charles Howling and Audrey Haynes.

Most of his arrangements were not entered for competitions although he did win prizes for several including the Tango Rosanna (1961), Kingston Quickstep (1962) and Tango Marisa (1967). He visited his friends in Scotland on several occasions and on June 17th, 1967 Bert and Isabel Finlay of Kirkcaldy arranged a dance at Colinswell House, Burntisland with a programme consisting entirely of his arrangements.

Starlight Waltz	*Victoria Quickstep*
Blues Foxtrot	*Doris Cha Cha Cha*
Waltz Cherie	*Border Tango*
Sunshire Swing	*Beverley Blues*
Waltz Michelle	*Ivory Rag*
Tango Marisa	*Embassy Foxtrot*
Cameron Quickstep	*Whispering Waltz*
Red Rose Tango	*Kingston Quickstep*

No-one can match his total of new dances - few have more than 100 dances to their credit. The report of James Wilson of Glasgow holding a party to celebrate his 800th dance described in 'Dance News' of December 23rd, 1965 is something of a leg-pull. In 1973 Ken was taken to task (perhaps unfairly) for adding to the profusion of sequence dances already available. In his spirited reply he said, "I fail to see why my new dances upset *(the correspondent)* as he need not dance them - surely he can find a hall where the dancers are of the same opinion as he is. If he cannot he must accept the fact that he is in a minority."

In general one might ask whether a musician can write too many tunes or a painter paint too many pictures!

PRESENTED IN 1971

Waltzes (Old-Time) (1971)

Alpine	Joan and Lewis Wilson (Heanor)	1st IDTA
Escort	Stan Pitcher and Ursula Allen	1st ADA Mid.
Gaynor	Doris Trail (Maidstone)	1st BATD
Hazela	Mrs. Glynis Barnes (Thornton Heath)	1st OTDA Brittania Shield
Samantha	Mr. and Mrs. Franklin (Bisley)	1st OTDA

Waltzes (Modern) (1971)

Birthday	G. A. Champion	
Danielle [Waltz]	Dennis and Alice Douglas	
Dawn	Joan and Lewis Wilson (Heanor)	1st Blackpool
Dorothy	Harry Bate	
Ivy	Stan Wheatley (Auckland, New Zealand)	
Newbury	Joe Collier	
Princess	Gerald Bell and Josephine Lubelska	1st NATD
Sarita	E. V. Wheale	1st OTDA
Twilight	J. and E. Richardson	
Willowdale	Ken Fuller (Worsley)	

Tangos (1971)

Cameo	Hazel Batty	1st SDF Yorks.
Cyrene [Tango]	Robert Stewart (Northampton)	OBBD O/T
Doreta	Derek Tonks and Beryl Bates	3rd Blackpool
Lorraine [Tango]	Harry Wells (London)	1st IDTA Mod.
Margot	Raymond Casey (Newcastle-upon-Tyne)	1st NCDTA
Olga	John Clifton	1st SDF Botham Trophy
Sorrento	John Whitty (Leicester)	3rd IDTA Mid.
Spanish Eyes	Ken Fuller (Worsley)	
Taboo	Ken Park (Newcastle)	1st ISDC IOM
Taluna	Harry and Eileen Toyer	1st NATD
Topkapi	Margaret Donald	1st BATD

Quicksteps (1971)

Britannia II	Les Sherwin and Joyce Ponting	1st ISTD
Hilton II	Jack Gaffney	
Imperial	Ken Fuller (Worsley)	1st NASD
Keeshie	Beryl and Alan Leavey	SDTA
Lisa	Ken Park (Newcastle)	1st ISDC
Marchetta	Bill and Maude Stevenson	1st ADA
Pasadena	Frank Short	

Quicksteps (1971) (continued)

Stanley	Jim Dalton	
Tipple	Robert Stewart	1st OBBD

Foxtrots (1971)

Moonraker	Harold Hulley	
Pandora	Joan and Lewis Wilson (Heanor)	OBBD
Protea	Carl Van Der Bank (Cape Town, S. Africa)	
Springtime	Peter Sharpe	ISTD
Verdon	Harry Dunkerton	1st ISTD

Swings (1971)

Champagne	Jeff and Muriel Aldren (Eastham)	2nd Blackpool
Honkytonk	Derek Tonks and Beryl Bates	2nd Blackpool
Maxi	Fred Dawson	1st UKAPTD

Miscellaneous (1971)

Balmoral Blues	Robert Stewart (Northampton)	1st Dance News Slough
Casino Cha Cha Cha	J. and E. Richardson	
Cecilia Cha Cha	Eddie Winfield	1st NCDTA
Esso Blues	Ken Park (Newcastle)	1st Blackpool
Glynn Stroll	Mr. and Mrs. J. Kelly (Northern Ireland)	
Keleta Sway	E. J. Pestell	2nd OTDA
Paso Seville	Archie Donald (Glasgow)	1st BATD
Rico [Rumba]	J. and E. Richardson (Huddersfield)	
Rumba One	Peter Varley (Leigh-on-Sea)	1st OBBD
Starlight Twinkle	Ron Davis (Hemel Hempstead)	1st SDF Blundell Trophy
Syon Saunter	Roger and Yvonne Corkery	1st Woolwich DTA
Tea Time Saunter	Bill Wait (Liverpool)	1st ADA
Vici	Vivian Carrie	1st ADA

Jack and Elsie Richardson [Twilight Waltz, Rumba Rico (1971)]

Jack Richardson was headmaster of Berry Brow County School in Huddersfield; he ran sequence dancing sessions there and elsewhere in the 1950's. He was Secretary of NASD in 1960 and later became Chairman. In 1968 he resigned to become Chairman of the Yorkshire Sequence Dance Federation - a post he held for more than 20 years. Jack and Elsie joined the Manchester MC's Club in 1962. They arranged more than 40 dances from 1958 to the 1980's; the Memory Rumba of 1985 is a late example.

PRESENTED IN 1972

Waltzes (Old-Time) (1972)

Boutique [Waltz]	Jeff and Muriel Aldren (Eastham)	1st Blackpool
Butterfly	Hugh and Mabel Jay	3rd SDTA
Tyrolean [Waltz]	Nora Bray	IDTA
Western	Don Franklin (Bisley)	2nd OTDA

Waltzes (Modern) (1972)

Airedale	S. Harrison	
Alice	Derek Tonks and Beryl Bates	1st Blackpool
Allendale	Jim Dalton	
Baronet	Brian and Betty Kirkham	1st ADA
Bluebell	Harry and Winnie Bate	
Cameo	Irene Watling and Bernard Wilding	1st Woolwich DTA
Carousel [Waltz]	Wendy and Bob Whelerton	2nd Dance Monthly
Cristallo	Les Clydesdale	1st UKAPTD
Disa	Carl van den Bank (Durban, South Africa)	
Evening Star	Hugh and Mabel Jay	1st SDTA
Jeannine [Waltz]	Eddie Ghys (Wembley)	Butlins Bognor Regis
Jozan [Waltz]	Elsie Platts	1st ISDC IOM
Juliette [Waltz]	Ken Fuller	
Marguerite II [Waltz]	Ken Fuller	
Matador	Tim Edmunds (Worsley)	1st NASD (North)
Maycliffe	John Clifton	1st SDF Botham Trophy
Silver	Miss Durley	1st IDTA
Sunset I	Ken Fuller	
Windsor II	Elizabeth Allen	1st NCDTA

Quicksteps (1972)

Adelaide	Tony and Denise Dyer	1st Dance Monthly
Alabama	Bill and Maude Stevenson	1st ADA (Mid.)
Brighton	Nancy Clarke and Eric Stonehouse	IDTA
Carlton II	Alwyn Leathley	2nd SDF Yorks.
Dixieland	David Bullen	1st OBBD
Eljay	Lewis and Joan Wilson	2nd Blackpool
Haviland	Sydney Tilbury	
Knokke	Mrs. E. Sharpe	1st BATD
Manhattan	Tony and Denise Dyer	1st IDTA
Seaside	Ted Burroughs	1st IDTA (SW)
Tracey	Eileen and Harry Toyer	1st NATD

Tangos (1972)

Accordian	Ken Fuller	
Alicante [Tango]	Ken Fuller	3rd NASD North
Caprice II [Tango]	Tony and Denise Dyer	1st IDTA London
Caprice III [Tango]	John Butler (Doncaster)	
Champagne	Edith Denton	1st NASD North
Chinchilla	Bill Wait	1st ADA
Firenza [Tango] (O/T)	Pat Hancock	1st SDF Blundell Trophy
Madame [Tango]	Lewis and Joan Wilson	2nd Blackpool
Mantilla II [Tango]	Nancy Clarke and Eric Stonehouse	IDTA
Park Lane	Ken Park	1st NCDTA
Scampari	Dorothy Vincent	1st OTDA
Tango for Two	Jeff and Muriel Aldren	Slough

Foxtrots (1972)

Alison	Jim Hutchinson	
Belrose	Bill and Louie Harvey	ISTD
Denalise	Dennis and Alice Douglas	
Dream II	J. and E. Richardson	
Harmony II	Betty Baker	
Louise [Foxtrot]	Lewis and Joan Wilson	2nd IDTA
Marcus	George Walton	4th NASD (North)
Maybelene	John and Rose Drinkwater	1st Butlins Bognor Regis
Phoenix	Alwyn Leathley	1st YSDF
Tara	Jack and Mary Taylor	1st YSDF
Tynedale	Nora Capps	1st NCDTA

Saunters (1972)

Andrea	Alf Hoskings	1st IDTA (SE)
Autumn II	Les and Freda Lancaster	1st YSDF
Rainbow	Robert Stewart	1st OBBD
Riverside	Arthur Lightfoot (Leeds)	1st ISDC IOM
Shell	Ted Burroughs	1st IDTA (SW)

Blues (1972)

Autumn	Ted and Olive Read	1st NATD
Barolan	Frank Torrance and Jimmie Fanning	
Benidorm	Ted Burroughs	1st IDTA (SW)
Lavender	Ken Fuller	
Midnight	David Bullen and Beverley Forsdike	1st ADA
Westminster	Sam and Irene Faultley	1st ISTD London

Sambas (1972)

April	Harry Wells	1st OBBD
Embee	Vivien Carrie	1st ADA
Katrina [Samba]	Mrs. Joan Wilson	1st IDTA

Miscellaneous (1972)

Bossa Nova Blues	Betty Croasdale and Fred Dawson	
Celebration Swing	Ken Fuller	
Cerma Sway	Beatrice Webster (Walsall)	2nd OTDA
Frenchy's Jive	Margaret Donald	1st BATD
Jubilee Glide	Glynnis Barnes (Thornton Heath)	1st OTDA
Martinique Cha Cha Cha	J. and E. Richardson	1st YSDF
Poco Pelo Cha Cha Cha	Doreen Edwards	
Summertime Stroll	Mr. R. Sharpe	1st BATD
Swanee Swing	Ken Fuller	

Harry Bate (Bluebell Waltz) ran most of his dancing classes in Irlam; he joined NASD with his wife, Winnie, in 1964. They arranged some half dozen dances from 1967 to 1972, the Katie Quickstep (1968) being the most popular. He moved to Poulton-Le-Fylde and died in April 1995.

The Bullen Family

The Bullen School of Dancing, established by John Bullen in Liverpool in 1896, was moved to Southport in 1936. Several sequence dances arranged by the son, Gerald Bullen, appear in the lists for the 1950's. These are mainly old-time and include the Corinthian Waltz (1953), Regency Stroll (1955) and Debonaire Saunter (1959).

The grandson, David Bullen (born May 1946), is a Carl Alan award winner and has had many successes in inventive dance competitions to his credit. Some of his earlier dances are the Saunter Martine (1968), Moulin Rouge Waltz (1970) and Dixieland Quickstep (1972). Dancing first with Denise Mayo and later with Iverna Corcoran he won many prizes in the 70's and 80's. The David Bullen Organisation provides scripts and other services for sequence dancers. He is the organiser of the elaborate North of Britain Festivals at Southport (and Bridlington) which include inventive dance competitions authorised by the Official Board.

PRESENTED IN 1973

Waltzes (Old-Time) (1973)

Almeda	Peter Sharpe	1st ISTD London
Dresden	Babs Gubbins	1st IDTA
Eddray	Ken and Vi Agar (Paignton)	1st UKAPTD
Ridgeway Progressive	Doris Gibbs	NATD

Waltzes (Modern) (1973)

Allenby	Alf and Dot Evans	
April	Harold Hammond	
Azalea	Betty Baker	1st NASD North
Capitol	Terry Cottrill	3rd NASD North
Cinderella	Ken and Vi Agar	2nd Butlins Bognor Regis
College	David Hogg	2nd UKAPTD
Cresta II	Tony and Denise Dyer	2nd OBBD Filey
Glenburn	Edna Collins	1st ADA
Glentore	Jack and Mary Taylor	
Hawaii [Waltz]	Ken Fuller	
Meridian	B. J. Peppiatt	3rd SDF London
Sequella	Nancy Clarke and Eric Stonehouse	IDTA
Springfield	Tim and Dorothy Edmunds	1st NASD North
Wishing	Lewis and Joan Wilson	1st Dancing Monthly

Tangos (1973)

Bonita II	David and Ivy Beevers	1st YSDF
Capri IV [Tango]	Ken and Vi Agar	Butlins
Clarendon	Derek Tonks and Beryl Bates	1st ISDC IOM
Granada [Tango]	Harry and Gladys Marsden	2nd SDF London
Juanita [Tango]	Ken Park	NCDTA
Kiro [Tango]	Denis and Alice Douglas	
Manhattan	Tony and Denise Dyer	1st Dance Monthly
Pablo [Tango]	Alf and Peggy Hoskings	1st SDF Botham Trophy
Romantica	Brian and Betty Kirkham	1st ADA Mid.
Russell [Tango]	John Jackson	UKAPTD
Santa Rosa	J. and E. Richardson	
Seville II	Jeff Robinson	4th NASD North
Star II	Ken and Barbara Street	1st ISTD
Topaz	Derek Tonks and Beryl Bates	1st OBBD
Tristar	Tom Liddiard	OTDA

Quicksteps (1973)

April	Helena Van Gaart	1ST OBBD
Cavalier	Alwyn Leathley	1st ISDC IOM
Cumberland	Ken Fuller	
Denton	Tony and Denise Dyer (Barnsley)	1st Blackpool
Dunster I	Tony and Denise Dyer	OBBD Filey
Dunster II	Bill and Dorothy Bestwick	1st ADA (Mid)
Emerald	J. and E. Richardson	
Lindon	Rose and Arthur Mills	
Melanie	George Walton	2nd NASD North
Presto	Elizabeth Allan	1st NCDTA
Reola	Ken and Vi Agar	2nd Dancing Monthly
Sovereign	Gerald Bell and Josephine Lubelska	NATD

Foxtrots (1973)

Carnaby	Yvonne and Roger Corkery	IDTA
Claringo	Clarry Clarke	
December	Alan and Brenda Holt	
Rosemount	Don Franklin (Bisley)	OTDA
Rosslyn	Arranged by OBBD	
Topaz	Bob and Wendy Whelerton	

Swings (1973)

Chantilly	Jeff and Muriel Aldren	Joint 1st Blackpool
Midway	Bernard Wilding and Irene Watling	1st BATD
Susie Rhyl	John and Susan Sommerin	1st Rhyl
Viennese II	Tony and Denise Dyer	1st OBBD Filey

Saunters (1973)

Buckingham	Jeff and Muriel Aldren (Wirral)	1st Dance News
Europa	David and Valierie Warren	1st BATD
Parfit [Saunter]	Maurice Tait	3rd OBBD Filey
Sea Breeze	Jeff and Muriel Aldren	Joint 1st Blackpool
Sentimental II	Wendy Whelerton	1st Dancing Monthly
Southwood	Winn and Bob Oliver	1st Butlins Bognor Regis

Blues (1973)

Harmony I	Ken and Barbara Street	ISTD
Marina	Jeff and Muriel Aldren	IDTA

Cha Cha Chas (1973)

| Duet [Cha Cha] | Percy Lane (Weymouth) | 1st BATD |
| Sally Ann | Ken and Barbara Street | 1st ISTD |

Miscellaneous (1973)

Alain [Rumba]	Les and Freda Lancaster	1st YSDF
Carisbrooke Gavotte	Len Brown	1st SDF London
Circle Conga (Party)	Ken Fuller	
Elizabeth Stroll	Ken and Vi Agar	2nd NDS
Follow Me (Party)	George Collings	1st ADA
Highland Caper (Party)	Iris Herd and Will Richardson	2nd SDF (London)
Jupiter Jive	Peter Varley	1st OBBD
Marquesa Rumba	Doris Latham	UKAPTD
Saucy Samba	Ken Park	1st NCDTA
Singalong Stroll (Party)	Ken Fuller	
Tico-Tico Samba	Tom and Doris Francis	NATD

Ted and Sue Burroughs [Seaside Quickstep (1972), Shell Saunter (1972), Benidorm Blues (1972)]

The dances listed above were prize-winners at the IDTA SW region competition. From 1975 onwards (latterly with his wife, Sue) Ted has had over 60 competition successes including 8 in 1982. The Burroughs have a school of dancing in Western-Super-Mare and are examiners and adjudicators. They act as guest MC's and organise festivals and dancing holidays.

Ken and Barbara Street [Star Tango (1973), Harmony Blues (1973), Sally Ann Cha Cha Cha (1973)]

This couple have had many successes (4 winners in 1990). Their Caribbean Rumba, Sally Ann Cha Cha Cha, Justa Jive and Jubilee Jive are ISTD championship dances.

The author regrets that many fine dancers and important personalities of the dancing world have not received special attention due to limitations of space. He would also have liked to have included Bernard Brooks, Monty Pearce and the other musicians who have given much joy to the sequence dancing fraternity.

PRESENTED IN 1974

Waltzes (Old-Time) (1974)

Ramonda	Gwendoline Blow (Stamford)	1st ADA (Midland)
Shamrock	Ken Fuller	
Winrick	Ron Davis	1st SDF London

Waltzes (1974)

Alexis	Derek Tonks and Beryl Bates	1st ISDC IOM
Belair [Waltz]	David Bullen and Denise Mayo (Southport)	1st Butlins OBBD
Benwell	Norma Bolton	1st NCDTA
Claisdale	Jack and Mary Taylor	2nd YSDF
De Mar [Waltz]	Bill and Mary Dean	3rd Southport
Emily Jane	Jim and Gwen Gordon Stewart (Bulkington)	2nd OTDA
Francine [Waltz]	F. E. Smith	1st ADA
Golden Wedding	Frank Torrance and J. Fanning	
Harmony II	Tony and Denise Dyer	1st NDS Pudsey
Jeanette [Waltz]	Fred and Pam Welham (Sutton-in-Ashfield)	1st OTDA
Julie Anne [Waltz]	Damien and Edna Norbury	2nd NASD (North)
Karen	Dennis and Alice Douglas	3rd Blackpool
Kendal	Alan and Joan Pye	4th NASD (North)
Mandalay [Waltz]	Ken and Vi Agar	UKAPTD
Marisse	David and Ivy Beevers	1st YSDF
Samantha	Ken Fuller	
Starlight II	Bill and Maude Stevenson	1st ADA
Sunset II	Joan Wilson	1st NATD

Tangos (1974)

Albeniz [Tango]	Ken Fuller	
Aragon	David Hogg	1st ISTD
Arloc	L. Cunningham	1st NASD Yorks.
Chanel [Tango]	David Bullen and Denise Mayo (Southport)	1st OBBD
Dolores II [Tango]	Ken Fuller	
El Torro [Tango]	Ken Fuller	
Glenavon	Derek Tonks and Beryl Bates	1st Blackpool (O/T)
Grenada [Tango]	Advisory Committee ISTD	ISTD
Jefferson	Jeff and Irene Robinson	3rd NASD (North)
Nigella [Tango]	Ken and Barbara Street	1st Bognor Regis
Rosella II [Tango]	Ken Fuller	
Verdad [Tango]	Ted and Ruth Emery	1st SDF Botham Trophy
Viola	Ken and Vi Agar	1st NDS Pudsey

140

Quicksteps (1974)

Ashton	Yvonne and Roger Corkery	1st IDTA
Crystal II	Committee for Medal Test	ISTD
Eivona	Mrs. E. M. Crompton (Derby)	1st Blackpool
Karneil	Phyllis and Norman Pitson	
Kestral	Bob and Wendy Whelerton	2nd NDS Pudsey
Lynwood	Ken Fuller	
Mynina	Ken and Vi Agar	3rd NDS Pudsey
Promenade	Tony Dyer	2nd Southport
Roscoe	Roy and Elaine Sharpe	1st BATD

Saunters (1974)

Astoria	Derek Tonks and Beryl Bates	1st IDTA
Marie [Saunter]	Edgar and Doris Holroyd	1st ISDC IOM
Michelle	Lesley Batty	1st YSDF
Mosside	Stephen and Christine Troke	Dance News
Shangri La	Ken Park	NCDTA
Soya	Ken Park	1st NCDTA
Susan	Dennis Douglas	2nd Blackpool

Cha Cha Chas (1974)

Chinchilla	Damien and Edna Norbury	NASD (North)
K.P.	Ken Park	1st NCDTA
Marina	Irene Wood	1st BATD
Medina [Cha Cha]	J. and E. Richardson	2nd YSDF
Paraguay [Cha Cha]	Ken Fuller	
Tahiti	David Bullen and Denise Mayo	1st ADA
Tutti Frutti	Vivien Carrie	1st ADA

Blues (1974)

Fiesta	Bob and Winn Oliver	2nd Butlins Bognor Regis
Harmony II	Tony and Denise Dyer	1st NDS Pudsey
Hawaiian	David Bullen and Denise Mayo	1st ADA
Imperial	Tony Eato	1st ISTD
Twilight	Frank Smith	2nd YSDF

Foxtrots (1974)

Benita	Derek Tonks and Beryl Bates	1st OBBD
Conmoore	Cliff and Gwen Abbot	NASD Yorks.
Debdon	Alf and Peggy Hoskings	3rd SDF London
Marlboro	J. and E. Richardson	
Nicola	Tim and Dorothy Edmonds	1st NASD (North)

Strolls (1974)

Blenheim	Ken and Barbara Street (Luton)	1st ISTD
Kimberley	Roy and Elaine Sharpe	1st BATD
Starlight II	R. H. Fowles (Surrey)	1st OTDA

Miscellaneous (1974)

Barbara Sway	Ken and Barbara Street	UKAPTD
Broadway Bounce	Ken Park	IDTA
Butterfly Rock	Jim Brennan	
Campbell Swing	Edna Collings (Ormskirk)	1st ADA
Festival Swing	Tony and Denise Dyer	2nd Butlins
Jenny Samba	Les and Freda Lancaster	1st YSDF
Kingfisher Swing	Keith Banton and Beverley Forsdike	1st Southport
Paso Deena	Lewis Wilson	1st IDTA
Paso Espanol	Maurice Tait and Yvonne Stanley	NATD
Paso Espana	Ken Fuller	
Penrose Two Step	David Bullen and Denise Mayo	1st PADC
Planet Jive	Peter Varley	1st OBBD
Ridgeway Gavotte	Doris Gibbs	1st NATD Worthing
Roulette [Rumba]	Peter Varley and Constance Nixon	
Rumbarba [Rumba]	Ken and Elaine Park	1st Blackpool
Sting-a-Ling (Fun dance)	Lewis and Joan Wilson (Heanor)	1st NATD Worthing

Numbers of Arrangements from 1946 - 1974

Waltzes O/T	278	Swings	40
Waltzes Modern	284	Glides	19
Tangos	326	Sways	17
Foxtrots	167	Mazurkas	13
Quicksteps	150	One Steps	14
Rumbas	16	Square Dances	8
Saunters	152	Schottisches	18
Cha Cha Chas	33	Strolls	21
Blues	78	Parades	13
Jives	6	Rags	7
Sambas	15	Bossa Novas	5
Gavottes	35	Miscellaneous	68
Two Steps	107	Total	1896
Paso Dobles	6		

Index of Dances (1946-1974)

Waltzes (O/T)

Lotus (1957)
Louise (1951)
Louise [Valse] (1957)
Lyndale (1954)
Majestic I (1950)
Majestic II (1957)
Malina [Waltz] (1969)
Malvern (1968)
Marguerite [Waltz] (1961)
Marietta [Waltz] (1954)
Martine [Valse] (1950)
Mavona (1961)
Mayfair (1957)
Mayflower (1958)
Maytime (1960)
Melody (1960)
Memoir (1968)
Mermaid (1953)
Merry Widow (1953)
Midland (1967)
Minerva (1967)
Miramar (1958)
Missouri (1957)
Mona Isle (1962)
Moonlight (1957)
Mysetta (1966)
Nannette [Waltz] (1952)
Northern Star (1965)
Oakley (1950)
Olympia [Waltz] (1956)
Opal (1968)
Orchid (1960)
Osborne (1968)
Petite [Valse] (1951)
Pink Lady (1955)
Pirouette [Waltz] (1957)
Primrose (1952)
Prince of Wales (1953)
Prince Consort (1952)
Princess Anne (1950)

Princess Margaret (1953)
Priory (1966)
Progressive II (1947)
Queen Elizabeth (Viennese)(53)
Queen's Own (1953)
Queens (1965)
Rainbow I (1951)
Rainbow II (1952)
Rainbow III (1957)
Ramon [Waltz] (1951)
Ramonda (1974)
Regal (1953)
Regency (1957)
Regency (1958)
Regis (1964)
Rendezvous (1955)
Richmond (1957)
Ridgeway Progressive (1973)
Roaming in the Gloaming (55)
Rock 'n' Roll (1956)
Romany (1961)
Rosary (1949)
Rosewood (1961)
Roulette (1958)
Samantha (1971)
Sandford (1964)
Saphena (1958)
Sapphire (1964)
Saturday (1951)
Serene [Waltz] (1955)
Shamrock (1974)
Shirley (1958)
Silver Wedding (1953)
Silverdor (1965)
Silvern (1956)
Sorrentino [Waltz] (1965)
Spanish (1960)
Springfield (1962)
Springtime I (1952)
Springtime II (1965)
St. Albans (1969)

St. Omer (1959)
Starlight (1963)
Starlit (1950)
Sunbeam (1952)
Susanne [Waltz] (1968)
Suzanne [Waltz] (1950)
Tina (1958)
Trecarn [Valse] (1954)
Treecia (1954)
Trudie (1957)
True Love (1961)
Tudor (1950)
Tulip (1955)
Tyrolean [Waltz] (1972)
University (1949)
Valentine (1957)
Venus (1961)
Victoria (1952)
Vienna [Waltz] (1949)
Viennese Flirtation (1954)
Virene (1965)
Waltheof (1956)
Waltz of the Bells (1958)
Waltz for the Queen (1953)
Waltz of Britain (1951)
Wearside (1969)
Wedding (1947)
Weekend (1961)
Wendy (1959)
Wessex (1953)
Western (1972)
Whitman (1969)
Willow (1964)
Windsor (1950)
Winifred [Valse] (1958)
Winrick (1974)
World Cup (1970)
Worral (1958)
Worrall (1961)
Wulfruna (1967)
Yvette [Waltz] (1962)

Zephyr (1963)

Waltzes (Mod)

Adoration I (1957)
Adoration II (1957)
Airedale (1972)
Alanric (1962)
Alback (1966)
Alexandra (1960)
Alexis (1974)
Alice (1972)
Alicia [Waltz] (1969)
Allenby (1973)
Allendale (1972)
Alpha (1969)
Amber (1970)
Anna Maria (1957)
Annabelle [Waltz] (1970)
Annette (1960)
Anniversary (1958)
April (1973)
Autumn (1963)
Azalea (1973)
Babette I [Waltz] (1957)
Babette II [Waltz] (1968)
Baronet (1972)
Barrita [Waltz] (1963)
Be Mine (1953)
Bedelia (1957)
Belair [Waltz] (1974)
Benwell (1974)
Bettina (1956)
Beverley (1969)
Birthday (1971)
Blue Lady (1968)
Blue Moon (1968)
Bluebell (1972)
Cameo (1972)
Candy (1960)
Capitol (1973)
Caravelle (1967)

144

Waltzes (Mod)

Carlton (Progressive) (1957)
Carolina (1958)
Carolyn (Progressive) (1965)
Carousel [Waltz] (1972)
Casino (1967)
Cathrine/Catherine [Waltz](56)
Cavalcade [Waltz] (1948)
Cavendish (1969)
Celebration (1964)
Chandelier (1964)
Charisse [Waltz] (1964)
Charmaine I [Waltz] (1955)
Charmaine II [Waltz] (1967)
Charming [Waltz] (1964)
Cherie [Waltz] (1959)
Chi-Co [Waltz] (1960)
Christine [Waltz] (1959)
Cinderella (1973)
Claisdale (1974)
College (1973)
Columbine [Waltz] (1968)
Cresta I (1955)
Cresta II (1973)
Crinoline (1966)
Cristallo (1972)
D'Laine (1969)
Danielle [Waltz] (1971)
Davidian (1969)
Dawn (1971)
De-Mar [Waltz] (1974)
Delight [Waltz] (1958)
Diane I [Waltz] (1955)
Diane II [Waltz] (1964)
Disa (1972)
Doreen (1962)
Doretta (1959)
Dorice [Waltz] (1962)
Dorissa [Waltz] (1958)
Dorothy (1971)

Dream (1967)
Dutch Spring (Party) (1958)
Eileen [Waltz] (1962)
Elaine I [Waltz] (1959)
Elaine II [Waltz] (1965)
Elise [Waltz] (1959)
Emily Jane (1974)
Empress (1966)
Engagement (1969)
English Rose (1967)
Etelle [Waltz] (1966)
Evening Star (1972)
Evening (1958)
Everlasting (1952)
Fernside (1968)
Festival of Britain (1951)
Festival (1950)
Forget Me Not (1965)
Francine [Waltz] (1974)
Frandor (1963)
Friendship (1958)
Geneve [Waltz] (1959)
Glenburn (1973)
Glentore (1973)
Golden Wedding (1974)
Greensleeves (1965)
Gwynne Circle (1950)
Harlequin (1969)
Harmony I (1968)
Harmony II (1974)
Harwinn (1965)
Hawaii [Waltz] (1973)
Hawthorns (1968)
Homecoming (1960)
Houghton (1970)
Idaho (1965)
International (1967)
Inverness (1959)
Isobel [Waltz] (1968)
Ivy (1971)
Jacqueline (1951)

Janette (1962)
Janine [Waltz] (1964)
Jasmin (1970)
Jasmine (1968)
Jeanette [Waltz] (1974)
Jeannine [Waltz] (1972)
Joanette (1965)
Josephine [Waltz] (1962)
Jozan [Waltz] (1972)
Juliana (1960)
Julie Anne [Waltz] (1974)
Julietta (1960)
Juliette [Waltz] (1972)
Karen (1974)
Kendal (1974)
Kentucky (1967)
Kildare (1965)
L'Aimant [Waltz] (1964)
Lanodale (1966)
Laura I (1966)
Laura II (1966)
Linda (1967)
Linden (1965)
Lindley (1962)
Loraine [Waltz] (1963)
Louise [Waltz] (1968)
Lucerne [Waltz] (1959)
Lullaby I (1952)
Lullaby II (1968)
Magenta (1951)
Magnolia (1969)
Maida (1963)
Mandalay [Waltz] (1974)
Marcella [Waltz] (1958)
Margaret (1960)
Marguerite I [Waltz] (1950)
Marguerite II [Waltz] (1972)
Marianne [Waltz] (1966)
Marie I [Waltz] (1948)
Marie II [Waltz] (1968)
Marigold (1966)

Marisse (1974)
Markette [Waltz] (1956)
Marlene [Waltz] (1958)
Matador (1972)
Maybelene (1966)
Maycliffe (1972)
Maytime (1965)
Melodrene (1967)
Melody (1952)
Melrose (1955)
Meridian (1973)
Merry Widow Waltz of 1952
Michelle [Waltz] (1966)
Moderna (1954)
Monterey (1966)
Moonglow (1955)
Moonlight (1967)
Morecambrian (1958)
Moulin Rouge [Waltz] (1970)
Newbury (1971)
Nocturne (1970)
Norma (1956)
Novella (1965)
Ozette (1970)
Parmela (Pamela) (1963)
Paradise (1954)
Parisienne (1966)
Patricia (1954)
Pennine (1969)
Prince Charles (1969)
Princess (1971)
Priory (1960)
Progress (1963)
Quorn (1961)
Ramona [Waltz] (1963)
Regent (1963)
Renown [Waltz] (1953)
Riley (1961)
Riversdale (1956)
Riverside (1968)
Ronde (1956)

Waltzes (Mod)

Ronet (1970)
Rose Lane (1963)
Rosemary (1964)
Roulette [Waltz] (1969)
Royale [Waltz] (1968)
Samantha (1974)
Sandra (1969)
Sarita (1971)
Savoy [Waltz] (1961)
Selby (1967)
September (1957)
Sequella (1973)
Serenade [Waltz] (1961)
Serene [Waltz] (1955)
Shadow (1954)
Siesta [Waltz] (1965)
Silver (1961)
Silver Wedding (1948)
Silver (1972)
Silverdor (1965)
Sincere [Waltz] (1959)
Soas (1960)
Somerville (1959)
Sorrento [Waltz] (1961)
Souvenir [Waltz] (1962)
Spire (1964)
Springfield (1973)
Springtime (1959)
Square (1970)
Star (1960)
Stardust (1970)
Starlight I (1960)
Starlight II (1974)
Summertime (1961)
Sunset I (1972)
Sunset II (1974)
Superbe [Waltz] (1960)
Suzanne (1961)
Sylvellen (1965)
Sylvia [Waltz] (1958)

Symphony (1951)
Tammy (1969)
Telestar (1962)
Telstar (1962)
Tennessee (1952)
Terre [Waltz] (1956)
Topaz (1965)
True Love (1957)
Tulip (1966)
Twilight (1971)
Variety (1956)
Venetia [Waltz] (1957)
Vienna (1967)
Viscount (1967)
Voice in the Night (1969)
Wallington (1970)
Waltz of the Moon (1969)
Waltz of the Valley (1969)
Waverley (1959)
Wayne (1967)
Welcome (1957)
Wentworth (1965)
Westminster (1953)
Westvale (1969)
Whispering I (1958)
Whispering II (1964)
White Rose I (1956)
White Rose II (1956)
Wild Rose (1957)
Willow (1958)
Willow Pattern (1959)
Willowdale (1971)
Windermere II (1955)
Windsor I (1965)
Windsor II (1972)
Winifred (1967)
Wishing (1973)
Woodlands (1965)
Woodside (1964)
Wyoming I (1953)
Wyoming II (1963)

Yvette (1969)
Yvonne (1965)

Tangos

Accordian (1972)
Alassio (1962)
Albany (1963)
Albenz [Tango] (1974)
Alemeda [Tango] (1964)
Alexandra (1955)
Alhambra (1957)
Alicante [Tango] (1972)
Alysia (1959)
Ameleon (1950)
Angelus (1958)
Anglesea (1959)
Annalita [Tango] (1967)
Apollo [Tango] (1969)
Aragon (1974)
Arloc (1974)
Arrogar (1970)
Autumn (1960)
Balalaika (1969)
Balmoral (1953)
Barcelona [Tango] (1955)
Bell (1961)
Belmont (1954)
Berkeley (1955)
Bermuda (1965)
Beryl [Tango] (1956)
Black Magic (1959)
Black Knight (1959)
Blue I (1952)
Blue II (1952)
Blue III [Tango] (1969)
Bluebell (1959)
Bon Bon (1951)
Bonita I (1959)
Bonita II (1973)
Brazil [Tango] (1966)
Buchanan (1954)

Butterfly (1951)
Cambria (1959)
Camellia (1952)
Cameo (1971)
Campari (1970)
Canasta [Tango] (1965)
Capri I [Tango] (1948)
Capri II [Tango] (1957)
Capri III [Tango] (1962)
Capri IV [Tango] (1973)
Caprice I [Tango] (1953)
Caprice II [Tango] (1972)
Caprice III [Tango] (1972)
Carlton (1956)
Carmenita (1954)
Castella (1968)
Celebration [Tango] (1953)
Champagne (1972)
Chanel [Tango] (1974)
Cherie [Tango] (1956)
Chinchilla (1972)
Clarendon (1973)
Collette [Tango] (1963)
Continental [Tango] (1970)
Coronation (1953)
Countessa [Tango] (1963)
Crown (1953)
Cyrene [Tango] (1971)
D'oro [Tango] (1957)
Dawn (1965)
De Reve (1950)
Del Mar (1964)
Del Sol [Tango] (1968)
Del Marina [Tango] (1958)
Del Rosa (1950)
Delano (1954)
Delilah [Tango] (1968)
Diablo [Tango] (1968)
Diana(e) [Tango] (1952)
Dolores I (1951)
Dolores II [Tango] (1974)

Tangos

Doreta (1971)
Dorian (1965)
Eastoke (1959)
Ectasy [Tango] (1956)
Eduanita [Tango] (1952)
El Cid (1967)
El Paseo (1968)
Elizabeth (1951)
El Torro (1974)
Encano [Tango] (1965)
Enchanteur (1950)
Enchantment (1952)
Espana [Tango] (1970)
Fantasy [Tango] (1951)
Fascination [Tango] (1946)
Fiesta I [Tango] (1951)
Fiesta II (1962)
Fiesta III (1964)
Fiesta IV (1966)
Firenza [Tango] (O/T) (1972)
Florenza (1959)
Florida [Tango] (1965)
Fredericka [Tango] (1958)
Gaytime (1968)
Geraldine (1970)
Glenavon (1974)
Glenmore (1952)
Glennifer (1958)
Golden Wedding (1969)
Golden I (1954)
Golden II (1963)
Golden Festival (1954)
Granada [Tango] (1973)
Granero [Tango] (1969)
Grenada [Tango] (1974)
Guitar (1965)
Harlequin I (1958)
Harlequin II (1959)
Havana (1954)
Hesitante [Tango] (1953)

Hevony (1955)
Invitation (1952)
Isabella (1965)
Isle of Man (1958)
Isola (1961)
Ivena (1956)
Janeen (1966)
Jealousy [Tango] (1959)
Jeannette [Tango] (1958)
Jefferson (1974)
Jose [Tango] (1959)
Juan [Tango] (1957)
Juanita [Tango] (1973)
Jubilee (1952)
Julian (1958)
Jupiter (1957)
Juroy (1962)
Katrina (1967)
Kensway (1970)
Kiro [Tango] (1973)
L'amour [Tango] (1957)
La Pree (1955)
La Cumparsita (1967)
La Ma (1958)
La Scala (1957)
La Dell (1951)
Lavelle [Tango] (1958)
Layton (1961)
Le Breton (1950)
Leona (1952)
Leonora [Tango] (1966)
Lilac (1961)
Lilani (1960)
Lilvina (1950)
Lloret (1964)
Lorraine [Tango] (1971)
Louetta (1954)
Lynwell (1965)
Madame [Tango] (1972)
Madelaine [Tango] (1958)
Madelena [Tango] (1967)

Madrid [Tango] (1954)
Magenta I [Tango] (1948)
Magenta II [Tango] (1954)
Magnolia (1957)
Majanah I (<1958?)
Majanah II (1958)
Majorca [Tango] (1964)
Maladetta [Tango] (1954)
Malayan (1948)
Malouine (1965)
Manhattan (1973)
Mantilla I [Tango] (1959)
Mantilla II [Tango] (1972)
Manyana (1967)
Marcelle [Tango] (1954)
Marella [Tango] (1968)
Margharita (1950)
Margot (1971)
Maria I [Tango] (1953)
Maria II [Tango] (1956)
Marianne (1958)
Marietta [Tango] (1951)
Marina I [Tango] (1959)
Marina II [Tango] (1959)
Marina III [Tango] (1963)
Marisa (1967)
Marlyn (1953)
Marquita (1951)
Matador (1950)
Mayfair (1958)
Maytime (1965)
Mexican (1970)
Mexicana [Tango] (1958)
Mia [Tango] (1959)
Michaelmas (1962)
Michelle [Tango] (1959)
Midnight (1952)
Minerva (1960)
Moderna [Tango] (1961)
Monaco (1958)
Moonlight (1957)

Moonstone (1968)
Morecambe (1948)
Morocco [Tango] (1973)
Myensa [Tango] (1970)
Myrvon (Progressive) (1958)
Nigella [Tango] (1974)
Olga (1971)
Olympic (1961)
Originaire [Tango] (1958)
Pablo [Tango] (1973)
Paraguay (1966)
Park Lane (1972)
Pierre [Tango] (1957)
Planet (1969)
Prince of Wales I (1955)
Prince of Wales II (1969)
Progressive (1951)
Raymonde [Tango] (1961)
Red Carnation (1952)
Red Rose (1963)
Red Moon (1957)
Ricardo (1953)
Rio I (1948)
Rio II (1968)
River (Guitar) (1969)
Riverside [Tango] (1960)
Rocola [Tango] (1968)
Romantica (1973)
Romero I [Tango] (1955)
Romero II [Tango] (1968)
Ronde I (1955)
Ronde II (1958)
Rosanna (1961)
Rosarie (1969)
Roseleigh (1965)
Rosella I (1966)
Rosella II (1974)
Rosita I [Tango] (1958)
Rosita II [Tango] (1960)
Roulette [Tango] (1963)
Rovero (1969)

Tangos

Royale [Tango] (1955)
Russell [Tango] (1973)
Sabena (1966)
Sabena [Tango] (1965)
San Rico (1967)
San Remo [Tango] (1952)
Santa Barbara [Tango] (1958)
Santa Rosa (1973)
Scampari (1972)
Scintilla [Tango] (1955)
Sebastian I (1953)
Sebastian II (1960)
Senorita [Tango] (1957)
Serena [Tango] (1959)
Serenade (1954)
Serida [Tango] (1961)
Seville I (1968)
Seville II (1973)
Silverside (1960)
Solair [Tango] (1970)
Sombrero [Tango] (1958)
Sorrento (1971)
Southern Star (1957)
Spanish Eyes (1971)
Spanish I (1958)
Spanish II (1969)
Springtime (1964)
Star I (1950)
Star II (1973)
Starcross (1965)
Stewart (1968)
Suhali [Tango] (1970)
Supreme [Tango] (1959)
Sweet Afton (1960)
Taboo (1971)
Tahiti [Tango] (1963)
Taluna (1971)
Tango for Two (1972)
Tango 'M' (1957)
Tango 65 (1965)

Tanya [Tango] (1968)
Tarragona (1964)
Telstar (1962)
Temptation [Tango] (1954)
Theresa (1968)
Tina (1963)
Tip Toe (1963)
Tivoli (1969)
Toledo I (1955)
Toledo II (1967)
Tongo (1954)
Topaz (1973)
Topkapi (1971)
Toreador (1963)
Torro (1970)
Trelawney (1954)
Trevan (1961)
Trident (1967)
Tristar (1973)
Troubador (1965)
Tudor (1950)
Twilight (1961)
Tyrolean I (1959)
Tyrolean II (1969)
Valencia I [Tango] (1964)
Valencia II [Tango] (1966)
Vee (1951)
Verdad [Tango] (1974)
Victor (1957)
Victoria [Tango] (1963)
Vienna [Tango] (1954)
Viola (1974)
Violetta I [Tango] (1957)
Violetta II [Tango] (1965)
Whispering (1961)
White Rose (1950)
Willows (1960)
Windsor I (1953)
Windsor II (1960)
Windsor III (1967)
Wyeland (1965)

Yellow Bird (1970)
Ysabelle (1957)
Yvonne (1970)
Zetland (1960)

Foxtrots

Adele (1957)
Adriana (1966)
Alana (1967)
Albertine (1967)
Alison (1972)
Amanda (1960)
Anita (1965)
April (1955)
Ashfield (1967)
Aud En El (1966)
Autumn (1953)
Avon (1953)
Avril I (<1958?)
Avril II (1958)
Azalea (1962)
Belrose (1972)
Benita (1974)
Bermuda (1965)
Blue Moon (1968)
Blue Star (1970)
Bluebell (1959)
Blues (1957)
Broadway (1959)
Broadwell (1967)
Caravelle (1964)
Carnaby (1973)
Celebration (1968)
Chiltern (1965)
Claringo (1973)
Colindor (1960)
Conmoore (1974)
Dale (1966)
Danuta (1961)
Debdon (1974)
December (1973)

Delamere (1958)
Delphine (1968)
Delwood (1970)
Denalise (1972)
Denholme (1968)
Diana (1957)
Dream I (1959)
Dream II (1972)
Dreamtime (1956)
Dunrich (1967)
Edwina (1954)
Eileen I (1957)
Eileen II (1959)
Embassy (1967)
Emerald (1965)
Empire (1956)
Eugene I (1957)
Eugene II (1957)
Fantail (1965)
Fawley (1969)
Felice (1957)
Filey (1970)
Flamingo (1966)
Flirtation (1961)
Franfield (1961)
Freda (1951)
Gaumont (1955)
Gaynor (1967)
Glad Rag (1961)
Glenavon (1969)
Gloria (1960)
Glynlee (1967)
Gwenneth (1961)
Harmony I (1964)
Harmony II (1972)
Harry Lime (1949)
Hasel (1956)
Hi-Fi (1957)
Highcroft (1964)
Hillary (1967)
Hillside (1959)

Foxtrots

Honey (1968)
Idaho (1959)
Indiana (1964)
Invicta (1956)
Iris (1958)
Jacqueline (1968)
Jameson (1969)
January (1962)
Jaunty (1958)
Jeffrey (1960)
Karen (1959)
Kathleen (1964)
Kingsmoor (1961)
La Renda (1968)
Laurigan (1959)
Locarno (1961)
Long Lea (1970)
Louise [Foxtrot] (1972)
Lucinda (1960)
Lydia (1958)
Malouine (1965)
Manhattan (1961)
Marcus (1972)
Mardale (1966)
Marina (1963)
Marlboro (1974)
Martin (1966)
Maryland (1950)
Maxie (1965)
Maybelene (1972)
Mayley (1958)
Melanie (1967)
Melody I (<1956)
Melody II (1956)
Merry (1958)
Millbrook (1960)
Millward (1967)
Mitzi (1961)
Moonraker (1971)
Nicola (1974)

Oasis (1965)
Olympic (1958)
Pandora (1971)
Parisienne (1964)
Pearl (1957)
Pee Gee (1964)
Peke (1958)
Pennanx (1958)
Phoenix (1972)
Piccadilly (1965)
Pins and Needles (1952)
Princess (1952)
Protea (1971)
Rainbow (1967)
Regnum (1959)
Roaming (1957)
Rosemount (1973)
Rosslyn (1973)
Royston (1965)
Sapphire (1960)
Sefton (1969)
Sherwood (1956)
Snaefell (1959)
Southern (1958)
Springtime (1971)
Sunbeam (1969)
Susanne (1958)
Swanee (1951)
Sylvan (1957)
Tara (1972)
Teatime (1953)
Tina (1964)
Topaz (1973)
Twilight (1970)
Twinkle (1958)
Tynedale (1972)
Unity (1957)
Variety (1949)
Venetian (1966)
Verdon (1971)
Venus (1959)

Viceroy (1959)
Vilia (1965)
Wandering Star (1970)
White Rose (1956)
Windsor (1957)
Winter (1967)
Zambra (1969)
Zeeta (1969)
Zeta (1958)

Quicksteps

Adelaide (1972)
Alabama (1972)
Alkirk (1955)
American (1952)
Annette (1970)
Apollo (1970)
April (1973)
Arizona (1959)
Ashton (1974)
Avon I (1959)
Avon II (1963)
Aztec (1962)
Beryldene (1969)
Beverley I (1964)
Beverley II (1964)
Bluebell (1961)
Bluebird (1966)
Brampton (1958)
Brighton (1972)
Britannia I (1960)
Britannia II (1971)
Broadway (1957)
Cabaret (1969)
Cairoli (1965)
Cameron (1965)
Carlton I (1963)
Carlton II (1972)
Caron (1965)
Cavalier (1973)
Claremont (1964)

Clarissa (1968)
Clifton (1968)
Clover (1965)
Club (1959)
Comet (1958)
Concorde (1968)
Congress (1966)
Conway (1968)
Coral (1970)
County (1958)
Crescent (1961)
Cresta (1967)
Crystal I (1958)
Crystal II (1974)
Cumberland (1973)
Dale (1965)
Dalston (1961)
Darktown Strutter (1955)
David (1958)
Delight (1970)
Delwood (1969)
Dena (1961)
Denry (1965)
Denton (1973)
Derby (1966)
Diddy (1966)
Dinsdale (1959)
Dixieland (1972)
Dunster I (1973)
Dunster II (1973)
Eivona (1974)
Elevera (1960)
Elizabeth (1961)
Eljay (1972)
Emerald (1973)
Empire (1966)
Fair Oak (1958)
Festival (1963)
Georgic (1957)
Glamis (1961)
Golunio (1959)

Quicksteps

Granada (1959)
Grosvenor (1957)
Happy Feet (1967)
Harlequin (1958)
Haviland (1972)
Helena (1962)
Hi-Fi (1963)
Hilton I (1968)
Hilton II (1971)
Holiday (1963)
Holyrood (1969)
Houghton (1969)
Imperial (1971)
Ivory (1951)
Jollity (1963)
Jovi (1961)
Jovial (1963)
Jubilee (1965)
Julie Ann (1958)
Karneil (1974)
Katie (1968)
Keeshie (1971)
Kelsus (1962)
Kentucky (1965)
Kerry (Kwickstep) (1956)
Kestral (1974)
Kevin (1967)
Kimberley (1969)
Kingston (1962)
Knokke (1972)
Koala (1968)
Lindon (1973)
Lisa (1971)
Lulu (1962)
Lynwood (1974)
M. T. (1968)
Manhattan (1972)
Marchetta (1971)
Marji (1969)
Maureen (1958)

Mayfair (1956)
Melanie (1973)
Mulvany (1962)
Mynina (1974)
Myric (1968)
Nelfield (1955)
Olympic (1968)
Omega (1966)
Pasadena (1971)
Patricia (1956)
Pauletta I (Party) (1961)
Pauletta II (1965)
Piccadilly (1960)
Presto (1973)
Promenade (1974)
Regent (1963)
Reola (1973)
Rock Around (1957)
Roscoe (1974)
Roylat (1969)
Ruby (1967)
S.B. (1970)
Seaside (1972)
Sentimental (1958)
Sequence (1958)
Seventy (1970)
Sovereign (1973)
Stanley (1971)
Susie (1958)
Tipple (1971)
Tipsy (Novelty) (1962)
Tracey (1972)
Twinkle (1968)
Ukandoit (1966)
Universal (1967)
Victoria (1966)
Virginia (1970)
Waverley (1965)
Winfield (1957)

Rumbas

Alain [Rumba] (1973)

Aquarius [Rumba] (1970)
Carioca Samba (1956)
Continental [Rumba] (1961)
Limbo (1963)
Lorrain (1968)
Marguerite [Rumba] (1968)
Marquesa (1973)
One [Rumba] (1971)
Rumbarba [Rumba] (1974)
Rico [Rumba] (1971)
Rio (1965)
Roulette [Rumba] (1974)
Royal (Royale) [Rumba] (1964)
South American Way (1958)
Variety (1949)

Saunters

Andrea (1972)
Annabelle (1959)
Anya (1970)
Astoria (1974)
Autumn I (1965)
Autumn II (1972)
Aviemore (1968)
Benson (1965)
Bewitched (1968)
Blue Nile (1959)
Blueberry (1967)
Britannia (1958)
Broadway (1956)
Brooklyn (1961)
Buckingham (1973)
Butterfly (1963)
Carolina (1970)
Catalina (1958)
Chevalier (1958)
Clarendon I (1952)
Clarendon II (1965)
Concorde (1970)
Coronation I (1953)
Coronation II (1953)

Crinoline (1955)
Dafny (1970)
Dakota (1967)
Debonaire [Saunter] (1959)
Doretta (1958)
Dream (1951)
Dunnwood (1961)
Eileen [Saunter] (1963)
Elise (1954)
Elite [Saunter] (1964)
Elizabeth (1953)
Empire (1956)
Ennerdale (1969)
Esseldo (1970)
Europa (1973)
Evelene (1957)
Evening (1960)
Evergreen (1958)
Foxtrot [Saunter] (1958)
Gossip (1955)
Granchester (1966)
Ilkley Moor (1961)
Jaunty (1958)
Jozan (1970)
Kayjon (1964)
Kelly's (1969)
Kingsway (1955)
La Rita (1950)
Liesl (1966)
Lover's (1953)
Lullaby (1952)
Lydia (1958)
Lynton (1968)
M (1958)
Maldor (1964)
Marelda (1970)
Marie [Saunter] (1974)
Marina (1961)
Marlessa (1964)
Martine [Saunter] (1968)
Memories (1957)

Saunters

Michelle (1974)
Millicent (1967)
Minx (1951)
Montrose (1958)
Mosside (1974)
Natalie (1967)
Parfit [Saunter] (1973)
Parisienne Tango (1952)
Pauline [Saunter] (1962)
Portchester (1958)
Prince of Wales (1956)
Progressive (1961)
Promenade I (1951)
Promenade II (1959)
Rainbow (1972)
Regalia [Saunter] (1956)
Regency (1969)
Reg 'n' M [Saunter] (1962)
Rendezvous [Saunter] (1953)
Revé [Saunter] (1961)
Riverside (1972)
Rock & Roll (1956)
Romantique (1968)
Rosemary (1959)
Royal Wedding I (1960)
Royal Wedding II (1963)
Royal (1953)
Ruby (1960)
Samantha (1963)
Santana [Saunter] (1964)
Saucy (1955)
Saunter 63 (1963)
Savannah (1964)
Sea Breeze (1973)
Seaburn (1954)
Seashore (1962)
Seaside (1951)
Sefton (1954)
Sentimental I [Saunter] (1958)
Sentimental II (1973)

September (1950)
Serenade I [Saunter] (1949)
Serenade II [Saunter] (1969)
Serene I (1959)
Serene II (1962)
Shadow (1959)
Shanakeill (1966)
Shangri La (1974)
Sharandon (1966)
Shell (1972)
Shenandoah (1965)
Sherrie (1949)
Sherwood (1963)
Silhouette (1969)
Silver I (1952)
Silver II (1963)
Sing-a-long (1965)
Sky Blue (1967)
Solwin (1966)
Southern (1954)
Southwood (1973)
Soya (1974)
Springtime (1958)
Starlight (1947)
Stroll Along (1950)
Stuart (1956)
Summertime (1964)
Sunnyside (1960)
Sunset I (1957)
Sunset II (1957)
Superbe (1950)
Supreme [Saunter] (1966)
Susan (1974)
Suzanne [Saunter] (1968)
Swanmore (1958)
Sway (1957)
Syon (1971)
Tea Time (1971)
Therese (1958)
Twilight (1950)
Wentworth (1955)

White Rose (1956)
Wilton (1968)
Windsor (1959)
Woodland (1954)
Woodside (1969)
Yucatan (1967)

Cha Cha Chas

Barn Dance (1961)
Burlington (1970)
Capri (1970)
Carousel (1969)
Casino (1971)
Cecilia (1971)
Charina (1963)
Cheery (1961)
Chiki (1966)
Chinchilla (1974)
Doris (1965)
Duet [Cha Cha] (1973)
Happy (1960)
Jacqueline (1961)
Jonida (1959)
K.P. (1974)
Kenton (1968)
L.A. (1962)
Looee (1963)
Margarite [Cha Cha] (1962)
Marina (1974)
Martinique (1972)
Medina [Cha Cha] (1974)
Paraguay [Cha Cha] (1974)
Poco Pelo (1972)
Rainbow (1970)
Rosita (1965)
Sally Ann (1973)
Saturday (1959)
Tahiti (1974)
Tutti Frutti (1974)
Victory (1967)
Warrington (1962)

Blues

Adrian (1960)
Autumn (1972)
Balmoral (1971)
Bambi (1962)
Barolan (1972)
Bee Bee (1963)
Belinda (1968)
Benidorm (1972)
Beverley (1965)
Bewitching (1953)
Blue Lady (1965)
Blues Glide (1950)
Bohemian (1952)
Breakaway (1946)
Cafuffule (1958)
Camelot (1964)
Carefree (1953)
Carolina (1957)
Charleston (1952)
Deep River (1960)
Delaville (1954)
Desmond (Jasmine) (1954)
Dolly (1964)
Drift (1969)
Eastham (1970)
Embassy (1956)
Empress (1954)
Esso (1971)
Fiesta (1974)
Frederika (1959)
Georgella (1950)
Graftonian (1953)
Harmony I (1973)
Harmony II (1974)
Hawaiian (1974)
Hyacinth (1962)
Imperial (1974)
Island (1957)
Karen (1955)
Kentucky (1969)

Blues

Lavender (1972)
Louise (1957)
Madison (1963)
Marie (1952)
Marina (1973)
Martino (1965)
Mercia (1968)
Merseyside (1964)
Midnight (1972)
Mona Lisa (1952)
Park Lane (1959)
Piccadilly (1960)
Plantation (1961)
Plemont (1968)
Priscilla (1958)
Rainbow (1966)
Richmond (1963)
Riversdale (1961)
Rock 'n' Roll Rhythm (1958)
Rock 'n' Roll I (1957)
Rock 'n' Roll II (1957)
Rossmore (1968)
Sapphire (1954)
Serenata (1950)
Sherrie (1959)
Southlands (1960)
St. Helens (1960)
Swinging (1958)
Swinging the Blues (1957)
Syland (1965)
Trudie (1958)
Twelfth Street (1954)
Twilight (1974)
Valentine (1968)
Vienna (1958)
Westbury (1966)
Westminster (1972)
Woodland (1969)

Jives

Frenchy's (1972)
Jim Jam (1962)
Jupiter (1973)
Peppermint (1970)
Planet (1974)
Rock (Barn Dance) (1969)

Sambas

Aggi (1968)
Amor (1967)
April (1972)
Dutch (1964)
Embee (1972)
Jenny (1974)
Katrina [Samba] (1972)
Margarette [Samba] (1956)
Miranda [Samba] (1961)
Party (1957)
Sapphire (1965)
Saucy (1973)
Sombrero [Samba] (1970)
Tico-Tico (1973)
Zeeta (1950)

Gavottes

Ballerina (1970)
Cameo (1967)
Carisbrooke (1973)
Classic (1961)
County (1965)
Crinoline (1952)
Cyrann (1956)
Devonaire (1958)
Elizabethan (1952)
Empire (1963)
Ena (1963)
Gaiety (1954)
Georgette (1955)
Godetia (1955)
Guadalajare (1970)

Hazel (1952)
Jade (1968)
Janina (1952)
Jasmine (1961)
La Marguerite (1952)
Leofric (1970)
Marina (1963)
Marlborough (1960)
My Fair Lady (1959)
Myrvon (1957)
Nanette (1956)
New Inspiration (1948)
Princess (1953)
Regal (1967)
Regency (1957)
Ridgeway (1974)
Shiralee (1960)
Victorian (1954)
Wedgewood Blue (1959)
Wesford (1952)

Two Steps

Adelaide (1962)
Alabama (1955)
Alexander (1956)
Alhambra (Progressive) (1956)
Anniversary (Prog.) (1951)
Averil (1957)
Baghdad (1950)
Balmoral (1966)
Brittania (1953)
Caribbean (1955)
Carnival (1953)
Casino (1964)
Cavalier (1968)
Cavendish (1949)
Clynol (1966)
Conference (1958)
Coronation (1953)
Courtesy (1956)
Crown (1957)

Dorian (1965)
Dot's (1968)
Eccles (1963)
Edinburgh (1960)
Elizabeth I (1953)
Elizabeth II (1958)
Equality (1953)
Federation (1959)
Fiesta (1957)
Filey Festival (1952)
Flirtation (1955)
Gaiety (1950)
Gay Step (1967)
Gazelle (1962)
Highland I (1954)
Highland II (1964)
Holiday (1956)
Honeywell (1956)
Howard (1961)
Imperial (Progressive) (1950)
Isle of Man (1957)
Jasfyl (1955)
JP (1958)
Kennan (1961)
Kentucky (1961)
Lancastrian (1956)
Lancelot (1951)
Liberty (1953)
Lightning (1954)
Lindy Lou (1960)
Lynx (1967)
Marigold (1955)
Marjon (1957)
Marlborough (1954)
Martine (1958)
Maxwell (1951)
McNamara's (1967)
Melody (1955)
Military (Prog.) (1952)
Millicent (1952)
New Rig (1955)

Two Steps

Newton (1960)
Nicholas (1955)
Olympia (1955)
Paris (1968)
Party (1957)
Pauletta (1957)
Pennine (1959)
Penrose (1974)
Peterton (1966)
Piccadilly (1954)
Pickwick (1957)
Premier (1958)
Pride of Britain (1953)
Prince (1960)
Prince of Wales (1954)
Queen's (1954)
Regency (1950)
Rene (1956)
Reylock (1966)
Rialto (1962)
Rosetta (1950)
Royal (1952)
Seaburn (1958)
Skegness (1958)
Social I (Party) (1958)
Social II (Party) (1958)
Sousa (1959)
Southern (1961)
Star (1959)
Stella Maris (1959)
Terry (Progressive) (1951)
Thames (Progressive) (1951)
Thanet (1955)
Thistle (1958)
Tiara (1964)
Tip Toe (1947)
Tivoli (1959)
Trafalgar (1952)
Trixie (1953)
Unity (1955)

Vanity (1956)
Victoria (1961)
Wardwick (1962)
Waverley (1956)
White Rose (1958)
Windsor (1953)
Zig Zag (1960)

Paso Dobles

El Paso (1961)
Paso Deena (1974)
Paso Espana (1974)
Paso Espanol (1974)
Paso Madrid (1964)
Paso Seville (1971)

Swings

Cabaret (1969)
Campbell (1974)
Celebration (1972)
Champagne (1971)
Chantilly (1973)
Cuban (1969)
Festival (1974)
Happytime (1969)
Honkytonk (1971)
International (1970)
Kingfisher (1974)
Lincoln (1964)
Lindy Lou (1958)
Londinium (1969)
Madison (1963)
Majong (1959)
Maxi (1971)
Melody (1965)
Mexican (1970)
Midnight (1962)
Midway (1973)
New Madison (1962)
Palais (1958)
Party (1970)

Patrol [Swing] (1950)
Ragtime (1969)
Saturday (1969)
Savoy (1963)
Sefton (1965)
Social (Novelty) (1967)
Somerset (1967)
Startime (1962)
Sunshine (1962)
Susie Rhyl (1973)
Swanee (1972)
Tio Pepe (1963)
Tower (1960)
Trixie (1966)
Viennese I (1965)
Viennese II (1973)

Glides

Albert (1957)
Anglia (1960)
Ascot (1968)
Cavendish (Progressive) (69)
Chelsea (1966)
Coronation (1953)
Festival (1957)
Gainsborough (1950)
Grosvenor (1964)
Guernsey (1966)
Hamilton (1961)
Hengist (1954)
Jubilee (1972)
Kingsley (Progressive) (1952)
Marion (1959)
Progressive Waltz (1962)
September (1962)
Silverdale (1968)
Trudie (1959)

Sways

April (1968)
Aron (1967)

Barbara (1974)
Cerma (1972)
Erimus (1969)
Franciscan (1963)
Islington (1950)
Jo-Ella (1964)
Kaymar (1965)
Keleta (1971)
Margerita (1967)
Panama (1967)
Sapphire (1968)
September (1952)
Shaftesbury (1969)
Silver (1967)
Whisky (1967)

Mazurkas

Bayfield (1960)
Cherry (1958)
Devon (1957)
Empress (1954)
Gaiety (1958)
Honey (1960)
Kathryn (1956)
Marguerite (1952)
Moonlight (1952)
Oriental (1962)
Petite (1959)
Phillipa (1965)
Royal (1955)

One Steps

Chin Chin (1950)
Christine (1959)
Columbia (1958)
Festival (1958)
Gay Paree (1957)
Glen Garry (1957)
Harlequin (1958)
Isle of Man (1958)
Jovial (1964)

One Steps

Party (1959)
Prince of Wales (1958)
Recreation (1958)
South West (1961)
Trampoline (1959)

Square Dances

Cotswold Cotillon (1961)
Dutch Foursome (1946)
Festival (1950)
Handel's Quadrille (1963)
Imperial Waltz Quadrille (1957)
Lancashire (1952)
Princess Progressive (1952)
Queens Quadrilles (1953)

Schottisches

Birthday (1953)
Blackpool (1954)
Bobette (1958)
County (1955)
Empress (1964)
Fredericka (1959)
Gay (1952)
Glydella (1956)
Hedley (1951)
Marigold (1952)
Mayfair (1956)
Road to the Isles I (1951)
Road to the Isles II (1957)
Rodney (1953)
Royale [Schottische] (1968)
Savoy (1950)
Shirley (1951)
Vanity Fair (1956)

Strolls

Autumn (1969)
Blenheim (1974)
Broadway (1969)

Elizabeth (1973)
Festival (1953)
Gaytime (1957)
Glynn (1971)
Kimberley (1974)
London (1969)
Lynton (1965)
Marian (1968)
Regency (1955)
Roban (1967)
Shadow (1970)
Siesta (1970)
Singalong (1973)
Somerset (1963)
Starlight I (1968)
Starlight II (1974)
Summertime (1972)
Sunshine (1966)

Parades

Easter (1968)
Festival (1963)
Holiday (1970)
Kentucky (1950)
Madison (1963)
New Empress (1956)
Northern (1958)
Pier (1950)
Silver (1958)
Trudie (1958)
Um-Pah (Novelty) (1961)
Westoe (1960)
White Rose (1957)

Rags

12th Street (1967)
Alexander (1958)
Crazy Otto ((1957)
Ivory (1965)
Kitchen (1953)
Rag Time (1959)

Ragtime Roll (1963)

Bossa Novas

'87 [Bossa Nova] (1987)
Bella (1992)
Blues [Bossa Nova] (1972)
Bossa Lou (1963)
Broadway (1969)

Miscellaneous

Aba Daba (1960)
Ballin the Jack (1948)
Bear Step (1959)
Black Domino (1964)
Blackpool Walk (1958)
Blues Twist (1962)
Bolerico (1950)
Broadway Bounce (1974)
Butterfly Rock (1974)
Californians (1961)
Calypso (1958)
Camelot (1964)
Caribbean (1955)
Cat Step (1967)
Chadwick (1951)
Children's Circle Dance (1959)
Circle Conga (1973)
Club Madison (1962)
Cokernut Hop (1968)
Coronation Polka (1963)
Dolly Weaver (1964)
Duetto (1952)
Elizabeth of England (1953)
Empress Walk (1950)
Fiesta (1960)
Fiona's Polka (1966)
Follow Me (1973)
Frisco Four Step (1965)
Harlequinade (1955)
Highland Caper (1973)
Jackpot Jinx (Novelty) (1969)

Jubilee Jinks (1964)
Kenjan Maze (1950)
La Belle Suzanne (1960)
La Brooke (1956)
Liberty Hornpipe (1957)
Liverpool Twinkle (1953)
Mambo Italiano (1955)
Masquerade (1950)
Midway [The] (1958)
Mini Step (1968)
New Charleston (1950)
Normansie (Foxtrot) (1961)
Oliver Twist (1962)
Palais Merry Go Round (1949)
Park Promenade (1951)
Party Fours (1959)
Party Twist (1960)
Royal Minuet (1947)
Scottish Ladbroke (1957)
Silhouette (1954)
Silver Fox (1960)
Skiffle (Novelty) (1950)
Starlight Twinkle (1971)
Sting-a-Ling (Fun dance) (74)
Strutter (1955)
Tantro (1955)
Tea For Two (1958)
Tiddley Jinks (1965)
Tipsy Two (1952)
Twilight Minuet (1950)
Verglas (Foxtrot) (1958)
Vermilion Charleston (1951)
Vici (1971)
Virginia Reel (1956)
Wandering Three Step (1957)
Yates A Four Step (1962)

THE MODERN ERA (1975 AND AFTER)

INDEX OF DANCES FROM 1975-1994

Numbers of New Sequence Dances

New sequence dances are essential to maintain interest, particularly for those who dance several times per week - on the other hand too many new dances cause problems for people who travel about. No-one likes to book up for a sequence dancing holiday and find a programme of dances largely unknown to them. Sydney Thompson, writing in 1956, put this in a nutshell, "reasoned variety leads to greater pleasure, uncontrolled variety leads to chaos".

By the 1970's there were too many inventive dance competitions and too many awards - up to 6 prizes per section in some cases. In 1975 the Official Board acted to control the number and nature of new dances. All new 'official' dances had to be winners at inventive dance competitions recognised by the Board. Dancing teachers and leaders were discouraged from including 'unofficial' (pirate) dances in their sessions. As the system operates at the present time, there are 15 competitions with one prize for a winning dance in the modern, old-time and Latin-American sections making 45 new official dances per year. Each organisation has to apply each year for permission to run an official inventive dance competition but there has not been too much change over the years after the initial settling-down period in the late 1970's.

This method of limiting dances is probably the best that could be achieved in the circumstances. It provides an adequate pool of new dances from which the ordinary sequence dancers will eventually choose their favourites and the dance competitors and organising bodies know where they stand. Minor disadvantages are the preponderance of tangos which appear in both the modern and old-time sections and the tendency to favour saunters, swings and blues rather than the more traditional old-time waltzes, two steps and gavottes. There are less prizes for the competitors to win as only first prizes count and the system has moved the competitions away from the ordinary dancing teachers - there is less discussion and comment in print concerning new dances than used to be the case.

Official Inventive Dance Competitions

In 1994 the bodies authorised to run official inventive sequence dance competitons are:-

1   The Official Board of Ballroom Dancing (OBBD) itself
2   Northern Counties Dance Teachers' Association (NCDTA)
3   International Dance Teachers' Association (IDTA)
4   Imperial Society of Teachers of Dancing (ISTD)
5   Allied Dancing Association Limited (ADA)
6   United Kingdom Alliance (UKA or UKAPTD)
7   British Association of Teachers of Dancing (BATD)
8   Scottish Dance Teachers' Association (SDTA)
9   National Association of Teachers of Dancing Ltd. (NATD)
10   International Sequence Dance Circle Limited (ISDC)
11/12 Butlins (Bognor Regis and Pwlheli)
13   Blackpool Tower Company (Blackpool)
14   'Dance News' Magazine (Slough)
15   David Bullen Enterprises (North of Britain)

Nos. 1-9 derive their authority from being members of the Offical Board. Not all the competitions are 'open' in the sense that some associations restrict entry to their own members.

Competitions in the three sections are not always held at the same venue at the same time, e.g. in 1994 the UKA held the modern competition at Weston Super Mare in February and the O/T and Latin-American sections at Blackpool in June.

Dance Lists from 1975 - 1980

It took some time for things to settle down after the Official Board ruling and from 1975 to 1980 the dance lists contain first (and some other) prize-winners from official competitions as well as winners from organisations such as OTDA and SDF.

Dance Lists from 1981 - 1994

From 1981 nearly all the dances are first prize winners at competitions authorised by the Board. (Many hundreds of 'unofficial' dances have been excluded.)

157

PRESENTED IN 1975

Waltzes (Old-Time) (1975)

Irena	David Bullen and Denise Mayo	IDTA

Waltzes (Modern) (1975)

Cara Mia	Alice Douglas	SDF London
Charade [Waltz]	Jeff and Muriel Aldren	Dance Monthly
Chelsea	Jack and Olive Fletcher	YSDF
Fleurette [Waltz]	Ken and Vi Agar	UKAPTD

Tangos (1975)

Aramis (O/T)	Joan Elstub	YSDF
Creole [Tango] (O/T)	Ken Park	OBBD
El-Mar [Tango] (O/T)	Derek Tonks	IDTA
Elandor [Tango] (O/T)	Thomas Liddiard	OTDA
Indigo (O/T)	Sandra Pickering	ISDC IOM
Mondello [Tango] (Mod)	Peter Sharpe	ISTD
Pearl (O/T)	David Bullen	ADA
Pedida (Mod)	Roy Sharpe	BATD

Quicksteps (1975)

Albany	Derek Tonks	IDTA
Bee Bee	Bill and Betty Hunter	YSDF
Corrie	Tom Francis	NATD
Florida	David Bullen and Denise Mayo	ADA
Ivan	Andy Noble	SDF London
J. M.	Jeff Aldren	OBBD
Supaul	Kit Hewitt (Bedford)	OTDA

Swings (1975)

Albama	Sam and Irene Faultley	ISTD
Bobtail	Ted Edmonds	NCDTA
Hipster	Muriel Aldren	2nd Blackpool
Soho	Ken and Elaine Park (Newcastle)	NCDTA
Sukie	Mrs. E. Sharpe	BATD

Rumbas (1975)

Casanova [Rumba]	Ken Park (Newcastle)	OBBD
Lisa [Rumba]	David Bullen and Denise Mayo	IDTA

Rumbas (1975) (continued)

Montego [Rumba]	Jack and Elsie Richardson	YSDF
Pandora	Ron Checketts	ADA

Saunters (1975)

Elaine	Sylvester Burrows	IDTA
Endean	Alf Hoskings	SDF London
Honeymoon	Linda and Fred Dudman	2nd NCDTA
Together [Saunter]	Bob and Wyn Oliver	Bognor Regis
Westminster	Tony and Denise Dyer	Dance News
Whispering	Denise Dyer	2rd Blackpool

Foxtrots (1975)

Elwyn	Alwyn Leathley (Leeds)	Blackpool
Flamenco	Alan Bolton	NCDTA
Florida	David Bullen	ADA

Blues (1975)

Alvaston	Tony and Denise Dyer	OBBD Filey
Harlequin	Ken and Barbara Street	2nd Bognor Regis

Cha Cha Chas (1975)

Chobe	Josephine Lubelska and Gerald Bell	NATD
Supreme	Linda and Fred Dudman	NCDTA

Gavottes (1975)

Moonlight	Roy and Elaine Sharpe (Bury)	Blackpool
Referendum	Ted Burroughs	UKAPTD

Miscellaneous (1975)

Bertha Bump (Party)	Tony and Denise Dyer	IDTA
Butlin Beat	Jeff and Muriel Aldren	2nd OBBD Filey
Campbell Swing (Party)	Edna Collins	ADA
Justa Jive	Pam and Eric Toulson	ISTD
Paso Nova (Paso Doble)	Roger and Yvonne Corkery	ISDC IOM
Sultana [Samba]	Bob and Winn Oliver	UKAPTD
Twyford Sway	Harry and Gwen James	NATD

Leading Arrangers:-

3 - David Bullen and Denise Mayo   2 - Bob and Winn Oliver   2 - Derek Tonks
3 - Tony and Denise Dyer   2 - Ken Park

PRESENTED IN 1976

Waltzes (Old-Time) (1976)

Capri [Waltz]	Roy Sharpe	BATD
La Ronde [Waltz]	Pamela Brown	SDF London
Wirral	Norman Yates and Christine Gallagher	ADA

Waltzes (Modern) (1976)

Alma	A. Champion	NASD Yorks.
Ashfield	Fred and Pam Welham	OTDA
Barcarolle	Winn and Bob Oliver	NATD
Britannia	Alf and Peggy Hoskings (Laughton)	SDF London
Daniela [Waltz]	Derek Tonks and Beryl Bates	IDTA
Fascination [Waltz]	Joan Elstub (Leeds)	YSDF
Goodnight	Ken Fuller	Manchester MC's
Lucille [Waltz]	Alice Douglas	3rd Blackpool
Pakefield	George Mott	Dance Monthly
Simone [Waltz]	Elsie Platts and Alwyn Leathley	2nd ISDC IOM

Tangos (1976)

Apache (Mod)	Edgar and Doris Holroyd	ISDC IOM
Christina (Mod)	Wilf Green	SDF LondonLondon
Firefly (O/T)	Wendy Whelerton (Middlesborough)	Blackpool
Flirtation	Ken Fuller	Manchester MC's
Hacienda (Mod)	Yvonne Carr	NATD
Imperial (Mod)	Muriel Burrell (Romford)	ISTD
Montreal	Dennis and Alice Douglas	Dancing Monthly
Sorelle (O/T)	Derek Tonks and Beryl Bates	IDTA
Sundance (O/T)	Bob and Wendy Whelerton	OBBD London
Topsy	Maurice Tait and Yvonne Stanley	3rd Butlins Filey
Westway (Mod)	Ted Burroughs	UKAPTD

Quicksteps (1976)

Alison	Ray and Christine Hogkinson	ISDC IOM
Flicker I	Elaine Sharpe	BATD
Honey	Norman and Olive Martin	NASD North
Plaza	Raymond Casey	NCDTA

Blues (1976)

International	D. and B. Tonks, D. and T. Dyer, D. Bullen	OBBD Filey
Marigold	Lavinia Thomas	NCDTA

Blues (1976) (continued)

Palma Nova	Derek Tonks and Beryl Bates	OBBD London
Virginia	Jeff and Muriel Aldren	2nd Butlins

Swings (1976)

1976	Pam and Eric Toulson	ISTD
Hawaiian	Peter and Sophie Galachas	ADA

Rumbas (1976)

Caribbean	Ken and Barbara Street	ISTD
Cinzano	David Bullen	OBBD
L'Amour [Rumba]	Raymond S. Addicott	UKAPTD

Saunters (1976)

Dawn	Ray Hemming	OTDA Brittain Shield
Kaybee	Bill and Louie Harvey	OBBD Filey
Louise [Saunter]	Jack and Olive Fletcher	YSDF

Sambas (1976)

Chalimar	Roy and Elaine Sharpe	BATD
Elegre [Samba]	Jim and Marie Barber	Blackpool
Siesta	David Bullen and Margaret Redmond	ADA

Cha Cha Chas (1976)

Acel	Mr. and Mrs. A. Lloyd	YSDF
Olympic	Lilian Aubrey	NCDTA
Silver	J. and E. Richardson	SDF
Y.C.	Yvonne Carr	NATD

Miscellaneous (1976)

Glenroy Foxtrot	Tom Turner and Florence E. Smith	ADA
Cameo Gavotte	Irene Watlling and Bernard Wilding	Dance News
Columbine Mazurka	Ted Burroughs	UKAPTD
Consort Two Step	Derek Tonks and Beryl Bates	IDTA
Rhythm Jive	Lewis and Joan Wilson	IDTA
Twenties Rag (Party)	Winn Oliver	UKAPTD
Valencia Paso	Dennis and Alice Douglas	

Leading Arrangers:-
4 - Derek Tonks and Beryl Bates   2 - Ted Burroughs
2 - Yvonne Carr

PRESENTED IN 1977

Waltzes (Old-Time) (1977)

Everglade	Tony and Denise Dyer	Blackpool
Sequence Time	Ted Burroughs	ISTD

Waltzes (Modern) (1977)

Ascar	Len Williams	BATD
Beverley Anne	Ted Burroughs	Dance News
Diane [Waltz]	Bill and Louie Harvey	2nd Bognor Regis
Eclaire [Waltz]	Ken Park	NCDTA
Jenette [Waltz]	Joan Elstub	YSDF
Mackinac	Jim Gordon	OTDA
Silver Jubilee	Bob and Wendy Whelerton	Dance Monthly
Silver Moon	Ted Burroughs	NATD
Solitaire [Waltz]	Alwyn Leathley and Elsie Platts	Southport
Springtime	Norman Martin	NASD North
St. Ledger	Derek and Joyce Ball	OBBD Filey

Tangos (1977)

Alfredo (O/T)	Alf and Margaret Redmond	ADA
Alpegho [Tango] (O/T)	Peggy and Alf Hoskings	SDF London
Flame (O/T)	Bob and Wendy Whelerton	OBBD
Segovia (Mod)	Ken Park	OBBD Blackpool
Silver Jubilee	Jeff and Muriel Aldren	Dance Monthly
Stevlyn (O/T)	Steve and Lyn Dewis	OTDA
Violetta [Tango] (O/T)	Lewis and Joan Wilson	NATD

Saunters (1977)

Blueberry	Reg and Betty Gregory	YSDF
Cheyenne	Ray Hodgkinson	NCDTA
d'Amour [Saunter]	Bob and Winn Oliver	Bognor Regis
Shanida	Wendy Whelerton	IDTA
Shemara	Ray and Christine Hodgkinson	ISDC IOM
Silverdale	Tony and Denise Dyer	UKAPTD
Tee Jay	Valerie and David Warren	BATD

Blues (1977)

Bye Bye	Arthur Lloyd	SDF
Jubilee	G. A. Champion	NASD Yorks.

Quicksteps (1977)

Canberra	Ted Burroughs	ISTD
Java	Joyce Marland	UKAPTD
Leighway	Peter Varley	OBBD
Silver Jubilee	Les and Gwen Du-Roy	Dance Monthly

Rumbas (1977)

Bianco	David Bullen and Margaret Redmond	OBBD
International	Derek Tonks and Beryl Bates	IDTA
Marbella	Sandra Pickering	ISDC IOM
Serenade [Rumba]	Dick Batty	YSDF
Zeeta	David and Valerie Warren	BATD

Jives (1977)

Jamboree	Norman Yates and Pamela Barcas	ADA
Jubilee	Ken and Barbara Street	
Tijuana	Yvonne Stanley and Maurice Tait	OBBD Filey
Womble	Tony and Denise Dyer	UKAPTD

Cha Cha Chas (1977)

Celebration	Ken Park	NCDTA
Shirlee	Shirley Cox	NATD

Foxtrots (1977)

Fenwick	Cliff and Gwen Abbot	NASD Yorks.
Marina	June Rudd	Manchester MC's
Silver Jubilee	Lewis and Joan Wilson	Dance Monthly

Miscellaneous (1977)

Allington Swing	David and Greta Darman	Southport
Blackpool Trot (Party)	Bob and Winn Oliver	IDTA
Cornish Capers (Party)	Oscar and Jennie Yellard	UKAPTD
Elizabethan Gavotte	Norman Yates and Pamela Barcas	ADA
Naval Capers (Party)	Ted Burroughs	UKAPTD

Leading Arrangers:-

5 - Ted Burroughs	2 - David and Valerie Warren
3 - Ken Park	2 - Norman Yates and Pamela Barcas
3 - Tony and Denise Dyer	2 - Jeff and Muriel Aldren
2 - Lewis and Joan Wilson	2 - Bob and Winn Oliver

PRESENTED IN 1978

Waltzes (Old-Time) (1978)

Golden Wedding	Ken Park (Special for Molly Affleck)	NCDTA
Westwood	Rod Wilson	OTDA

Waltzes (Modern) (1978)

Acora	Ken Park	NCDTA
Concordia	Ray Hemming (Worcester)	OTDA
Dior [Waltz]	David Bullen	ISDC IOM
Marrella [Waltz]	Ken and Vi Agar	UKAPTD
Michelle [Waltz]	Tony and Denise Dyer	Blackpool
Nanette	June Rudd (Atherton)	NASD North
Willow	Reg and Betty Gregory	SDF London

Tangos (1978)

Cordoba [Tango] (Mod)	Margaret Donald	BATD
Crimson (O/T)	Bob and Wendy Whelerton	OBBD Brean Sands
El-Kantara (Mod)	Raymond Addicott	'All England' Rosendale Festival
El-Torro (O/T)	Ted Burroughs	'All England' Rossendale Festival
Las Vegas [Tango] (O/T)	David Bullen	ADA
Martinella (O/T)	Pat Hancock	SDF London
Tania (Mod)	Tony and Denise Dyer	UKAPTD
Tarquilla [Tango] (Mod)	Ken Park	OBBD Pudsey
Valentino [Tango] (O/T)	Yvonne Carr	OBBD Pudsey

Quicksteps (1978)

Ellesmere	Ted Burroughs	Southport
Gemini	Bob and Wendy Whelerton	OBBD Brean Sands
Glenhelen	Tom and Flo Turner	ADA
International	Eileen Crompton	IDTA
Quincey	Derek and Karen Brough	Bognor Regis

Saunters (1978)

Charmaine [Saunter]	Ray and Christine Hodgkinson	ISDC IOM
Coral	Elaine and Ken Park	IDTA
Eljay	Joan and Lewis Wilson	NATD
Forget-Me-Not	Winn and Bob Oliver	BATD
Kitikat	J. Cunningham	NASD Yorks.
Rockford	J. Gordon Stuart (Bulkington)	OTDA
Sharon	Roger and Yvonne Corkery	Dance News Slough

Sambas (1978)

Astoria	Ted Burroughs	'All England' Rossendale Festival
Petite	Bob and Winn Oliver	IDTA
Suzanne [Samba]	Tony and Denise Dyer	UKAPTD
Swinging	Maurice Tait and Yvonne Stanley	OBBD Filey

Cha Cha Chas (1978)

Cheeky Cheeky	Lavinia Thomas	NCDTA
Chicory	Muriel Burrell	ISTD

Swings (1978)

Lulu	Dennis Douglas	Blackpool
Panama	Steve and Morna White	NCDTA
Tippy Top	Ken and Vi Agar	UKAPTD

Blues (1978)

Cuddling	David and Greta Darman	Southport
Jonnelen	Len and Pearl Puckett	NATD
Tremaine	Ken and Barbara Street	ISTD

Foxtrots (1978)

Amanda	Tony and Denise Dyer	2nd Blackpool
Denham	Dorothy Moxon	NATD
Valerie	Ken and Barbara Street	ISTD

Rumbas (1978)

Playa [Rumba]	Jacqueline Ward	ADA
Rosette [Rumba]	Peter Varley	OBBD Pudsey
Sayonara [Rumba]	Maurice Tait and Yvonne Stanley	NATD
Sombrero [Rumba]	Freda and Arthur Blincoe	OBBD Brean Sands

Jives (1978)

Fiesta	Maurice Tait and Yvonne Stanley	Southport
Kelvin	Winn and Bob Oliver	BATD

Party Dances (1978)

Penguin Rock	Ted Burroughs	UKAPTD
Smurff Dance	Michael and Jackie Hough	IDTA

Leading Arrangers:-

4 - Ted Burroughs	3 - Maurice Tait and Yvonne Stanley	2 - David Bullen
3 - Ken Park	3 - Bob and Winn Oliver	2 - Bob and Wendy Whelerton
3 - Tony and Denise Dyer	2 - Ken and Vi Agar	2 - Ken and Barbara Street

PRESENTED IN 1979

Waltzes (Old-Time) (1979)

Madeira	Beryl Bates	3rd IDTA

Waltzes (Modern) (1979)

Acacia	Dorothy and Cyril Vincent	OTDA
Emmerdale	W. J. Crook	
Estelle I [Waltz]	Bob and Lily Jackson	NASD Pennine Trophy
Helenbrooke	Dorothy Moxon	NATD
Kingsmere	Roger and Yvonne Corkery	OBBD
Maritime	Jim Brennan	ADA
Paradise	Olive R. McFarlane	UKAPTD
Phencia	David Bullen	2nd IDTA
Rayen	Ray and Helen Wilson	ISTD
Silhouette	Ray and Elaine Sharpe	BATD

Tangos (1979)

Capella [Tango] (Mod)	Jeff and Muriel Aldren	OBBD Filey
Casani [Tango] (Mod)	Bill and Louie Harvey	Bognor Regis
Estelle [Tango] (O/T)	Alice and Dennis Douglas	UKAPTD
Nakoma [Tango] (Mod)	Ray and Christine Hodgkinson	NCDTA
Rosetta [Tango] (O/T)	Edgar and Doris Holroyd	ISDC IOM
Sherrie (O/T)	David Bullen	IDTA Blackpool

Saunters (1979)

Alpine	Wendy Whelerton	2nd IDTA
Edinburgh	Annette Sheridan	BATD
Grenville	David and Greta Darman	OBBD
Shelley	Tony and Denise Dyer	Blackpool
Therese [Saunter]	Margaret and Frank Westbrook	ISTD
Viv'Ann	Bert French	1st OTDA

Quicksteps (1979)

Bernice	Lesley Reaney	Southport
Quando	Christine Hodgkinson	NCDTA
Video	Tony and Denise Dyer	Blackpool

Blues (1979)

Barbarella	David Bullen	ADA
Beechwood	Yvonne Carr	NATD
Tuesday	Patricia Jay and Gary Fleetwood	Dance News Slough

Jives (1979)

City	Frank and Margaret Westbrook	ISDC
Embassy	David Hipshaw	ADA
Rock-On	Ray and Dorothy Casey	NCDTA

Cha Cha Chas (1979)

Canberra	Derek Tonks and Beryl Bates	IDTA Blackpool
Disco	Ted and Sue Burroughs	OBBD
Echo	Ray and Christine Hodgkinson	UKAPTD
Yvette	Steve and Morna White	Southport

Rumbas (1979)

Blue Mosque	Ted Burroughs and Sue Hillman	ISDC IOM
Santana [Rumba]	Colin Gear and Lavinia Thomas	

Sambas (1979)

Holiday	Winn and Bob Oliver	BATD
Laughing (Party)	J. Watson	

Miscellaneous (1979)

Carlton Foxtrot	J. and L. Cunningham	NASD Yorks.
Daffodil Gavotte	Jeff and Muriel Aldren	Southport
Golden Swing	Alf and Peggy Hoskings	SDF London
Hallelujah Sway	Dorothy Collins	SDF London
International Foxtrot	Joan Wilson	3rd IDTA

Leading Arrangers:-

3 - David Bullen	2 - Ray and Christine Hodgkinson
3 - Ted Burroughs	2 - Frank and Margaret Westbrook
2 - Tony and Denise Dyer	2 - Jeff and Muriel Aldren

PRESENTED IN 1980

Waltzes (Old-Time) (1980)

Sunshine	John and Susan Sommerin	UKAPTD

Waltzes (Modern) (1980)

Cavatina [Waltz]	Ken and Barbara Street	ISTD
Champagne [Waltz]	David Bullen	IDTA
Ferness	Jim and Ellen Truffet	NASD North
Misty Moon	Jack and Flo Howard	NASD Yorks.
President's	Ken Park (Special for N. Clarke)	IDTA
Sapphire	Maurice Tait and Yvonne Stanley	ADA
Silver	Alf and Peggy Hoskings	SDF London
Tahitian	Michael Davies	ISDC
Tennessee Waltz '80	Patricia Jay and Gary Fleetwood	Blackpool

Tangos (1980)

Antrim	Olive Martin	Manchester MC's
Dallas (Mod)	Jeff and Muriel Aldren	Southport
Del Mar [Tango]	Stan Haines	SDF London
España [Tango] (O/T)	Arthur Lightfoot	BATD
Leonora [Tango] (O/T)	Bob Waite	NCDTA
Ricardo [Tango] (O/T)	Tony and Denise Dyer	OBBD
San Anton [Tango] (Mod)	Dorothy Moxon	NATD
Delgada [Tango] (O/T)	Derek Tonks and Beryl Bates	Blackpool
Yvette [Tango] (Mod)	Roger and Yvonne Corkery	OBBD

Saunters (1980)

Babalu [Saunter]	David Bullen	IDTA
Celia	Tom Liddiard	OTDA
Chiffon [Saunter]	Edgar and Doris Holroyd	ISDC
Royale [Saunter]	Yvonne Corkery	ISTD
Sandara [Saunter]	Sandra and Ivor Griffiths	Dance News

Rumbas (1980)

Duet [Rumba]	Yvonne Stanley and Maurice Tait	OBBD Filey
Marguerite [Rumba]	Margaret Redmond	ADA
Presidente [Rumba]	David Bullen	IDTA
Romantica [Rumba]	Winn and Bob Oliver	BATD
Roundabout	Ted and Sue Burroughs	NATD

Foxtrots (1980)

Aljulay	Annette Sheridan	BATD
Metro	Ray and Dorothy Casey	NCDTA
R & R	Ray Hemming	OTDA

Blues (1980)

Baracuda	Ted and Sue Burroughs	NATD
Belinda	Margaret and Norman Yates	ADA

Swings (1980)

Boogie	Patricia Jay	Bognor Regis
Boulevard	Ted and Sue Burroughs	Southport

Sambas (1980)

Manyana [Samba]	Bob and Winn Oliver	UKAPTD
Shadow	Frances and Yvonne Carr	OBBD

Quicksteps (1980)

Deejay	Lewis and Joan Wilson	UKAPTD

Cha Cha Chas (1980)

Juanita [Cha Cha]	Colin Gear and Lavinia Thomas	NCDTA

Paso Dobles (1980)

Paso Del Sol	Roger and Yvonne Corkery	ISTD

Leading Arrangers:-
3 - David Bullen   2 - Roger and Yvonne Corkery
3 - Ted and Sue Burroughs   2 - Bob and Winn Oliver
2 - Maurice Tate and Yvonne Stanley

PRESENTED IN 1981

Waltzes (Old-Time) (1981)

Lehar [Waltz]	Jeff and Muriel Aldren	IDTA

Waltzes (Modern) (1981)

Aquilla	Ted and Sue Burroughs	NATD
Diana [Waltz]	Ken Park	NCDTA
Esmi	Ray and Helen Wilson	ISTD
La Reve [Waltz]	Joseph Wareing	ADA
Lifetime	Annette Sheridan	UKAPTD
Royal Wedding	Alan and Mary MacKay	BATD
Violetta [Waltz]	James Hargreaves	Southport

Tangos (1981)

Avocado [Tango] (O/T)	Ray and Christine Hodgkinson	Butlins, Filey
Conroy (O/T)	Ted and Sue Burroughs	UKAPTD
Terrel (Mod)	Terry and Ethel Grundy	Butlins Bognor Regis
Tucan (O/T)	Ken and Elaine Park	Southport

Saunters (1981)

Anita	Terry and Ethel Grundy	Butlins, Bognor Regis
Aquarius [Saunter]	Edgar Holroyd	NCDTA
Beverley	Norman and Margaret Yates	ADA
Christina [Saunter]	Morris Langham	ISDC
Crystal	Lewis and Joan Wilson	OBBD
Nirvana [Saunter]	David Bullen and Iverna Corcoran	Blackpool
Saxton	Elaine Sharpe (Conference)	BATD

Jives (1981)

Charlie's	Ken Park	NCDTA
Honeysuckle	Peter Varley	OBBD
Jennifer	Yvonne and Frances Carr	NATD
Susie	Bob and Winn Oliver	BATD

Cha Cha Chas (1981)

Barbados	Ted and Sue Burroughs	Blackpool
Cadiz	Roger and Yvonne Corkery	ISTD
Casino	Steve White	Butlins, Filey
M.Y.	Yvonne Stanley and Maurice Tait	ADA

Rumbas (1981)

Maria [Rumba]	Annette Sheridan	UKAPTD
Rose [Rumba]	David and Angela Ford (Salisbury)	Butlins, Bognor Regis
Topazine [Rumba]	Jill Bush	IDTA

Quicksteps (1981)

Flicker II	Jill Bush	OBBD
Kestral	Michael Davies	IDTA
L.A.	Neil Marshall and Lesley Reaney	Butlins, Filey

Foxtrots (1981)

Falcon	Michael Davies	ISDC
Moor Park	J. Denton	Slough

Gavottes (1981)

Edwardian	Ken and Barbara Street	ISTD

Party Dances (1981)

Dolce Vita	Norman and Margaret Yates	ADA
Glyn-Gary Swing	A. Ford	

Two Steps (1981)

Tammy	Dorothy Moxon	NATD

Leading Arrangers:-
3 - Ted and Sue Burroughs
2 - Ken Park
2 - Annette Sheridan
2 - Terry and Ethel Grundy

2 - Norman and Margaret Yates
2 - Jill Bush
2 - Michael Davies

PRESENTED IN 1982

Waltzes (Old-Time) (1982)

Willow	Roger and Yvonne Corkery	ISTD

Waltzes (Modern) (1982)

Bluebird	Michael Davies	ISDC
Gillion	Paul and Alison Platts	Southport
La Fleur [Waltz]	Ted and Sue Burroughs	Slough
Waikiki	Maurice Tait and Yvonne Stanley	ISTD

Tangos (1982)

Burgundy (O/T)	Jeff and Muriel Aldren	ADA
Caprina (Capri) [Tango] (Mod)	Annette Sheridan	BATD
Cascade [Tango] (O/T)	Ted and Sue Burroughs	UKAPTD
Lorenzo [Tango] (O/T)	Michael Davies	Southport
Montoya [Tango] (O/T)	Morris Langham (Gateshead)	NCDTA
Tamara [Tango] (Mod)	Barry Jones and Elaine Starkey	IDTA
Tenerife [Tango] (Mod)	Bob and Wendy Whelerton	OBBD
Zara (O/T)	Muriel Burrell	IDTA

Saunters (1982)

Cherry Tree	Ted and Sue Burroughs	Slough
Clifton	Jeff and Muriel Aldren	OBBD
Fairview	Ted and Sue Burroughs	Butlins, Bognor Regis
Hyland	Derek and Irene Stevens	Butlins, Filey
September	Annette Sheridan	NATD

Rumbas (1982)

Amour [Rumba]	Peter Varley	IDTA
Blue Orchid	Ted and Sue Burroughs	OBBD
Cuban Rock	Frances and Yvonne Carr	NATD
Red	Ken Park	NCDTA
Topaz [Rumba]	Ernie and Marjorie Hague	ADA

Quicksteps (1982)

Caroline	Morris Langham (Gateshead)	NCDTA
Corsa	Paul and Alison Platts (Rotherham)	Butlins, Filey
National	Annette Sheridan	NATD
Queensway	Ted and Sue Burroughs	Butlins, Bognor Regis

Foxtrots (1982)

Karen Foxtrot	Derek and Irene Stevens	Blackpool
Marlborough	Joseph Wareing	ADA
U.K.	Annette Sheridan	UKAPTD

Sambas (1982)

Salsa (Party Progressive)	Bob and Winn Oliver	
Sierra	Yvonne and Roger Corkery	ISTD
Simple	Reg and Sylvia Dart	Butlins, Bognor Regis

Jives (1982)

| Jemma | Norman Cavin and Norma Morris | Butlins, Filey |
| Juke Box | Ted and Sue Burroughs | UKAPTD |

Cha Cha Chas (1982)

| Cognac | David Bullen | Slough |
| Grand Prix | Ted Burroughs | BATD |

Swings (1982)

| Dixie | Michael Davies | ISDC |

Blues (1982)

| Elizabethan | David Bullen and Iverna Corcoran | Blackpool |

Party Dances (1982)

| Heidi Hop | Eric and Marjorie Dyer | ADA |

Gavottes (1982)

| Royal | Ted and Sue Burroughs | BATD |

Leading Arrangers:-
8 - Ted and Sue Burroughs
4 - Annette Sheridan
3 - Michael Davies
2 - Jeff and Muriel Aldren

2 - Morris Langham
2 - Paul and Alison Platts
2 - Derek and Irene Stevens
2 - Yvonne and Roger Corkery

PRESENTED IN 1983

Waltzes (Modern) (1983)

Aquaintance	Annette Sheridan	Slough
Estelle II [Waltz]	David Hipshaw and Pauline Griffiths	ADA
Fantasy	Patricia Jay and Gary Fleetwood	BCBD
Martell [Waltz]	Neil and Lesley Marshall	Butlins, Filey
Minstrel	Allan and Audrey Bainbridge	Butlins, Bognor Regis
Mornay [Waltz]	David Bullen and Iverna Corcoran	Blackpool
Wiclif	Barry and Julie Earnshaw	ISTD

Tangos (1983)

Ambassador (O/T)	Ted and Sue Burroughs	UKAPTD
Carradale (Mod)	Harold Lonyon	ISDC
Mimosa [Tango] (O/T)	Morris Langham	ISDC
Remar [Tango] (O/T)	Neil and Lesley Marshall	Southport

Swings (1983)

Candy	Ted and Sue Burroughs	IDTA
Juju	Barry and Julie Earnshaw	BCBD
Savoy	Betty Baker and Michael Davies	Blackpool
Sierra	Neil and Lesley Marshall	Butlins, Filey

Rumbas (1983)

Blue Bayou	Ted and Sue Burroughs	IDTA
Blue Moon	Ted and Sue Burroughs	NATD
Bolero [Rumba]	Yvonne and Roger Corkery	Slough
Mitzy	Annette Sheridan	UKAPTD Blackpool

Jives (1983)

Galaxy	Denness and Millie Garraway	BCBD
Georgia	Roger and Yvonne Corkery	ISTD
Glen Rock	Annette Sheridan	BATD
Gypsy	Steve and Morna White	Southport

Quicksteps (1983)

Maestro	Ken Park	NCDTA
Rothesay	Audrey and Allan Bainbridge	BATD
Twinkle	Michael Shilstone and Wendy Bates	NATD

Cha Cha Chas (1983)

Casbud	Neil and Lesley Marshall	Butlins, Filey
Cherry B	Ken and Elaine Park	NCDTA
Montego	David Hipshaw and Pauline Griffiths	ADA

Saunters (1983)

E.T.	Ken and Elaine Park	NCDTA
J.R.	Annette Sheridan	Slough
Sue Ellen	David and May Ewart	BATD

Blues (1983)

Blue Eyes	Annette Sheridan	ADA
Domino	Reg Dart	Butlins, Bognor Regis
Dynasty	Ted and Sue Burroughs	NATD

Foxtrots (1983)

Abbeydale	Neil and Lesley Marshall	Southport
Ferrari	David Bullen and Iverna Corcoran	UKAPTD

Sambas (1983)

Concorde [Samba]	Michael Pharaoh and Julie Williams	Butlins, Bognor Regis

Leading Arrangers:-

5 - Annette Sheridan
5 - Neil and Lesley Marshall
5 - Ted and Sue Burroughs
2 - Allan and Audrey Bainbridge
2 - David Bullen and Iverna Corcoran

2 - Barry and Julie Earnshaw
2 - David Hipshaw and Pauline Griffiths
2 - Yvonne and Roger Corkery
2 - Ken Park

PRESENTED IN 1984

Waltzes (Old-Time) (1984)

Candy	Yvonne Stanley and Maurice Tait	ADA
Wentworth	Barry Jones and Elaine Starkey	Blackpool

Waltzes (Modern) (1984)

Blue Heather	Ken and Barbara Street	BCBD
Caprice [Waltz]	Jill Bush	ISTD
Chantelle [Waltz]	Ted and Sue Burroughs	NATD
Emma	Annette Sheridan and Ray Reeves	UKAPTD

Tangos (1984)

Cordilia [Tango] (O/T)	Ray Hodgkinson	NCDTA
Eismere (O/T)	Ted Burroughs	UKAPTD
Gabicci [Tango] (O/T)	Jeff and Muriel Aldren	Butlins, Pwllheli
Malibu (O/T)	Edgar and Doris Holroyd	ISDC IOM
Mayfield (Mod)	Ted and Sue Burroughs	Southport
Santa Anna (Mod)	Allan and Audrey Bainbridge	BATD
Telex (O/T)	Ted and Sue Burroughs	IDTA
Temptation (Mod)	Patricia Jay and Gary Fleetwood	Bognor Regis

Rumbas (1984)

Beguine [Rumba]	Annette Sheridan and Ray Reeves	Butlins, Minehead
Blandford	Vernon Kemp	ISTD
Blue Sapphire	Ted Burroughs	UKAPTD (Blackpool)
Charmaine [Rumba]	Barry and Julie Earnshaw	Southport
Hawaiian	Barry and Julie Earnshaw	BCBD
Torvil	Enid Eglinton	NCDTA

Foxtrots (1984)

Dream	Annette Sheridan and Ray Reeves	Slough
Evening	Edgar and Doris Holroyd	ISDC IOM
Feather	Edgar and Doris Holroyd	NCDTA
Surprise	Ted and Sue Burroughs	Butlins, Minehead

Saunters (1984)

Adele [Saunter]	Michael and Ann Morris	Southport
Ceefax	Joyce Marland	BATD
Jasmin	Yvonne and Roger Corkery	BCBD

Quicksteps (1984)

Cameron	Michael Davies and Betty Baker	Blackpool
Kempston	Ken and Barbara Street	IDTA
Natasha	Michael Beetham	ADA

Swings (1984)

Sindy	Patricia Jay and Gary Fleetwood	Butlins, Minehead
Tropicano	Ted and Sue Burroughs	Slough

Gavottes (1984)

Shadow	Terry and Ethel Grundy	Bognor Regis
Twilight	Jill Bush	ISTD

Jives (1984)

Karand	Audrey Bromage and Michelle Webster	NATD
Klaxon	Joyce Marland	BATD

Sambas (1984)

Pepsi	Maurice Tait and Yvonne Stanley	ADA
Simplicity	Audrey and Allan Bainbridge	Bognor Regis

Blues (1984)

Indiana	Ted and Sue Burroughs	NATD

Cha Cha Chas (1984)

Niki	Barry and Julie Earnshaw	Slough

Leading Arrangers:-
6 - Ted and Sue Burroughs   2 - Patricia Jay and Gary Fleetwood
3 - Edgar and Doris Holroyd   2 - Ken and Barbara Street
3 - Annette Sheridan and Ray Reeves   2 - Yvonne Stanley and Maurice Tait
3 - Barry and Julie Earnshaw   2 - Jill Bush
2 - Allan and Audrey Bainbridge   2 - Joyce Marland

PRESENTED IN 1985

Waltzes (Modern) (1985)

Cradle	Annette Sheridan and Ray Reeves	BATD
Honeysuckle	Graham and Avril Watkins	Butlins, Pwllheli
William's	Graham Thomson and Kathy Bugler	Southport
Wynette [Waltz]	Edgar and Doris Holroyd	NCDTA

Tangos (1985)

Alma (O/T)	Lewis and Joan Wilson	Slough
Glenaire (O/T)	Graham Thompson and Kathy Bugler	Southport
Malvern (O/T)	Barry and Julie Earnshaw	BCBD
Martini (O/T)	David Hipshaw	ADA
Schiehallion [Tango] (Mod)	Graham Thomson and Kathy Bugler	BCBD
Ventura [Tango] (Mod)	Barry Jones and Elaine Starkey	IDTA
Winter (Mod)	Jill Bush	ISTD

Saunters (1985)

Celica [Saunter]	Patricia Jay and Gary Fleetwood	Butlins, Bognor Regis
Ebony	Yvonne and Roger Corkery	ISTD
Lenalan	Howard Cookson	BATD
Misty Isle	Graham Thomson and Kathy Bugler	Blackpool
Seashell	Avril and Graham Watkins	IDTA
Selina	Jeff and Muriel Aldren	NATD
Si Bon [Saunter]	Morris Langham	NCDTA

Rumbas (1985)

Apricot	Patricia Jay and Gary Fleetwood	Butlins, Bognor Regis
Jamaican	Julie Earnshaw	BCBD
Mustique [Rumba]	Michael and Enid Eglinton	NCDTA
Rainbow	Jeff and Muriel Aldren	UKAPTD
Regatta [Rumba]	Paul and Allison Platts	Southport

Foxtrots (1985)

Fairview	Lewis and Joan Wilson	Slough
Fiesta	Michael Davies	ISDC
Raynette	Annette Sheridan and Ray Reeves	Butlins, Bognor Regis
Valentine	Ray Reeves and Annette Sheridan	UKAPTD

Quicksteps (1985)

Carr-Naze	Ted and Sue Burroughs	NATD
Catchy	Graham Thomson and Kathy Bugler	Blackpool
Sophie	Jeff and Muriel Aldren	ADA

Cha Cha Chas (1985)

Chico	Neil and Lesley Marshall	Butlins, Pwllheli
Cocktail	Jeff and Muriel Aldren	NATD
El Tel	Margaret Yates	ADA

Jives (1985)

Jollery	Reg and Sylvia Dart	Slough
Springtime	Jill Bush	ISTD
Sunridge	Ted and Sue Burroughs	BATD

Gavottes (1985)

Crystal	Barry and Julie Earnshaw	Butlins, Pwllheli

Two Steps (1985)

Hampton	Clive Hurt	UKAPTD

Swings (1985)

Miami	Michael Davies	ISDC

Miscellaneous (1985)

National Fling	Jeff and Muriel Aldren	NATD (Fun)

Leading Arrangers:-

5 - Graham Thomson and Kathy Bugler 2 - Jill Bush
5 - Jeff and Muriel Aldren 2 - Patricia Jay and Gary Fleetwood
3 - Annette Sheridan and Ray Reeves 2 - Lewis and Joan Wilson
2 - Michael Davies 2 - Avril and Graham Watkins
2 - Barry and Julie Earnshaw 2 - Ted and Sue Burroughs

PRESENTED IN 1986

Waltzes (Old-Time) (1986)

Evergreen	Ken and Barbara Street	ISTD
Moon Glow	Joseph Wareing	ADA

Waltzes (Modern) (1986)

Eden	Michael and Angela Hayton	Blackpool
Geisha	Barry Jones and Elaine Starkey	IDTA
Nichole [Waltz]	Miss Joan Shields	ISDC
Snowbird	Michael Beetham	ADA

Tangos (1986)

Andross (Mod)	Margaret Anderson	NATD
Croft (O/T)	Barry and Julie Earnshaw	Southport
Dragon (O/T)	Michael Pharaoh and Julie Williams	Butlins, Bognor Regis
Givenchy [Tango] (Mod)	Elizabeth Atkinson and David Howker	UKAPTD
Highland (Mod)	Audrey and Allan Bainbridge	BATD
Masumi [Tango] (Mod)	Patricia Jay and Gary Fleetwood	Butlins, Pwllheli
Oakfield (O/T)	Morris Langham and Joan Shields	ISDC
Panama (O/T)	Alwyn Leathley and Elsie Platts	IDTA
Tianavaig (O/T)	Graham and Kathy Thomson	SDTA
Tina (O/T)	Terry and Ethel Grundy	Slough

Rumbas (1986)

Charisma [Rumba]	Elizabeth Atkinson and David Howker	Blackpool
Memory	Annette Sheridan and Ray Reeves	BATD
Neon	Ted and Sue Burroughs	NATD
Renato [Rumba]	Sid and Shirley Robson	NCDTA
Rosas	Norman and Margaret Yates	UKAPTD
Roulette	Jill Bush	ISTD

Quicksteps (1986)

Comet	Denness and Millie Garraway	NCDTA
Jomar	Reg and Sylvia Dart	Butlins, Bognor Regis
Kira	Pat Sharkey and Lorraine Heron	Southport
Knightsbridge	Audrey Bromage and Michelle Webster	ISTD
Kontiki	Neil and Lesley Marshall	SDTA

Jives (1986)

Normandy	Bill and Grace McMillan	SDTA
Tandy	David Howker and Elizabeth Atkinson	Southport
Tommy's	Cliff and Hazel Browning	BCBD
Woodstock	Neil and Lesley Marshall	Butlins, Pwllheli

Saunters (1986)

Blue Nile	Morris Langham	BCBD
Sorrento [Saunter]	Sid and Shirley Robson	NCDTA

Foxtrots (1986)

Caribbean	Alwyn Leathley and Elsie Platts	BCBD
Fergie	Annette Sheridan and Ray Reeves	Slough

Blues (1986)

Broadway	Ted and Sue Burroughs	Butlins, Pwllheli
Desi	Annette Sheridan and Ray Reeves	UKAPTD

Sambas (1986)

Sunlight	Jeff and Muriel Aldren	ADA
Tico	Ken and Barbara Street	Slough

Swings (1986)

Bavarian	Yvonne and Frances Carr	NATD (Fun dance)
Debonair [Swing]	Jeff and Muriel Aldren	Blackpool

Miscellaneous (1986)

Edinburgh Gavotte	Ted and Sue Burroughs	NATD
Pepi Paso	Annette Sheridan and Ray Reeves	Butlins, Bognor Regis
Red Dragon Cha Cha Cha	Martyn Gallagher and Averina Trahar	IDTA
Telemark Two Step	Alan and Kay Wainwright	BATD

Leading Arrangers:-
4 - Annette Sheridan and Ray Reeves
3 - Ted and Sue Burrough
3 - Elizabeth Atkinson and David Howker
2 - Alwyn Leathley and Elsie Platts

2 - Ken and Barbara Street
2 - Sid and Shirley Robson
2 - Neil and Lesley Marshall
2 - Jeff and Muriel Aldren

PRESENTED IN 1987

Waltzes (Old-Time) (1987)

Magnolia	Joan and Lewis Wilson	BCBD

Waltzes (Modern) (1987)

Alana	Jackie Sanderson	UKAPTD
Chez Elle [Waltz]	Graham and Kathy Thomson	Blackpool
Madeira	Ray Hodgkinson and Jean Robson	NCDTA
Monique [Waltz]	Elsie Platts and Alwyn Leathley	BCBD
Rochelle [Waltz]	David Hipshaw	ADA
Ryan	Audrey Bromage and Michelle Webster	NATD
Westgate	Jeff and Muriel Aldren	Butlins, Pwllheli

Tangos (1987)

'87 [Tango] (O/T)	Roy Hopkinson	ADA
Amigo [Tango] (O/T)	Ray Hodgkinson and Jean Robson	SDTA
Berlina [Tango] (O/T)	Barry Jones and Elaine Starkey	Southport
Chelsea (O/T)	Don and Jan Nicolson	NCDTA
Lancaster (Mod)	Annette Sheridan and Ray Reeves	IDTA
Tiffany (O/T)	Ted and Sue Burroughs	BATD
Tracy (Mod)	Sylvester Burrows	BATD

Cha Cha Chas (1987)

39 [Cha Cha]	Audrey Bromage and Michelle Webster	BATD
Calypso	Ray Hodgkinson and Jean Robson	Butlins, Pwllheli
Caravelle	Philip and Yvonne Ainsley	NCDTA
Chirpy	Ted and Sue Burroughs	Slough
Karina	Patricia Jay and Gary Fleetwood	IDTA
Oriental	Barry and Julie Earnshaw	BCBD
Pepito	Neil and Lesley Marshall	ADA

Saunters (1987)

Shalimar	Ted and Sue Burroughs	ISTD
Solara [Saunter]	Graham and Kathy Thomson	Blackpool
Summer	Graham and Avril Watkins	IDTA
Supreme [Saunter]	Derek and Irene Stevens	NATD

Rumbas (1987)

Blue Maze	Ted and Sue Burroughs	Southport
Ravelle [Rumba]	Sue and Ted Burroughs	ISDC
Romance	Patricia Jay and Gary Fleetwood	Bognor Regis
Sunrise	Graham and Kathy Thomson	Blackpool

Jives (1987)

Cameo	Ken and Barbara Street	ISTD
Edinburgh Rock	Morris and Joan Langham	SDTA
Jade	Ted and Sue Burroughs	BATD
Minnie	Annette Sheridan and Ray Reeves	UKAPTD

Swings (1987)

Michigan	David Howker and Elizabeth Atkinson	UKAPTD
Saucey	Michael and Ann Morris	Pwllheli
Sophie	Ivor and Sandra Griffiths	Slough

Foxtrots (1987)

Brookside	Audrey Bromage and Michelle Webster	ISDC
Festival	Barry and Julie Earnshaw	Southport
Jayde	Derek and Irene Stevens	Slough

Quicksteps (1987)

Etone	Barry and Julie Earnshaw	ISTD
Fishtail	Audrey and Allan Bainbridge	Bognor Regis
Hayley	Neil Marshall	SDTA

Blues (1987)

| April | Annette Sheridan and Ray Reeves | Bognor Regis |
| Branson | Morris and Jean Langham | ISDC |

Leading Arrangers:-

6 - Ted and Sue Burroughs

3 - Graham and Kathy Thomson

3 - Ray Hodgkinson and Jean Robson

3 - Audrey Bromage and Michelle Webster

3 - Annette Sheridan and Ray Reeves

3 - Barry and Julie Earnshaw

2 - Patricia Jay and Gary Fleetwood

2 - Derek and Irene StevensIrene Stevens

2 - Morris and Joan Langham

PRESENTED IN 1988

Waltzes (Modern) (1988)

Candleglow	Jill Bush	BCBD
Esther	Sid and Shirley Robson	NCDTA
Francesco	Barry and Julie Earnshaw	Slough
Graffton	Michael Pharaoh and Julie Williams	Bognor Regis
Jamie	Jim and Madge Curley	SDTA
Montrose [Waltz]	Barry and Julie Earnshaw	Butlins, Pwllheli
Saga	Michael Pharaoh and Julie Williams	Saga Holiday

Tangos (1988)

Fajara [Tango] (O/T)	Barry and Julie Earnshaw	Butlins, Pwllheli
Merlin (Mod)	Jeff and Muriel Aldren	ADA
Miramar (O/T)	Philip Ainsley	IDTA
Panache [Tango] (O/T)	Michael Beetham and Rita Carradus	SDTA
Rioch [Tango] (Mod)	Bob and Wendy Whelerton	IDTA
Texas (O/T)	Ted and Sue Burroughs	NATD
Trimpell (O/T	Don and Jan Nicolson	NCTDA
Tropical (O/T)	Ted and Sue Burroughs	Southport

Cha Cha Chas (1988)

Cameo	Ted and Sue Burroughs	BATD
Carnival	Ted and Sue Burroughs	Southport
Carvoeiro	Ray Hodgkinson and Jean Robson	UKAPTD
Cassandra	Michael and Ann Morris	Butlins, Pwllheli
Cherokee	Reg and Joyce Bentley	Bognor Regis
Flo-Jo	Neil and Lesley Marshall	Slough
Handshake	Margaret Preedy	ISTD
Orpheo	Jackie Sanderson	Blackpool

Saunters (1988)

Bamboo	Patricia Jay and Gary Fleetwood	ISDC
Bettina	David Howker and Elizabeth Atkinson	UKAPTD
Mandarin	David Bullen and Iverna Corcoran	BCBD
Manhatten	Annette Sheridan	ADA
Solitaire [Saunter]	Marilyn Pugsley and Claire Linden	ISTD
Twilight	Barry and Julie Earnshaw	Slough

Rumbas (1988)

Havanna	Michael Beetham	ADA
Malibu [Rumba]	David Bullen and Iverna Corcoran	BCBD
Paradise	Yvonne Ainsley	IDTA
Rhapsody	Ted and Sue Burroughs	ISDC
Sapphire	Audrey Bromage and Michelle Webster	NATD

Quicksteps (1988)

Abax	Annette Sheridan and Ray Reeves	BATD
Cresta	Michael Davies and Betty Baker	ISDC
Santa Fe	Audrey Bromage and Michelle Webster	ISTD
Woodspring	Ted and Sue Burroughs	NATD

Foxtrots (1988)

Lullaby	David Howker and Elizabeth Atkinson	UKAPTD
Phoenix	Barry and Julie Earnshaw	Blackpool
Stephanie	Graham and Kathy Thomson	Southport

Miscellaneous (1988)

Ascot Gavotte	Ted and Sue Burroughs	Blackpool
Brazilian Samba	Michael Beetham and Rita Carradus	SDTA
Dalton Swing	Ted and Sue Burroughs	BATD
Jingle Jive	Jean Robson and Ray Hodgkinson	NCDTA
Sapphire Blues	Patricia Jay and Gary Fleetwood	Bognor Regis
Six-Twenty Two Step	David Barrett and Dorothy Hudson	UKAPTD
Sixties Swing	Audrey Bromage and Michelle Webster	NATD

Leading Arrangers:-

8 - Ted and Sue Burroughs
5 - Barry and Julie Earnshaw
2 - Michael Beetham and Rita Carradus
2 - Ray Hodgkinson and Jean Robson
2 - Michael Pharaoh and Julie Williams

2 - Patricia Jay and Gary Fleetwood
2 - David Howker and Elizabeth Atkinson
2 - David Bullen and Iverna Corcoran
2 - Audrey Bromage and Michelle Webster
2 - Annette Sheridan

PRESENTED IN 1989

Waltzes (Old-Time) (1989)

Velvet	Patricia Jay and Gary Fleetwood	IDTA

Waltzes (Modern) (1989)

Autumn Mist	Audrey Bromage and Michelle Webster	ISTD
Camilla [Waltz]	Paticia Jay and Gary Fleetwood	UKAPTD
Charminster	Ken and Barbara Street	Butlins, Bognor Regis
Finesse [Waltz]	Alwyn Leathley and Elsie Platts	ISDC
Louise [Waltz]	Neil and Leslie Marshall	SDTA
Stardust	Michael Beetham and Rita Carradus	ADA
Suzanne [Waltz]	Graham and Kathy Thomson	BCBD
Westmount	Philip Ainsley and Lorraine Heron	Blackpool

Tangos (1989)

Armadale (Mod)	Annette Sheridan and Ray Reeves	BATD
Blue Haven (O/T)	Joseph Wareing and Margaret Littler	ADA
Cerise [Tango] (O/T)	Jim and Madge Curley	BATD
Cleopatra [Tango] (O/T)	Sid and Shirley Robson	NCDTA
Executive (O/T)	Audrey Bromage and Michelle Webster	NATD
Manhatten (O/T)	Philip Ainsley and Lorraine Heron	Blackpool

Rumbas (1989)

Adore [Rumba]	Audrey Bromage and Michelle Webster	NATD
Classique [Rumba]	Michael Beetham and Rita Carradus	ADA
Divine [Rumba]	Audrey Bromage and Michelle Webster	BCBD
Forever [Rumba]	Audrey Bromage and Michelle Webster	ISTD
Passat [Rumba]	Graham Crookes and Doreen Wareing	Blackpool
Ruby	Graham and Avril Watkins	ISDC
Sweetheart	Ken and Barbara Street	IDTA

Cha Cha Chas (1989)

Chino	Michael and Ann Morris	Butlins, Pwllheli
Mardi Gras	John and Christine Harrison	SDTA
Orlando	Sid and Shirley Robson	NCDTA
Rainbow	Graham and Kathy Thomson	Southport

Blues (1989)

Debbie	Michael and Ann Morris	Butlins, Pwllheli
Harvestime	Michael Beetham and Rita Carradus	BCBD
Misty	David Howker and Elizabeth Atkinson	UKAPTD

Foxtrots (1989)

Aurora	Lewis and Joan Wilson	Slough Dance News
Ellis	Annette Sheridan and Ray Reeves	NATD
Freesia	John and Christine Harrison	Southport
Mondrago	Jim and Mary Mallon	NCDTA

Jives (1989)

Boogie Beat	Bill and Grace McMillan	BATD
Fantasy	Roy and Jean Hopkinson	Slough Dance News
Ginger	Dorothy Hudson and Eric Taylor	UKAPTD
Jody's	Reg and Joyce Bentley	Butlins, Bognor Regis

Swings (1989)

Bobbie	Jim and Madge Curley	SDTA
Supra	Patricia Jay and Gary Fleetwood	Butlins, Bognor Regis
Willow	Graham and Avril Watkins	Slough

Saunters (1989)

Katrina	Michael and Ann Morris	Southport
Simone [Saunter]	Alwyn Leathley and Elsie Platts	ISDC

Quicksteps (1989)

Alay	Alwyn Leathley and Elsie Platts	IDTA
Kirsty	Michael and Ann Morris	Butlins, Pwllheli

Gavottes (1989)

Victorian	Ken and Barbara Street	ISTD

Leading Arrangers:-

5 - Audrey Bromage and Michelle Webster
4 - Michael and Ann Morris
3 - Patricia Jay and Gary Fleetwood
3 - Ken and Barbara Street
3 - Alwyn Leathley and Elsie Platts
3 - Michael Beetham and Rita Carradus
2 - Graham and Kathy Thomson

2 - Graham and Avril Watkins
2 - Philip Ainsley and Lorraine Heron
2 - Annette Sheridan and Ray Reeves
2 - Sid and Shirley Robson
2 - John and Christine Harrison
2 - Jim and Madge CurleyMadge Curley

PRESENTED IN 1990

Waltzes (Old-Time) (1990)

Galaxy	Mark Paton and Jacquie Davies	Dance News

Waltzes (Modern) (1990)

Callam's	Graham and Kathy Thomson	IDTA
Omega	David Howker and Elizabeth Atkinson	Southport
Sheridan	Audrey Bromage and Michelle Webster	NATD
Wensley	Philip Ainsley and Lorraine Heron	BCBD
Westlynn	Howard and Joanne Cookson	BATD
Wetheral	Michael and Angela Hayton	Butlins, Pwllheli

Tangos (1990)

Debonaire [Tango] (Mod)	Ken and Barbara Street	ISTD
Edor [Tango] (O/T)	Edgar and Doris Holroyd	NCDTA
Nadine [Tango] (O/T)	Philip Ainsley and Lorraine Heron	UKAPTD
Newfield (Mod)	Michael and Angela Hayton	SDTA
Tony (O/T)	Jim and Madge Curley	SDTA
Vilamoura [Tango] (O/T)	Michael and Angela Hayton	Butlins, Pwllheli

Cha Cha Chas (1990)

Carley	Michael and Ann Morris	ISDC
Chilli	Albert and Florence Clark	NCDTA
Chinchilla	Graham Crooks and Doreen Wareing	SDTA
Continental	Nicola Twigg and David Barrett	IDTA
Corrida	Michael and Ann Morris	ADA
Sarah's	Audrey Bromage and Michelle Webster	NATD

Rumbas (1990)

Charlene [Rumba]	Philip Ainsley and Lorraine Heron	Southport
Delight [Rumba]	Patricia Jay and Gary Fleetwood	Butlins, Bognor Regis
Dominique [Rumba]	David Bullen and Iverna Corcoran	Blackpool
Poldhu	Audrey and Allan Bainbridge	BATD
Sabor [Rumba]	Graham Crookes and Doreen Wareing	UKAPTD

Saunters (1990)

Bel-Air [Saunter]	Michael and Ann Morris	ADA
Kingfisher	Graham and Kathy Thomson	Blackpool
Kirsty	Howard and Joanne Cookson	BATD
Samara [Saunter]	Philip Ainsley and Lorraine Heron	Southport

Foxtrots (1990)

Felicity	Albert and Florence Clark	NCDTA
Fortuna	Mark Paton and Jacquie Davis	Dance News
Harlequin	Ken and Barbara Street	Butlins, Bognor Regis
Nevada	David Howker and Elizabeth Atkinson	ISDC

Quicksteps (1990)

Appleby	Jeff and Muriel Aldren	ADA
Chandella	Philip Ainsley and Lorraine Heron	UKAPTD
Margie	Jim and Madge Curley	Blackpool

Gavottes (1990)

Gwendoline	Ken and Barbara Street	Bognor Regis
Regency	Nicola Twigg and David Barrett	NATD
Sunset	Barry and Julie Earnshaw	BCBD

Jives (1990)

Alphabet	Steve and Diane Shaw	Dance News
Jetta	Graham Crookes and Doreen Wareing	BCBD
Shelley	Audrey Bromage and Michelle Webster	ISTD

Blues (1990)

Berkeley	Peter Sharpe	ISTD

Sambas (1990)

Marina [Samba]	Michael and Ann Morris	Butlins, Pwllheli

Swings (1990)

Savana	Graham Crookes and Doreen Wareing	ISDC
Sharron	Ken and Barbara Street	IDTA

Leading Arrangers:-

4 - Philip Ainsley and Lorraine Heron   2 - Mark Paton and Jacquie Davies
4 - Ken and Barbara Street   2 - David Howker and Elizabeth Atkinson
4 - Michael and Ann Morris   2 - Howard and Joanne Cookson
4 - Graham Crookes and Doreen Wareing   2 - Jim and Madge Curley
3 - Audrey Bromage and Michelle Webster   2 - Albert and Florence Clark
3 - Michael and Angela Hayton   2 - Nicola Twigg and David Barrett
2 - Graham and Kathy Thomson

PRESENTED IN 1991

Waltzes (Modern) (1991)

Bellerby	Philip Ainsley and Lorraine Heron	Blackpool
Blue Dawn	Mary Cruickshank	ISTD
Blue Lace	Ken and Barbara Street	IDTA
Claudia's	Graham and Kathy Thomson	North of Britain
Clinique [Waltz]	David Hipshaw and Pauline Griffiths	ADA
Granby	Flora Millar	Ireland East Coast
Washington	Mark Paton and Jacquie Davis	Slough

Tangos (1991)

Glendale (Mod)	Graham and Kathy Thomson	BCBD
Mirage (O/T)	Barry and Julie Earnshaw	North of Britain
Taurus (O/T)	Mark Paton and Jacquie Davis	Slough
Torque (Mod)	Albert and Florence Clark	NCDTA
Tripoli (O/T)	Philip Ainsley and Lorraine Heron	NCDTA
Tuscany (O/T)	Audrey Bromage and Ron Lane	NATD

Saunters (1991)

Carousel	Howard and Joanne Cookson	Blackpool
Columbine	Ken and Barbara Street	ISDC
Feline [Saunter]	Ken and Enid Smith	Butlins, Bognor Regis
Princess	Michael and Ann Morris	ADA
Redrose	Steven and Diane Shaw	Butlins, Pwllheli
Sateen [Saunter]	Robert and Kathleen Pickering	ISTD

Rumbas (1991)

Lakeside	Barry and Julie Earnshaw	Butlins, Pwllheli
Louise [Rumba]	Graham and Kathy Thomson	BCBD
Riverdale	Sid and Shirley Robson	NCDTA
Rosemount	Philip Ainsley and Lorraine Heron	Blackpool
Ruskin	Andrew Pigg and Doreen Wareing	Slough

Cha Cha Chas (1991)

Anitra	Alwyn Leathley and Elsie Platts	IDTA
Claymore	Graham and Kathy Thomson	SDTA
Clio	David Hipshaw and Pauline Griffiths	ADA
Dominion	Mary Cruickshank	ISTD
Susie Q	Arthur and Jean Parr	North of Britain

Jives (1991)

Bee Hive	John and Jean Moody	ISDC
Disney	David Barrett and Nicola Twigg	NATD
Jimpy	Reg and Sylvia Dart	Butlins, Bognor Regis
Joplin	Ray Bulpitt and Doreen Wareing	UKA

Foxtrots (1991)

Grosvenor	Muriel Aldren	Butlins, Pwllheli
Nicola	Norman and Linda Briggs	Butlins, Bognor Regis
Sahara	Audrey Bromage and Ron Lane	NATD
White Heather	Graham and Kathy Thomson	SDTA

Quicksteps (1991)

Kay's	Jim and Madge Curley	BATD
Quatro	Graham Crookes and Doreen Wareing	ISDC
Roxy	David Howker and Elizabeth Atkinson	UKA

Swings (1991)

Sacha	Michael and Ann Morris	UKA
Sandown	Howard and Joanne Cookson	BATD

Gavottes (1991)

Primrose	Patricia Jay and Gary Fleetwood	IDTA
Shimmering	Graham and Kathy Thomson	SDTA

Sambas (1991)

Popcorn	Audrey and Allan Bainbridge	BATD

Two Steps (1991)

Solara	Mike and Sheree Savory	BCBD

Leading Arrangers:-

6 - Graham and Kathy Thomson
2 - Philip Ainsley and Lorraine Heron
2 - Ken and Barbara Street
2 - Mary Cruickshank
2 - David Hipshaw and Pauline Griffiths

2 - Mark Paton and Jacquie Davis
2 - Barry and Julie Earnshaw
2 - Audrey Bromage and Ron Lane
2 - Howard and Joanne Cookson
2 - Michael and Ann Morris

PRESENTED IN 1992

Waltzes (Modern) (1992)

Apple Blossom	Samantha Haywood	ISTD
Border	Michael and Angela Hayton	SDTA
Chambellan [Waltz]	Philip Ainsley and Lorraine Heron	Blackpool
Denverdale	Steven and Diane Shaw	Butlins, Pwllheli
Hadrians	Michael and Angela Hayton	UKA
Highfield	Steven and Diane Shaw	Slough
Rabanne [Waltz]	Elsie Platts and Alwyn Leathley	ISDC

Tangos (1992)

Leanne [Tango] (O/T)	Philip Ainsley and Lorraine Heron	UKA
Negro [Tango] (O/T	Don and Jan Nicolson	NCDTA
Nightfire (O/T)	Ian and Sue Webster	ISDC, Llandudno
Telecon (Mod)	Alwyn Leathley	ADA
Tornado (O/T)	Ted and Sue Burroughs	Blackpool
Torviscas [Tango] (Mod)	Philip Ainsley and Lorraine Heron	BCBD
Trafalgar (O/T)	Michael and Ann Morris	ADA

Rumbas (1992)

Atlanta [Rumba]	Elizabeth Atkinson and Paul Wallace	ISDC
Fantasia [Rumba]	Graham and Kathy Thomson	North of Britain
Noir [Rumba]	Pat Sharkey and Yvonne White	SDTA
Pineapple	Michael Beetham	UKA
Rafiki [Rumba]	Colin Taylor and Carol Thirlaway	NCDTA
Regency	Ted and Sue Burroughs	BATD
Renaissance	Audrey Bromage and Ron Lane	ISTD
Richard's	Flora Millar	Blackpool

Saunters (1992)

Centenary	Jim and Madge Curley	BATD
Cerise	Graham and Avril Watkins	Butlins, Bognor Regis
Sandringham	John and Maureen Dack	Slough
Shakara [Saunter]	Graham and Kathy Thomson	North of Britain
Solazur [Saunter]	Philip Ainsley and Lorraine Heron	BCBD
St. Clair [Saunter]	Michael and Ann Morris	SDTA

Quicksteps (1992)

Florentine	Graham and Kathy Thomson	North of Britain
Katrina	Joanne and Howard Cookson	BATD
Quality	Ted and Sue Burroughs	NATD
Queslett	Mark Paton and Jacquie Davis	IDTA

Cha Cha Chas (1992)

CJ	Clive and Jennifer Hurt	Butlins, Bognor Regis
Commador	Michael and Ann Morris	ADA
Ebony	Ian and Sue Webster	Butlins, Pwllheli
Mahogany	Ian and Sue Webster	Slough

Foxtrots (1992)

April	Graham and Avril Watkins	Butlins, Bognor Regis
Tempro	Margaret Halliday	NCDTA

Swings (1992)

Linden	Ken and Barbara Street	ISTD
Singapore	Theo and Doreen Ball	IDTA

Bossa Novas (1992)

Bella	June Macready and Don Millington	NATD

Blues (1992)

Cheney	Patricia Jay and Gary Fleetwood	Butlins, Pwllheli

Jives (1992)

Jessica	Eric and Jean Taylor	BCBD

Gavottes (1992)

Lladro	Jeff and Muriel Aldren	NATD

Sambas (1992)

Social	Pat Sharkey and Yvonne White	IDTA
Studio	Jeff and Muriel Aldren	Ireland East Coast

Leading Arrangers:-

4 - Philip Ainsley and Lorraine Heron
3 - Graham and Kathy Thomson
3 - Ted and Sue Burroughs
3 - Ian and Sue Webster
3 - Michael and Ann Morriss

2 - Michael and Angela Hayton
2 - Steven and Diane Shaw
2 - Graham and Avril Watkins
2 - Pat Sharkey and Yvonne White

PRESENTED IN 1993

Waltzes (Modern) (1993)

Carliol	Michael and Angela Hayton	Butlins, Pwllheli
Cerise [Waltz]	Michael Beetham and Doreen Wareing	ADA
Lovely Lady	Steve and Kathleen Wright	ISDC
Sophie's	Graham and Kathy Thomson	IDTA
Windsor	Stuart and Karen Wright	Blackpool

Tangos (1993)

Danielle [Tango] (Mod)	Don Millington and June MacReady	NATD
Gibson (O/T)	Stuart and Karen Wright	Blackpool
Merrick (Mod)	Bob and Veronica Ryan	ISTD
Nocturne [Tango] (Mod)	Don Millington and June Macready	Slough
Renoir [Tango] (O/T)	Pat Sharkey and Yvonne White	ISDC
Samarnie (O/T)	Neil and Lesley Marshall	SDTA
Tanya (Mod)	Paul Wallace	BATD
Thirlmere (O/T)	Michael and Angela Hayton	Butlins, Pwllheli
Troodos (O/T)	Howard and Joanne Cookson	BATD
Turnberry (O/T)	Philip Ainsley and Lorraine Heron	North of Britain
Vienna [Tango] (Mod)	Graham and Kathy Thomson	BCBD

Rumbas (1993)

Apollo [Rumba]	Paul Wallace and Elizabeth Atkinson	Butlins, Pwllheli
Invicta	Bill and Gay Pugh	UKA
Miami	Audrey Bromage and Ron Lane	ISTD
Raynham	Philip Ainsley and Lorraine Heron	North of Britain
Venezia [Rumba]	Philip Ainsley and Lorraine Heron	Blackpool

Cha Cha Chas (1993)

Charlie's	Dorothy Hudson and Jean Taylor	ADA
Katie	Michelle Webster and David Howker	NATD
Mario	Graham and Avril Watkins	Butlins, Bognor Regis
Rachel	Margaret and Edwin Halliday	IDTA
Waikiki	Paul Wallace	BATD

Saunters (1993)

Azalia	Dorothy Hudson and Jean Taylor	ADA
Melrose	David and Ann Lavery	Dance News, Slough
Oxbury	Michelle Webster and David Howker	NATD
Romero [Saunter]	Patricia Jay and Gary Fleetwood	UKA

Jives (1993)

Jambo	Colin Taylor and Carol Thirlaway	SDTA
Julie's	Margaret and Edwin Halliday	NCDTA
Jurassic	Roy and Jean Hopkinson	Slough
Let's	Ray and Bridget Fenton-Storey	BCBD

Foxtrots (1993)

Jasmine	David Belshaw and Karen Kelly	NCDTA
Philishar	Jim and Madge Curley	SDTA
Stardust	Graham and Avril Watkins	Butlins, Bognor Regis

Quicksteps (1993)

Katy	Ross and Shirley Hillman	North of Britain
Richmond	Michael Beetham and Doreen Wareing	UKA

Swings (1993)

Chevy	Colin Taylor and Carol Thirlaway	NCDTA
Ivory	Patricia Jay and Gary Fleetwood	IDTA

Miscellaneous (1993)

Grenadier Two Step	Ken and Barbara Street	ISTD
Scirocco Samba	Roy and Jean Hopkinson	ISDC
Starlight Gavotte	Maureen and John Dack	Butlins, Bognor Regis
Stephanne Blues	Pat Sharkey and Yvonne White	BCBD

Leading Arrangers:-

3 - Philip Ainsley and Lorraine Heron
2 - Stuart and Karen Wright
2 - June Macready and Don Millington
2 - Pat Sharkey and Yvonne White
2 - Paul Wallace
2 - Michael and Angela Hayton
2 - Graham and Kathy Thomson
2 - Michael Beetham and Doreen Wareing

2 - Dorothy Hudson and Jean Taylor
2 - Michelle Webster and David Howker
2 - Graham and Avril Watkins
2 - Margaret and Edwin Halliday
2 - Patricia Jay and Gary Fleetwood
2 - Colin Taylor and Carol Thirlaway
2 - Roy and Jean Hopkinson

PRESENTED IN 1994

Waltzes (Old-Time) (1994)

Sovereign	John and Maureen Dack	UKA
Waltz of Vienna	Jeff and Muriel Aldren	SDTA
Wednesday	Rachel Wadey	ISTD

Waltzes (Modern) (1994)

Aurora	Michelle Webster and David Howker	ISTD
Centenary	Malcolm T. Brister (Ann Green)	Blackpool
Parkgate	Jeff and Muriel Aldren	Butlins, Pwllheli
Springside	Howard and Joanne Cookson	BATD
Stacey Ann	Neil and Lesley Marshall	SDTA

Tangos (1994)

Blackpool Tower (Mod)	Arthur and Jean Parr	IDTA
Cassanova [Tango] (Mod)	Don Millington and June McReady	NATD
Devoran (O/T)	Michael and Ann Morris	Slough
Heartbeat (O/T)	Graham and Avril Watkins	IDTA
Lanercost (O/T)	Michael and Angela Hayton	Butlins, Pwllheli
Moderato [Tango] (Mod)	Margaret Yates and Carol Parry	ADA
Teak (O/T)	Ian and Sue Webster	Blackpool
Trevini (O/T)	Philip Ainsley and Lorraine Heron	North of Britain

Rumbas (1994)

Caprice [Rumba]	Ken and Barbara Street	ISTD
Cosmopolitan	David Howker and Michelle Webster	NATD
Dorice [Rumba]	David Bullen and Iverna Corcoran	BCBD
Elise [Rumba]	Graham and Kathy Thomson	Blackpool
Headlands	Audrey and Allan Bainbridge	BATD
Raquel [Rumba]	Bob and Diane Smith	ADA
Rosewood	Ian and Sue Webster	ISDC
Samantha [Rumba]	Lesley Hawthorne	IDTA
Tamara [Rumba]	Ian and Sue Webster	NCDTA

Foxtrots (1994)

Cheslyn	Terry and Ethel Grundy	Slough
Emerald	Graham and Avril Watkins	Butlins, Bognor Regis
Maple	Ian and Sue Webster	NCDTA
Mirror Glass	Malcolm Brister (Ann Green)	BCBD

Saunters (1994)

Navidia	June Day and Deborah Long	BATD
Sandalwood	Ian and Sue Webster	ISDC
Sonata [Saunter]	Bob and Diane Smith	ADA
Sovereign	Ian and Sue Webster	NCDTA

Cha Cha Chas (1994)

Caroland	Andrew Pigg and Caroline Roberts	Butlins, Pwllheli
Par [Cha Cha]	Arthur and Jean Parr	North of Britain
Paradise	Roy Randall and Heather Pitman	Slough

Quicksteps (1994)

Bernena	Neil and Lesley Marshall	ISDC
Somerset	Malcolm Brister (Ann Green)	UKA
Trojan	David Howker and Michelle Webster	North of Britain

Jives (1994)

Coca Rola	Arthur and Jean Parr	UKA
Jennie	Michael and Anne Morris	SDTA

Blues(1994)

Aqua	Graham and Avril Watkins	BCBD

Gavottes (1994)

Charlotte	John and Maureen Dack	Butlins, Bognor Regis

Sambas (1994)

Miami	Steven and Diane Shaw	Butlins, Bognor Regis

Swings (1994)

Shamrock	David Trowbridge and Beverley Crowder	NATD

Leading Arrangers:-
6 - Ian and Sue Webster   2 - Bob and Diane Smith
3 - David Howker and Michelle Webster 2 - Jeff and Muriel Aldren
3 - Arthur and Jean Parr   2 - John and Maureen Dack
3 - Graham and Avril Watkins   2 - Neil and Lesley Marshall
3 - Malcolm Brister   2 - Michael and Ann Morris

Index of Dances (1975-1994)

Waltzes (Mod)

Windsor (1993)
Wynette (1985)

Tangos

'87 (O/T) (1987)
Alfredo (O/T) (1977)
Alma (O/T) (1985)
Alpegho (O/T) (1977)
Ambassador (O/T) (1983)
Amigo (O/T) (1987)
Andross (Mod) (1986)
Antrim (1980)
Apache (Mod) (1976)
Aramis (O/T) (1975)
Armadale (Mod) (1989)
Avocado (O/T) (1981)
Berlina (O/T) (1987)
Blackpool Tower (Mod) (1994)
Blue Haven (O/T) (1989)
Burgundy (O/T) (1982)
Capella (Mod) (1979)
Caprina (Capri) (M)(82)
Carradale (Mod) (1983)
Casani (Mod) (1979)
Cascade (O/T) (1982)
Cassanova (Mod) (94)
Cerise (O/T) (1989)
Chelsea (O/T) (1987)
Christina (Mod) (1976)
Cleopatra (O/T) (1989)
Conroy (O/T) (1981)
Cordilia (O/T) (1984)
Cordoba (Mod) (1978)
Creole (O/T) (1975)
Crimson (O/T) (1978)
Croft (O/T) (1986)
Dallas (Mod) (1980)
Danielle (Mod) (1993)
Debonaire (Mod) (90)
Delgada (O/T) (1980)

Del Mar (1980)
Devoran (O/T) (1994)
Dragon (O/T) (1986)
Edor (O/T) (1990)
Eismere (O/T) (1984)
Elandor (O/T) (1975)
El-Kantara (Mod) (1978)
El-Mar (O/T) (1975)
El-Torro (O/T) (1978)
España (O/T) (1980)
Estelle (O/T) (1979)
Executive (O/T) (1989)
Fajara (O/T) (1988)
Firefly (O/T) (1976)
Flame (O/T) (1977)
Flirtation (1976)
Gabicci (O/T) (1984)
Gibson (O/T) (1993)
Givenchy (Mod) (1986)
Glenaire (O/T) (1985)
Glendale (Mod) (1991)
Hacienda (Mod) (1976)
Heartbeart (O/T) (1994)
Highland (Mod) (1986)
Imperial (Mod) (1976)
Indigo (O/T) (1975)
Lancaster (Mod) (1987)
Lanercost (O/T) (1994)
Las Vegas (O/T) (78)
Leanne (O/T) (1992)
Leonora (O/T) (1980)
Lorenzo (O/T) (1982)
Malibu (O/T) (1984)
Malvern (O/T) (1985)
Manhatten (O/T) (1989)
Martinella (O/T) (1978)
Martini (O/T) (1985)
Masumi (Mod) (1986)
Mayfield (Mod) (1984)
Merlin (Mod) (1988)
Merrick (Mod) (1993)

Mimosa (O/T) (1983)
Mirage (O/T) (1991)
Miramar (O/T) (1988)
Moderato (Mod) (1994)
Mondello (Mod) (1975)
Montoya (O/T) (1982)
Montreal (1976)
Nadine (O/T) (1990)
Nakoma (Mod) (1979)
Negro (O/T) (1992)
Newfield (Mod) (1990)
Nightfire (O/T) (1992)
Nocturne (Mod) (1993)
Oakfield (O/T) (1986)
Panache (O/T) (1988)
Panama (O/T) (1986)
Pearl (O/T) (1975)
Pedida (Mod) (1975)
Remar (O/T) (1983)
Renoir (O/T) (1993)
Ricardo (O/T) (1980)
Rioch (Mod) (1988)
Rosetta (O/T) (1979)
Samarnie (O/T) (1993)
San Anton (Mod) (80)
Santa Anna (Mod) (1984)
Schiehallion (Mod)(85)
Segovia (Mod) (1977)
Sherrie (O/T) (1979)
Silver Jubilee (1977)
Sorelle (O/T) (1976)
Stevlyn (O/T) (1977)
Sundance (O/T) (1976)
Tamara (Mod) (1982)
Tania (Mod) (1978)
Tanya (Mod) (1993)
Tarquilla (Mod) (1978)
Taurus (O/T) (1991)
Teak (O/T) (1994)
Telecon (Mod) (1992)
Telex (O/T) (1984)

Temptation (Mod) (1984)
Tenerife (Mod) (1982)
Terrel (Mod) (1981)
Texas (O/T) (1988)
Thirlmere (O/T) (1993)
Tianavaig (O/T) (1986)
Tiffany (O/T) (1987)
Tina (O/T) (1986)
Tony (O/T) (1990)
Topsy (1976)
Tornado (O/T) (1992)
Torque (Mod) (1991)
Torviscas (Mod) (92)
Tracy (Mod) (1987)
Trafalgar (O/T) (1992)
Trevini (O/T) (1994)
Trimpell (O/T) (1988)
Tripoli (O/T) (1991)
Troodos (O/T) (1993)
Tropical (O/T) (1988)
Tucan (O/T) (1981)
Turnberry (O/T) (1993)
Tuscany (O/T) (1991)
Valentino (O/T) (1978)
Ventura (Mod) (1985)
Vienna (Mod) (1993)
Vilamoura (O/T) (1990)
Violetta (O/T) (1977)
Westway (Mod) (1976)
Winter (Mod) (1985)
Yvette (Mod) (1980)
Zara (O/T) (1982)

Foxtrots

Abbeydale (1983)
Aljulay (1980)
Amanda (1978)
April (1992)
Aurora (1989)
Brookside (1987)
Caribbean (1986)

Foxtrots

Carlton (1979)
Cheslyn (1994)
Denham (1978)
Dream (1984)
Ellis (1989)
Elwyn (1975)
Emerald (1994)
Evening (1984)
Fairview (1985)
Falcon (1981)
Feather (1984)
Felicity (1990)
Fenwick (1977)
Fergie (1986)
Ferrari (1983)
Festival (1987)
Fiesta (1985)
Flamenco (1975)
Florida (1975)
Fortuna (1990)
Freesia (1989)
Glenroy (1976)
Grosvenor (1991)
Harlequin (1990)
International (1979)
Jasmine (1993)
Jayde (1987)
Karen Foxtrot (1982)
Lullaby (1988)
Maple (1994)
Marina (1977)
Marlborough (1982)
Metro (1980)
Mirror Glass (1994)
Mondrago (1989)
Moor Park (1981)
Nevada (1990)
Nicola (1991)
Philishar (1993)
Phoenix (1988)

R & R (1980)
Raynette (1985)
Sahara (1991)
Silver Jubilee (1977)
Stardust (1993)
Stephanie (1988)
Surprise (1984)
Tempro (1992)
U.K. (1982)
Valentine (1985)
Valerie (1978)
White Heather (1991)

Quicksteps

Abax (1988)
Alay (1989)
Albany (1975)
Alison (1976)
Appleby (1990)
Bee Bee (1975)
Bernena (1994)
Bernice (1979)
Cameron (1984)
Canberra (1977)
Caroline (1982)
Carr-Naze (1985)
Catchy (1985)
Chandella (1990)
Comet (1986)
Corrie (1975)
Corsa (1982)
Cresta (1988)
Deejay (1980)
Ellesmere (1978)
Etone (1987)
Fishtail (1987)
Flicker I (1976)
Flicker II (1981)
Florentine (1992)
Florida (1975)
Gemini (1978)

Glenhelen (1978)
Hayley (1987)
Honey (1976)
International (1978)
Ivan (1975)
J.M. (1975)
Java (1977)
Jomar (1986)
Katrina (1992)
Katy (1993)
Kay's (1991)
Kempston (1984)
Kestral (1981)
Kira (1986)
Kirsty (1989)
Knightsbridge (1986)
Kontiki (1986)
L.A. (1981)
Leighway (1977)
Maestro (1983)
Margie (1990)
Natasha (1984)
National (1982)
Plaza (1976)
Quality (1992)
Quando (1979)
Quatro (1991)
Queensway (1982)
Queslett (1992)
Quincey (1978)
Richmond (1993)
Rothesay (1983)
Roxy (1991)
Santa Fe (1988)
Silver Jubilee (1977)
Somerset (1994)
Sophie (1985)
Supaul (1975)
Trojan (1994)
Twinkle (1983)
Video (1979)

Woodspring (1988)

Rumbas

Adore (1989)
Amour (1982)
Apollo (1993)
Apricot (1985)
Atlanta (1992)
Beguine (1984)
Bianco (1977)
Blandford (1984)
Blue Bayou (1983)
Blue Maze (1987)
Blue Moon (1983)
Blue Mosque (1979)
Blue Orchid (1982)
Blue Sapphire (1984)
Bolero (1983)
Caprice (1994)
Caribbean (1976)
Casanova (1975)
Charisma (1986)
Charlene (1990)
Charmaine (1984)
Cinzano (1976)
Classique (1989)
Cosmopolitan (1994)
Cuban Rock (1982)
Delight (1990)
Divine (1989)
Dominique (1990)
Dorice (1994)
Duet (1980)
Elise (1994)
Fantasia (1992)
Forever (1989)
Havanna (1988)
Hawaiian (1984)
Headlands (1994)
International (1977)
Invicta (1993)

Rumbas

Jamaican (1985)
L'Amour (1976)
Lakeside (1991)
Lisa (1975)
Louise (1991)
Malibu (1988)
Marbella (1977)
Marguerite (1980)
Maria (1981)
Memory (1986)
Miami (1993)
Mitzy (1983)
Montego (1975)
Mustique (1985)
Neon (1986)
Noir (1992)
Pandora (1975)
Paradise (1988)
Passat (1989)
Pineapple (1992)
Playa (1978)
Poldhu (1990)
Presidente (1980)
Rafiki (1992)
Rainbow (1985)
Raquel (1994)
Ravelle (1987)
Raynham (1993)
Red (1982)
Regatta (1985)
Regency (1992)
Renaissance (1992)
Renato (1986)
Rhapsody (1988)
Richard's (1992)
Riverdale (1991)
Romance (1987)
Romantica (1980)
Rosas (1986)
Rose (1981)

Rosemount (1991)
Rosette (1978)
Rosewood (1994)
Roulette (1986)
Roundabout (1980)
Ruby (1989)
Ruskin (1991)
Sabor (1990)
Samantha (1994)
Santana (1979)
Sapphire (1988)
Sayonara (1978)
Serenade (1977)
Sombrero (1978)
Sunrise (1987)
Sweetheart (1989)
Tamara (1994)
Topaz (1982)
Topazine (1981)
Torvil (1984)
Venezia (1993)
Zeeta (1977)

Saunters

Adele (1984)
Alpine (1979)
Anita (1981)
Aquarius (1981)
Azalia (1993)
Babalu (1980)
Bamboo (1988)
Bel-Air (1990)
Bettina (1988)
Beverley (1981)
Blueberry (1977)
Blue Nile (1986)
Carousel (1991)
Ceefax (1984)
Celia (1980)
Celica (1985)
Centenary (1992)

Cerise (1992)
Charmaine (1978)
Cherry Tree (1982)
Cheyenne (1977)
Chiffon (1980)
Christina (1981)
Clifton (1982)
Columbine (1991)
Coral (1978)
Crystal (1981)
d'Amour (1977)
Dawn (1976)
E.T. (1983)
Ebony (1985)
Edinburgh (1979)
Elaine (1975)
Eljay (1978)
Endean (1975)
Fairview (1982)
Feline (1991)
Forget-Me-Not (1978)
Grenville (1979)
Honeymoon (1975)
Hyland (1982)
J.R. (1983)
Jasmin (1984)
Katrina (1989)
Kaybee (1976)
Kingfisher (1990)
Kirsty (1990)
Kitikat (1978)
Lenalan (1985)
Louise (1976)
Mandarin (1988)
Manhatten (1988)
Melrose (1993)
Misty Isle (1985)
Navidia (1994)
Nirvana (1981)
Oxbury (1993)
Princess (1991)

Redrose (1991)
Rockford (1978)
Romero (1993)
Royale (1980)
Samara (1990)
Sandalwood (1994)
Sandara (1980)
Sandringham (1992)
Sateen (1991)
Saxton (1981)
Seashell (1985)
Selina (1985)
September (1982)
Shakara (1992)
Shalimar (1987)
Shanida (1977)
Sharon (1978)
Shelley (1979)
Shemara (1977)
Si Bon (1985)
Silverdale (1977)
Simone (1989)
Solara (1987)
Solazur (1992)
Solitaire (1988)
Sonata (1994)
Sorrento (1986)
Sovereign (1994)
St. Clair (1992)
Sue Ellen (1983)
Summer (1987)
Supreme (1987)
Tee Jay (1977)
Therese (1979)
Together (1975)
Twilight (1988)
Viv'Ann (1979)
Westminster (1975)
Whispering (1975)

Cha Cha Chas

39 [Cha Cha] (1987)
Acel (1976)
Anitra (1991)
Barbados (1981)
Cadiz (1981)
Calypso (1987)
Cameo (1988)
Canberra (1979)
Caravelle (1987)
Carley (1990)
Carnival (1988)
Caroland (1994)
Carvoeiro (1988)
Casbud (1983)
Casino (1981)
Cassandra (1988)
Celebration (1977)
Charlie's (1993)
Cheeky Cheeky (1978)
Cherokee (1988)
Cherry B (1983)
Chico (1985)
Chicory (1978)
Chilli (1990)
Chinchilla (1990)
Chino (1989)
Chirpy (1987)
Chobe (1975)
CJ (1992)
Claymore (1991)
Clio (1991)
Cocktail (1985)
Cognac (1982)
Commador (1992)
Continental (1990)
Corrida (1990)
Disco (1979)
Dominion (1991)
Ebony (1992)
Echo (1979)

El Tel (1985)
Flo-Jo (1988)
Grand Prix (1982)
Handshake (1988)
Juanita [Cha Cha] (1980)
Karina (1987)
Katie (1993)
M.Y. (1981)
Mahogany (1992)
Mardi Gras (1989)
Mario (1993)
Montego (1983)
Niki (1984)
Olympic (1976)
Oriental (1987)
Orlando (1989)
Orpheo (1988)
Par [Cha Cha] (1994)
Paradise (1994)
Pepito (1987)
Rachel (1993)
Rainbow (1989)
Red Dragon (1986)
Sarah's (1990)
Shirlee (1977)
Silver (1976)
Supreme (1975)
Susie Q (1991)
Waikiki (1993)
Y.C. (1976)
Yvette (1979)

Blues

Alvaston (1975)
April (1987)
Aqua (1994)
Baracuda (1980)
Barbarella (1979)
Beechwood (1979)
Belinda (1980)
Berkeley (1990)

Blue Eyes (1983)
Branson (1987)
Broadway (1986)
Bye Bye (1977)
Cheney (1992)
Cuddling (1978)
Debbie (1989)
Desi (1986)
Domino (1983)
Dynasty (1983)
Elizabethan (1982)
Harlequin (1975)
Harvestime (1989)
Indiana (1984)
International (1976)
Jonnelen (1978)
Jubilee (1977)
Marigold (1976)
Misty (1989)
Palma Nova (1976)
Sapphire (1988)
Stephanne (1993)
Tremaine (1978)
Tuesday (1979)
Virginia (1976)

Jives

Alphabet (1990)
Bee Hive (1991)
Boogie Beat (1989)
Cameo (1987)
Charlie's (1981)
City (1979)
Coca Rola (1994)
Disney (1991)
Edinburgh Rock (1987)
Embassy (1979)
Fantasy (1989)
Fiesta (1978)
Galaxy (1983)
Georgia (1983)

Ginger (1989)
Glen Rock (1983)
Gypsy (1983)
Honeysuckle (1981)
Jade (1987)
Jambo (1993)
Jamboree (1977)
Jemma (1982)
Jennie (1994)
Jennifer (1981)
Jessica (1992)
Jetta (1990)
Jimpy (1991)
Jingle (1988)
Jody's (1989)
Jollery (1985)
Joplin (1991)
Jubilee (1979)
Juke Box (1982)
Julie's (1993)
Jurassic (1993)
Justa (1975)
Karand (1984)
Kelvin (1978)
Klaxon (1984)
Let's (1993)
Minnie (1987)
Normandy (1986)
Rhythm (1976)
Rock-On (1979)
Shelley (1990)
Springtime (1985)
Sunridge (1985)
Susie (1981)
Tandy (1986)
Tijuana (1977)
Tommy's (1986)
Womble (1977)
Woodstock (1986)

Sambas

Astoria (1978)
Brazilian (1988)
Chalimar (1976)
Concorde (1983)
Elegre (1976)
Holiday (1979)
Laughing (Party) (1979)
Manyana (1980)
Marina (1990)
Miami (1994)
Pepsi (1984)
Petite (1978)
Popcorn (1990)
Salsa (Partr Prog.) (1982)
Scirocco (1993)
Shadow (1980)
Sierra (1982)
Siesta (1976)
Simple (1982)
Simplicity (1984)
Social (1992)
Studio (1992)
Sultana (1975)
Sunlight (1986)
Suzanne (1978)
Swinging (1978)
Tico (1986)

Gavottes

Ascot (1988)
Cameo (1976)
Charlotte (1994)
Crystal (1985)
Daffodil (1979)
Edinburgh (1986)
Edwardian (1981)
Elizabethan (1977)
Gwendoline (1990)
Lladro (1992)
Moonlight (1975)

Primrose (1991)
Referendum (1975)
Regency (1990)
Royal (1982)
Shadow (1984)
Shimmering (1991)
Starlight (1993)
Sunset (1990)
Twilight (1984)
Victorian (1989)

Two Steps

Consort (1976)
Grenadier (1993)
Hampton (1985)
Six-Twenty (1988)
Solara (1991)
Tammy (1981)
Telemark (1986)

Paso Dobles

Paso Del Sol (1980)
Paso Nova (1975)
Pepi Paso (1986)
Valencia Paso (1976)

Swings

1976 (1976)
Albama (1975)
Allington (1977)
Bavarian (1986)
Bobbie (1989)
Bobtail (1975)
Boogie (1980)
Boulevard (1980)
Campbell (1975)
Candy (1983)
Chevy (1993)
Dalton (1988)
Debonair (1986)
Dixie (1982)

Glyn-Gary (1981)
Golden (1979)
Hawaiian (1976)
Hipster (1975)
Ivory (1993)
Juju (1983)
Linden (1992)
Lulu (1978)
Miami (1985)
Michigan (1987)
Panama (1978)
Sacha (1991)
Sandown (1991)
Saucey (1987)
Savana (1990)
Savoy (1983)
Shamrock (1994)
Sharron (1990)
Sierra (1983)
Sindy (1984)
Singapore (1992)
Sixties (1988)
Soho (1975)
Sophie (1987)
Sukie (1975)
Supra (1989)
Tippy Top (1978)
Tropicano (1984)
Willow (1989)

Miscellaneous

Bella Bosa Nova (1992)
Bertha Bump (1975)
Blackpool Trot (1977)
Butlin Beat (1975)
Columbine Mazurka (1976)
Cornish Capers (1977)
Dolce Vita (1981)
Halleluja Sway (1979)
Heidi Hop (1982)
National Fling (1985)

Naval Capers (1977)
Penguin Rock (1978)
Smurff Dance (1978)
Twenties Rag (1976)
Tyford Sway (1975)

Summary

Waltzes O/T	22
Waltzes Modern	133
Tangos	150
Foxtrots	59
Quicksteps	69
Rumbas	100
Saunters	97
Cha Cha Chas	71
Blues	33
Jives	53
Sambas	27
Gavottes	21
Two Steps	7
Paso Dobles	4
Swings	43
Mazurkas	1
Rags	1
Bossa Novas	1
Miscellaneous	12
	904

Changes in Sequence Dancing Over the Years

The Top Ten in order of popularity:-

Up to 1945		1946-1974		1975-1994	
1. Waltzes O/T	32.0%	Tangos	17.0%	Tangos	16.5%
2. Two Steps	7.5%	Waltzes Modern	15.0%	Waltzes Modern	14.5%
3. Tangos	7.0%	Waltzes O/T	14.5%	Rumbas	11.0%
4. Square Dances	5.0%	Foxtrots	9.0%	Saunters	11.0%
5. Barn Dances	2.5%	Saunters	8.0%	Cha Cha Chas	8.0%
6. Mazurkas	2.5%	Quicksteps	8.0%	Quicksteps	7.5%
7. Gavottes	2.5%	Two Steps	5.5%	Foxtrots	6.5%
8. Schottisches	2.5%	Blues	4.0%	Jives	6.0%
9. Saunters	2.5%	Swings	2.0%	Swings	4.5%
10. One Steps	2.0%	Gavottes	2.0%	Blues	3.5%

More than two thirds of early sequence dances made some use of old-time waltz figures; since the revival the slower modern waltz has gained ground. Ratios of old-time to modern waltz sequences are roughly as follows:-

Early 1950's	5:1
Early 1960's	1:1
Early 1970's	1:3
Early 1990's	1:6

Tangos, saunters and to a lesser extent blues and gavottes have retained their popularity over the years; dances with hopping steps such as polkas, mazurkas and schottisches have fallen from favour. The swing is an old-time dance played in quickstep tempo; swings date from 1961. From 1957 onwards two steps were displaced by quicksteps and foxtrots.

	1950-54	1960-64	1970-74	1990-94
Two Steps	31	17	0	2
Quicksteps	0	28	48	15
Foxtrots	4	24	25	17

Since 1975 one third of new official sequence dances are Latin-American. Dates at which these dances began to appear more frequently are: Cha Cha Cha 1971; Samba 1975; Rumba 1975; and Jive 1977.

SEQUENCE DANCING IN PERSPECTIVE

Sequence and Ballroom Dancing

The virtues and limitations of sequence dancing are seen more clearly by looking at ballroom dancing which is the main alternative form of round dancing. This comparison is particularly important since the higher reaches of sequence dancing are controlled by the various ballroom associations and the Official Board who monitor the inventive dance competitions, award qualifications for teachers and legislate on matters of professional interest. Although the sequence and ballroom dancers use the same dancing figures, technique and almost the same music, the freedom of the ballroom dancer to choose his own order of steps has far-reaching consequences. In ballroom dancing the man leads and the lady follows as best she can. In theory any dancing figure can be indicated by the use of subtle signals by the man - in practice this tends to limit the range of figures used, particularly if the man is not highly trained or has to dance with a number of different partners. In sequence dancing the lady knows the order as well as the man (and often whispers to him what to do next!). Considerations of this kind lead to differences in approach:-

In **sequence dancing** a wide range of figures is used and the emphasis is on correct steps and accurately remembering the order of the sequence - technique has to take second place to some extent, particularly in the early stages.

In **ballroom dancing** the aim is to execute a limited number of dancing figures with good style according to the principles laid down by the various associations; the dancers work towards awards, enter competitions and give exhibitions. As well as correct foot movements, attention is directed to movements of the body as a whole. Good social ballroom dancers will thus tend to perform fewer figures with better technique.

Other consequences of the difference between sequence and go-as-you-please are examined in the following sections.

Dancing as a Spectacle

The 'English' style of dancing, developed from 1923 onwards, with its rise and fall, sway, footwork and contrary body movement, sets a standard for ballroom dancing the world over. It is very attractive to watch and the festivals, demonstrations and dance competitions attract large audiences. Ballroom dancing has great glamour and cult figures emerge whose activities are followed with great interest. Acquiring a good technique for a relatively small number of dancing figures from a teacher of dancing will permit children and adult learners to move about gracefully and be well prepared for the social occasions which need dancing skills. Keen students will be able to progress to medal awards and enter competitions. Emphasis on training and technique does produce, however, a small elite of experts and a correspondingly larger number of spectators. This is seen in more extreme form in ballet where many watch but few perform.

Sequence dancing, in contrast, is less attractive to the viewer since all follow the sequence for the particular dance and there is less scope for freedom of expression. In any case, the dancers need to make an effort to remember the sequences accurately and this militates against too much concentration on technique. Nevertheless, the sight of many elderly couples moving round in harmony, and obviously enjoying themselves, is not without its appeal.

Space Required

Ballroom dancers move in a somewhat unpredictable manner and are trained to take long steps. They thus need more space than sequence dancers - a dozen pairs of competition dancers will fill an average size ballroom! Ballroom dancing sessions are, therefore, more expensive since the dance promoter has to recover his costs from less dancers. Sequence dancers take up less room since they are all (hopefully!) moving in the same direction and expenses are lower - an important factor to some retired people wishing to dance 4 or 5 nights per week.

Variety

As well as low cost, variety and challenge in the dancing programme are essential to persuade people to dance several times per week. As Cowper says, "Variety's the very spice of life, that gives it all its flavour." Unfortunately, ballroom dancing is somewhat lacking in this essential requirement since performing a limited number of figures time and time again with the same partner soon loses its appeal. In social dancing monotony is relieved by including free-style dancing like the jive, rock 'n' roll and disco dances as well as elementary sequence and novelty dances. At advanced levels the partners agree on a sequence of their own to include figures of their choice - the lady knows what is to come and is well prepared. Sequences of this type are used by ballroom dancers in demonstrations, exhibitions and competitions.

If anything, sequence dancers have too much variety! - with 20 basic dances and hundreds of sequences they have much to think about. They may be challenged, puzzled or frustrated but they are rarely bored.

Ease of Learning

It is not too difficult to learn the basic steps for social dancing by observation and practice. There are also many excellent manuals, charts and videos available for beginners. To extend the repertoire of figures and acquire a good style, however, lessons from a trained teacher are essential. Sequence dancing is easier to learn from this point of view since a wide range of figures is performed time and time again. In all sequence dancing sessions there is a learning element as the dancers watch one another perform and sometimes hear the MC calling out the order of figures. To master a figure like the hover cross in the slow foxtrot would be almost impossible by watching ballroom dancers - it might never be performed and certainly would not be repeated several times. A sequence dancing couple, in contrast, could take note of a slow foxtrot sequence containing the figure, watch carefully and then take to the floor and compare their performance with that of those around them.

By practising other sequence slow foxtrots they would eventually come to know the hover cross in all its variations.

The learning system for the modern sequence dancer who masters the new dances as they appear is cheap, effective and based on sound educational principles. Within days of winning an official inventive dance competition the dance is taught to sequence dancers all over the country. They can see the sequence performed (often by different teachers on different nights), practise the dance on numerous occasions and obtain the script if they so desire. Successful dancers need to discipline themselves by attending regularly and watching the demonstration with great care. The system keeps them up-to-date - if a new paso doble, mazurka or sequence lambada appears in no time at all it will be added to the repertoire of the faithful!

Community Spirit

Dancing sessions are happy occasions where one can move in time to music and converse with others. The go-as-you-please nature of ballroom dancing leads to a close bond between the partners and a more distant relationship with other couples - within the limits of the dance each pair performs its own order of steps. In sequence dancing all couples perform the same sequence and there is a much greater feeling of togetherness - a community spirit is developed by the dancers having the common aim of performing the given sequence correctly. Each couple (perhaps subconsciously) watches the others and they often compare notes after the dance; this is particularly the case when new dances appear or old ones are revived from the past. This community spirit is strengthened by the fact that many sequence dancers attend several nights per week for years on end - firm friendships develop and they often meet up outside the dances or go on holiday together. Modern sequence dancing is practised largely in the UK - it seems to have just the right amount of togetherness for our island race. American square dancing in special dress has perhaps too much social interaction for our type of dancer!

Standards of Performance

The expertise of ballroom dancers covers a wide range from social and nightclub dancers who merely rock about in time to the music to demonstration and competition dancers who have affinities with gymnasts and ballet artistes. Sequence dancers form a more homogeneous group. There are really no poor sequence dancers - anyone who has acquired the minimum repertoire of the 10-15 sequence dances necessary to attend even the simplest session must have some degree of dancing skill.

There is no doubt that trained ballroom dancers have better technique than the average sequence dancer - their primary aim is to move round with grace and style according to the principles developed by the schools and ballroom associations. They devise routines of their own to show off their capabilities and are a delight to the eye. Sequence dancers have other preoccupations - they have to perform a wide range of figures in many dances and they cannot give the same time and thought to technique. Their emphasis must be on remembering and performing the steps in correct sequence to avoid hindering neighbouring couples. They are by no means, however, unappreciative of good technique, and watch the leaders and other dancers with great interest to learn what they can. Many sequence dancers have considerable natural ability and would have made good ballroom dancers if their inclinations had happened to lie in this direction.

Standard ballroom technique tends to be modified by sequence dancers to take account of the following factors: - less need for the man to lead; less ballroom space available; dancers more mature and sometimes physically handicapped; a need to economise on energy if performing all dances in a 2-3 hour dancing session. The main differences in style are: - less body contact; arms held lower; smaller steps; less exaggerated arm movements in the Latin-American dances. Ballroom dancers who attend sequence dances for a change should bear these factors in mind - it is very easy for them to crowd elderly couples (and others) by taking long steps and expecting others to fit round them.

Frequency of Sessions

Persons trained to a high level in a pastime or sport may find only limited opportunities to exercise their skills - ice skaters and ski jumpers have to travel about a bit! Qualified ballroom dancers often fall into this category. In his address given to the 1964 ISTD Diamond Jubilee Dinner, Victor Sylvester said:-

> *"I get numerous enquiries from people who come up to London and want an evening out with what I could call our kind of dancing. I have to tell them that such a ballroom does not exist. Why? Because everything is a question of supply and demand, and unfortunately there is not a big enough demand for it, otherwise there would be a ballroom to cater for them ... The fact is that the general public will never dance with long gliding steps, it is too difficult, and it takes up too much room. It is as simple as that."*

(Quoted in 'The Dancing Master', Frank Burrows, 1978)

It is doubtful if this situation has improved in the last 30 years and the keen ballroom dancer may often have to choose between social dancing sessions (ballroom with simple sequence) or taking up sequence dancing.

Sequence dancers often have a large choice of venues since many dance leaders will run 3-4 sessions per week; there may be 30 or more sessions per week within a 5 mile radius in some urban areas. The dancers are not altogether popular with proprietors of ballrooms and licensed premises since they expect to pay very little (and have tea and biscuits included!) and are not great drinkers. A disco dance for the younger element (with all its problems) is often a more profitable venture!

Old-Time Sequence Dancing

Old-time sequence dancing is still popular today although much less so than the modern style. It is practised by those who place great store on order, formality, politeness and appreciation of the values of the past. It has considerable aesthetic appeal - to see the Varsovianna or Wedgewood Blue Gavotte performed in proper style is a memorable experience. Formal or evening dress is worn, the partners bow and curtsey and the national anthem is played. The programmes consist mainly of dances arranged before 1958 with some square dances; there are a few early modern but no Latin-American dances. Some later dances such as the Balmoral Blues, Saunter Together, Tango Serida or Sindy Swing are often played but care is taken to see that the programmes do not become too modern. The introduction of new dances is a relatively slow process and it is not too difficult for a couple to pick up the threads after an absence due to holidays or illness.

Modern Sequence Dancing

Keen sequence dancers attend sessions where most dances are from the current year. Programmes change month by month as new winners of inventive dance competitions appear and any prolonged absence involves a considerable catching-up operation. Some couples need 4-5 nights per week to keep on top, more experienced dancers can get by with 1 or 2 sessions. Attendances increase as the new dances appear and fall off when there are no competitions at the turn of the year. Fewer new dances per year might well reduce numbers and lead to less dancing sessions. There is no doubt that the new dances give life and interest to the movement and prevent stagnation. Sequence dancing at this level has been compared to a comet moving forward and shedding a trail of once-popular dances! These dancers know their dances and dancing figures and sequence dancing is a way of life to them - they dance regularly anything up to 15 hours per week.

There are other sessions where only some of the new dances are taught along with favourites from other years - these are useful stepping stones for learners, giving them opportunities to practise their skills without feeling under too much pressure. Programmes are more settled and couples who attend regularly soon master the repertoire. Requiring still less attendance and commitment are the social (club) dances where new sequences rarely appear. The programmes contain old favourites like the Square Tango, Lingering Blues, Saunter Together, Melody Foxtrot, Mayfair Quickstep and Emmerdale Waltz with other sequences established by the traditions of the club. Dancing clubs meeting in schools or church halls have a leader and recorded music; in licensed premises an organist usually announces and plays the sequences. These clubs have a small membership fee and a committee which will often organise meals, outings and other activities. Aspiring sequence dancers often join these clubs and feel genuine regret at having to leave the atmosphere of good fellowship to move higher up the ladder.

Line Dancing

Line dancing is a more recent form of sequence which may modify the modern sequence dancing of the future - will its devotees turn to partner sequence dancing when they get older? It has American roots being often performed in cowboy dress to country-western music. Most dances are for individuals facing the same way and performing the steps in unison (somethiing like the slosh). It has figures from disco dancing and elsewhere like the chug, grapevine and shuffle; there are hundreds of sequences like the Tennesee Stroll, Country Strut, Cowboy Hustle and Alley Cat (a few are for pairs usually standing in side-by-side position). The dances are performed without any bounce with the legs slightly flexed; the upper body and head move about while the arms often accentuate the motions of the feet.

Line dancing was given great impetus by the dancing of John Travolta in 'Saturday Night Fever' in 1978. The country-western 'Achy Breaky Heart' became the most popular song in 1993 and its accompanying line dance script swept the country. A recommended book is 'Christy Lane's Complete Book of Line Dancing', Human Kinetics (1995).

The Future of Modern Sequence Dancing

At present sequence dancing is practised mainly by older people who can spare the time necessary to master its intricacies. Many of the present dancers were active in the period of great popularity of social ballroom dancing in the 1940's and acquired the ability to dance with a partner in ballroom hold at a relatively early stage. With the coming of rock and disco and the individual mode of free-style dancing, will the present generation take so readily to sequence in their later years? On the other hand, with progress in medical science and a rise in the standard of living, there are relatively more old and reasonably fit people looking for some healthy social activity for their declining years. It is difficult to think of any other pastime which brings out elderly couples so frequently. Sequence dancing has the great attraction of moving about with a partner to the tunes of the past and the present in an atmosphere of friendship - for those having the skill and persistence to perform it is greatly superior to playing dominoes, whist or bingo, or watching cabaret in the clubs.

In the 1900's the technique of sequence dancing was somewhat stylised and artificial although it was simplified by social dancers. With the development of the modern style based on a walking action it seems likely to persist for many years. Unless there is some great national catastrophe any decline will take the form of gradually decreasing numbers of sessions and dancers and this will be a lengthy process as things are at present. Sequence dancing in one form or another has survived since 1900 and its adherents are strongly motivated - some have been dancing 3 or 4 nights per week for 20 years or more. The question is, are new younger people joining as fast as the older people are retiring from the scene? There does not seem to be much evidence either way at present but who can foretell the future? Who would have thought in the 1950's that the older generation would be spending weeks at a time in marble hotels in the winter sun in places like Benidorm with sequence dancing most afternoons and evenings?

Some Useful Addresses

Dance Scripts

1. North Star Publishers, P.O. Box 20, Otley, West Yorkshire, LS21 2SA. 01943 462269. Publisher of "Sequence Dancing World" (10 issues per year). Supplier of scripts, script collections and other books on sequence dancing.

2. Brockbank Lane Sequence Script Service, P.O. Box 2341, Weymouth, Dorset, DT4 9YZ. 01345 770157. Supplier of scripts (list available) and script accessories. Many scripts have the lady's in addition to the man's steps. Dance records.

3. The Dave Bullen Script Service, 24 Lyndhurst Road, Birkdale, Southport, PR8 4JT. 01704 66922. Scripts, dance records, dancing holidays.

4. Northern Dance Services (NDS), 18 Commercial Street, Shipley, West Yorkshire, BD18 3SP. 01274 586829. Large collection of scripts, dance records.

Suppliers of Books on Dancing

5. Imperial Society of Teachers of Dancing (ISTD), Euston Hall, Birkenhead Street, London, WC1H 8BE. 0171 837 9967. Their list includes books on dancing (some on sequence dancing as well as some scripts) and various dancing accessories.

6. Ballroom Dancing Times Book Service, 45-47 Clerkenwell Green, London, EC1R 0BE. 0171 250 3006.

Old-Time Dancing

7. The Society for the Preservation and Appreciation of Old-Time Music and Dancing. (The Old-Time Society)

    Secretary: F. Boast, 8 Bourne Way, Addlestone, Surrey, KT15 2BT, 01932 843475.

Bally Dancing!

What's the name of that little dance?
You know, the one we used to do!
It had a little twiddly bit,
And then a turn or two.

You must remember that little dance!
It went sort of slow, with quick steps.
It had that funny three point turn,
And then some lockwards backsteps.

Oh! What's the name of that little dance?
It was my favourite thing!
I think it had a oozit ...
And then a wrong side wing.

You know! We danced it all the time!
And you always partnered me!
It had a two, and three, and four,
And then a one, two, three!

I'm sure it's not a tango,
And I don't think it was a rumba.
It might have been a cha-cha-cha ...
What was its name I wonder?

Tomorrow, I'll ask our teacher,
And request another chance
To dance again the 'wotsitsname' -
My very favourite dance!

By Pat Price - poet, cartoonist and sequence dancer. Her publications are 'Smile When You Dance' and 'Modern Sequence Dancing with a Funny Bone'.